Born and Raised in Sawdust

My Journey Around The World in Eighty Years

Lewis Thigpen, Ph. D., PE

authorHOUSE

AuthorHouse™
1663 Liberty Drive
Bloomington, IN 47403
www.authorhouse.com
Phone: 1 (800) 839-8640

© 2019 Lewis Thigpen, Ph. D., PE. All rights reserved.

No part of this book may be reproduced, stored in a retrieval system, or transmitted by any means without the written permission of the author.

Published by AuthorHouse 11/14/2019

ISBN: 978-1-7283-2961-1 (sc)
ISBN: 978-1-7283-2960-4 (hc)
ISBN: 978-1-7283-2959-8 (e)

Library of Congress Control Number: 2019915329

Print information available on the last page.

Any people depicted in stock imagery provided by Getty Images are models, and such images are being used for illustrative purposes only.
Certain stock imagery © Getty Images.

This book is printed on acid-free paper.

Because of the dynamic nature of the Internet, any web addresses or links contained in this book may have changed since publication and may no longer be valid. The views expressed in this work are solely those of the author and do not necessarily reflect the views of the publisher, and the publisher hereby disclaims any responsibility for them.

*To members of my family . . . past and present,
and to the others who helped me on my journey*

Contents

Preface ix
Acknowledgements xi

PART I   THE EARLY YEARS   1

Chapter 1   The Family 3
Chapter 2   My Early Years 16
Chapter 3   School Years 30

PART II   TEEN YEARS AFTER HIGH SCHOOL   65

Chapter 4   Farm and Construction Work 67
Chapter 5   Life in the U.S. Army 70

PART III   YOUNG ADULT   89

Chapter 6   My First Year after Active Duty in the Army 91
Chapter 7   Undergraduate Student at FAMU 96
Chapter 8   Undergraduate Student at Howard University 104
Chapter 9   Summer Job at Sandia Corporation 114
Chapter 10   Graduate Student at Illinois Institute of Technology 116

PART IV   PROFESSIONAL LIFE   129

Chapter 11   My Employers 131
Chapter 12   Major Achievements 178
Chapter 13   Activities and Retirement 183

Chapter 14	My Travels	196
Chapter 15	Natural Environmental Events	221
Chapter 16	Family Get-Together	225
Chapter 17	Friends	254
Chapter 18	Some of My Favorite Things	261

PART V   EMBRACING A CHANGING WORLD   267

Chapter 19	National Leadership	269
Chapter 20	Military Service in the Family	278
Chapter 21	Continuing Education	280
Chapter 22	Technology Developments and Advancements	283

Epilogue	291
Appendix	297
Index	305

Preface

I have had a life filled with challenges which I had to overcome to become successful. I had not thought about writing my memoirs until after I ran into my former barber in a hardware store in Quincy, Florida, during my Christmas visit with the family in 2009 after I had retired. He was considering developing an archive on black people from Gadsden County who he thought were successful. He wanted some information on my accomplishments. After returning home to Alexandria, Virginia, I began to outline thoughts on my life and accomplishments. There was no follow up before my former barber passed away.

As I wrote that outline, the idea came to me that I should write my memoirs. Several years later, I definitively decided to write my life story.

My story is of a black child who grew up in the Jim Crow South in the rural community of Sawdust in Gadsden County, Florida, in the late 1930s, 1940s and early 1950s. It is the story of a black child in a poor family that had few resources, who goes on to be recognized nationally and internationally for significant contributions in science, engineering, and engineering education.

I am presenting my story in as much detail that I think is needed to let present and future generations of the family know what life was like for their parents and grandparents in the rural South. A very large part of my life has been outside of the South. Through my experiences, family members and others will know what life has been like for a black person not only in the Jim Crow South, but also in other areas of the United States and around the world.

For more than three decades before deciding to write my story, I gathered information on my family. This began when I learned the origin of my family name from a co-worker who was searching genealogy of his family through records in Salt Lake City, Utah. He brought me an article on my last name indicating that Thigpen means "Beggar of Coins" in German. I began to chase down the history of my family in the U.S. At that time, my Aunt Addie Thigpen Hall was the only living child of my grandfather, Alonzo Thigpen, Sr. She said that her grandfather was Ed Thigpen. I also obtained information about my grandparents and great-grandparents from the U.S. Census and other members of my immediate family.

This memoir covers my life including education; hard work and dedication; relationships with relatives, friends and others; and opportunities I have had. It includes good things and bad from my early years to retirement and beyond ... so far.

Acknowledgements

First, I thank Franklin Jones who instilled in me the idea to write my memoirs. Franklin was my former barber and a businessman who wanted to showcase accomplishments of African Americans in Gadsden County, Florida. He had followed my career and wanted to include me in his archives, but he passed away before we connected on my accomplishments. I retired in 2008 and decided in 2010 to write my memoirs, beginning with the outline of my accomplishments that I had prepared for him. Without Franklin's interest in my career and accomplishments, this memoir may never have been written.

I am extremely grateful to members of my family. My parents taught me rules of conduct, core family values, and how to survive in a rural community in the Jim Crow South. Without those rules and family values, and given my attitude and reaction toward those who denigrated me as a person, I probably would not have survived past teenage.

My mother, Emma Ray Thigpen, must have seen something special in me. When I was a young child, she protected me from work that my older brother and sisters were assigned to do by my father and she taught me so much about living. I thank you Mother for your teachings and for taking care of me. I hope that I have done you justice in this book.

I am indebted to my sisters and brothers who have helped me throughout my life in more ways than they know. My sisters Leatrice Thigpen Green, Gladys Thigpen Rhowe, and Isabel Thigpen also deserve credit for helping me with the family history.

Gladys is also the family Historian. Anytime I needed information related to family members she was always there to help me search for that information during the writing of my memoirs.

Isabel was always exceedingly helpful to me in gathering needed information on my paternal and maternal sides of the family, providing dates of events that I needed, and the spelling of names during my writing of these memoirs.

I thank my brother Amos Thigpen for jogging my memory of the years when we were growing up. My brother James Woodrow Thigpen, niece Traci Thigpen Weatherspoon, and her daughter Lindsey Nicole Weatherspoon continued to encourage me to complete these memoirs.

I was especially thrilled that my grandniece Lindsey, a member of the next generation of our family, was extremely interested to know what my life was like during my childhood.

I further thank my brother James Woodrow Thigpen for his work in obtaining and providing photos of parents and grandparents. And I thank him for his painting of replicas of the house that I was born in and the schoolhouse that I attended in Sawdust. His artistic talent is awesome!

My first-cousins Essie Gunn Nealy, Willie Mae Gunn Ford, Adell Gunn Gilliam, and Ruby Gunn Clark, who were like sisters to me, played an important role in my life. I learned information from Adell regarding my paternal great-grandmother and the relationship between the Thigpen and Gunn families in Sawdust.

I acknowledge Amanda Rolax, who had a significant impact on my life from the time I was ten years old and she was a senior in high school. Other than my mother and my sister Leatrice, Amanda was another person who must have seen something special in me. She assured that I had a seat on an overcrowded school bus when I was a young child and encouraged me to attend college when, as a young adult, I was on a path to return to active duty in the Army. Without Amanda's encouragement, I may never have attended college. My whole life would have taken a different path and these memoirs would not have been written. Thank you, Amanda, for helping me put my life on a different but successful path when I needed encouragement the most.

I thank my friends Hailey Baker, John Owens, and Ray B. Stout for jogging my memory regarding years in college and graduate school.

I am fortunate to have had friends Ray B. Stout and Raymond C. Y. Chin; members of my family James Woodrow Thigpen and his daughter

Stephanie Renfroe; and my surrogate daughter Kashira Turner read my manuscript. I thank them sincerely for their comments.

I thank Mary Frances Stubbs, Ph.D., and Thelma Austin for their superb editing which clarified my writing and caught the inconsistencies. Thelma Austin, MyFamilyVoices/Praise Press, also deserves special thanks for guiding the manuscript through the process from editing to publication.

PART I
The Early Years

Chapter 1

The Family

I am the son of Alonzo Thigpen, Jr. and Emma Adaline Ray Thigpen. My father, Alonzo, was a farmer who farmed the home place of his father, Alonzo Thigpen Sr., and sharecropped other farms to care for his family. He was born in 1907 and raised on his father's farm in the rural Sawdust Community in Gadsden County, Florida. Both he and my mother completed only the sixth-grade. For black people with only a sixth-grade education in the segregated South, there were very few job opportunities other than working on farms.

While working on the farm, my father wore tan khaki work pants and shirts, and brogans (heavy ankle-high work boots with steel toes). His pipe and hat were his signature; he would never go anywhere without them. He was always lighting his pipe—I don't think he ever learned how to pack it. The tobacco he smoked was Prince Albert Pipe and Cigarette Tobacco, a loose tobacco that included small, thin, oblong sheets of cigarette paper to roll into cigarettes. He carried the metal tobacco can in a back pocket of his pants. There were <u>always</u> crushed cans in our house still containing small amounts of tobacco. My brother Amos and I took the crushed cans and cigarette paper to the corn field to hide and roll our own cigarettes to smoke.

Alonzo Thigpen, Jr. was an even-tempered man. He hardly ever got upset with the behavior of others. Family members told me the one incident in which he showed severe anger was when a white man left the gate open, allowing the cows to get out of our pasture and leave our farm. This had happened before; this man did not respect a black man. He had a route to his property that ran through the Thigpen family farm and would leave our gate open. This time, when our cows got out, my father got exceedingly upset with the man.

When my father heard about the cows, he was at his first cousin Trudy Campbell's house across the road from our farm. He told his cousins that he was going to end this disrespect. They got worried about what my father would do. After all, this man was white. Campbell's daughter Susie took my father's hat and hid it, knowing that he would go nowhere without it. No one at that time wore hats in anyone's house, so it was easy for Susie to just take and hide it. My father searched for his hat until Susie gave it back to him—after she saw that the white man had left the area.

The white man owned the property on the south side of our farm. His property had been originally owned by the Fergusons, a black family who had lost it through unpaid taxes. The man did not live on this property.

In later years, we worked on his small shade tobacco (tobacco grown in a field covered with cheese cloth) farm at his home place. He had Clydesdale horses, and I drove one of them, pulling the barge "sled" to haul the tobacco from the tobacco shade to the barn for stringing and curing. Driving the horse pulling the sled was a favorite job for young boys. Shade tobacco is used to wrap other tobacco fillings during the process of rolling cigars.

Most of the men in Sawdust who could find moonshine (strong liquor produced and sold illegally)—and Alonzo Thigpen Jr. was one of them—would drink it. However, he drank only on weekends during the farming and harvesting season, from spring through early January of the next year. During the period when there was no harvesting or planting, he drank moonshine during weekdays as well. In late December, all farmers who grew sugar cane had their own home-made liquor, commonly called "buck." My father, like the other farmers, made his buck using skimmings from making molasses syrup from sugar cane.

My father loved to drive cars. He would drive anyone who wanted him to take them shopping, or to places where they could get alcoholic drinks. He did this until his last days. He passed away at home on September 8, 1976, at sixty-nine years old.

I cannot talk about anything that I would call a hobby of my father. However, he taught my oldest brother, Amos, and me to hunt, trap, and fish. For families in the rural South, hunting, trapping, and fishing were necessary to provide additional food that was not grown on the farm. One key thing that he taught us about hunting and fishing was trailblazing. Trailblazing prevented you from getting lost in the woods. As I recall, trailblazing was most important at night when we went into the woods. We would break bushes—blaze a trail—to show a way out of the woods. We also blazed a trail in the woods during the day when we searched for a new place on Juniper Creek to fish during daylight.

My father assigned tasks to his children for farm work after we came home from school. There were specific tasks for us boys, other tasks for the girls, and common tasks for both. It was expected that these tasks would be completed whether he was home or away sharecropping on another farm. I think all of us learned from this responsibility. I learned that any job worth doing is a job worth doing to the best of your ability. I have lived with this all my working days, and I have tried to apply that in the writing of this autobiography.

In the early 1950s, my father began experimenting with new money crops. His major money crops prior to that time had been tobacco, sugar cane, corn, and sweet potatoes. Each year he would try a new crop: cucumbers, pimentos, cotton, and eggplant. Over a period of four years he only lost money with those new crops—except cotton. I think he lost not because of his experiments but because he had not obtained a written contract from a buyer. He probably had taken a handshake from someone who said that they would buy those crops—but no contract. Remember: my father had only a sixth-grade education. When the crop was ready to harvest, he had no buyer.

His experimentations inspired his sons to experiment with new crops on a small scale. I grew popcorn and carrots during the early 1950s, and my brother James Woodrow began experimenting and growing vegetables and fruits in the late 1990s and early 2000s that had not previously been considered suitable to the climate in Gadsden County.

My mother, Emma Adaline Ray Thigpen, was born in 1907, in Donaldsonville, Georgia. Her parents, my maternal grandparents, were George Ray and Emma Brown Ray. In 1918, Grandma Emma died from the Spanish flu when my mother was eleven years old. Consequently, my mother and her siblings went to live with their grandparents—my maternal great-grandparents, Allen Brown and Betty Goodsen Brown—who raised them on their 205-acre farm in Gadsden County near Sawdust. After Great-Grandpa Allen Brown passed away, the farm was called the "Betty Brown Place" by people in the Sawdust Community who worked on the farm.

My grandparents Emma and George Ray had three children. My mother was the oldest, followed by her sister, Ezella, and brother, Allen. Later, my grandmother separated from my grandfather. The family had no contact with him after the separation or in later years.

When she was young, my mother had several types of employment. Like all young children in the rural South, she worked on the farm. Later, she rolled cigars by hand for a cigar company and worked as a cook for a family in Gadsden County. She was an excellent cook and seamstress, and loved reading.

After my parents got married, my mother continued to develop her cooking skills with her women friends. One of these friends was Miss Rendy, who served as a cook on Maxwell Strom's farm in Sawdust. I do not know Miss Rendy's last name because, in the 1940s, most people were called only by first names or pseudonyms— what we called "nicknames." Another friend was Mrs. Amelia Jackson, who also lived on Maxwell Strom's farm when I was a young child. We would walk more than a mile to visit them—or they would visit us—and the ladies would make new recipes and cook up fancy desserts. My mother's children and Mrs. Amelia's children became good friends. Miss Rendy had no husband or children that I know of.

My mother continued her cooking skills by preserving foods in Mason jars using her large pressure cooker. The process was called canning. She would can enough vegetables, fruits, and preserves to last the whole year. She could make excellent jelly and fruit preserves out of any cultivated or wild fruit in the area. Cultivated or planted fruits included peaches, pears, and figs. Wild fruits included crab apples, grapes, plums, blackberries, blueberries, and mayhaw berries.

There was an area against the wall in the kitchen with shelves similar to a book case. It was more than eight feet tall and about the same width. This is where my mother placed canned Mason jars of fruits and vegetables.

As a small child, I would wonder each year whether she would fill those shelves with canned goods—and she always did.

My mother also canned vegetables grown on our farm for Robert Parramore, who had a rolling store, a traveling convenience store that delivered products to our rural area on Mondays. I believe that my mother had cooked for one of the Parramore families before she got married, and Robert Parramore knew of her cooking and canning prowess.

The wild game that my mother cooked was so good that I wish I had her recipes now, especially for squirrel, rabbit, quail, and other game. Game was a delicacy and a change from mostly chicken, pork, fish, and sometimes beefs.

There were certain ingredients that she used in cooking that were scarce or unavailable during World War II. This did not affect her excellent cooking. She would just change her recipes. If she did not have lard to fry fish or chicken, she would make great fish stews and the best perlau (chicken and rice) that I have ever eaten. Her perlau was made using a hen that was laying eggs; the developing eggs inside the hen were part of the dish. She also made the best beef soup that I have ever had—with a cheap beef bone (soup bone) that contained marrow, and adding rice and tomatoes along with her spices.

My mother had a cloth bag containing numerous unprocessed spices. I remember helping her breakdown and process her spices for her recipes for meats, vegetables, soups, and desserts. She also took charge of smoking the pork that was butchered on the farm. The pork was cured at the ice plant in town with salt to draw out the liquid for forty days and brought home for smoking.

Many rural communities did not have electricity, so ice plants in Quincy, Florida, made ice and supplied it to rural areas. The ice plants, which had huge ice-box containers not available on farm, also cured the meat for the local farmers. The farmers had smokehouses for the meat to continue the curing process by smoking it with oak, black walnut, pecan, or hickory wood. This cured pork meat, supplemented with fish and chickens grown on the farm, along with hunted game, would last throughout the year.

My mother was a great seamstress who made clothes for the children and quilts for the beds. She made many of the children's clothes, especially dresses, shirts, and underwear, from flour sacks or other inexpensive materials. In those days, people purchased large sacks of flour for making bread. The sacks had flower designs or other designs suitable for making clothes. My mother used a foot-powered pedal-driven sewing machine.

She would also take leftover scraps of cloth to sew designs for the cover of a quilt. When the cover was completed, the ladies in the community would get together for a quilting party. They set up a rack on the back porch and spread the quilt cover, interior filling ("batting"), and inside liner over the rack. The ladies would then stand around the rack and sew the three components together. These regular quilting parties largely ended in our community in the late 1940s. But women continued to make quilts. The quilts provided warm covering for beds and lasted for decades.

In addition, my mother could crochet—she made small items such as placemats for a table. Her talent also included tatting and knitting. If you name a process related to sewing or making an item that used thread, my mother could do it. She passed her knowledge to any of her children who showed an interest to learn. As a young boy, I observed her activities and tried to do some of the things that she did, but I was unsuccessful. However, my sister Mildred learned to sew and crochet; she even crocheted a bedspread. Mildred taught her daughter Janice Maxwell to sew. Janice made a dashiki for me when they were in style in the 1970s. My other three sisters, Leatrice, Gladys, and Isabel, have excelled in my mother's cooking prowess.

My mother loved to read. Maybe that is what encouraged her to save certain things that are important to the family today. She kept her grandfather's hat, her grandmother's clock, the blade that she used to cut wrappers to make cigars by hand, and the ration books used to buy products during World War II.

My mother protected her young children. During the winter, my father wanted all of us who were four or more years old to work on the farm covering up sugar cane or other chores. My mother would protect me by sending me to Aunt Lucy Rolax's house to take a flour sack. She knew that I would follow my first cousin William Rolax all day and William would bring me home that evening. Aunt Lucy lived on the farm next to our farm, on our eastern border. As a child of four or five years old, I would walk to Aunt Lucy's house through the fields and not on the road, as we were taught. My mother would let me sleep late when my older siblings had to get out of bed. My sister Gladys must have been jealous because she has reminded me of this throughout my life. I believe that my mother saw something in me that would highlight the family in the future, and understood that supporting my needs as a young child would help me prepare for success.

On September 24, 2006—less than four months from reaching one hundred years old—my mother passed away in a hospital in Tallahassee. The cause was complications from a broken hip endured in a fall while she was trying to sit down in a chair. She lived thirty years after my father passed away.

My parents faced major challenges feeding and clothing their family and protecting us from white racism. Several things come to memory. One day Amos and I worked on Kennon Sheppard's family farm picking up sweet potatoes that had been plowed up in the field. He gave us a few sweet potatoes to take home. When Sheppard brought us home and we got out of the back of the truck, he asked if we had taken the potatoes. I responded, "Yeah." My father heard me and said that we should say "yahsur," meaning "yes sir," even though white men's children, no matter how young, called my father by his first name. Whenever Amos and I worked on the Sheppard farm alone all day, they would provide lunch. Amos and I were served on the back porch next to their kitchen. Black people had to always communicate with white people at the back of their house. My father sharecropped shade tobacco with Kennon and maintained a good relationship with him throughout his life.

My father also sharecropped growing shade tobacco with another white farmer, Edward Rudd, in the late 1940s. Amos and I played with his three sons, Willard, Byron, and George, when we were working on the farm during the summer. One day I had a confrontation with the oldest son in the tobacco barn. I was nine years old and he was at least five years older than me. My father scolded me for this incident. I did not understand my father's behavior toward me but I did not question it. In retrospect, I understood that my father was only trying to protect me, because it didn't matter that the white boy was older or in the wrong. If that white family chose to punish me—or my family for that matter—the law was not going to protect us. Raising black children in the Jim Crow

South, our parents walked a thin line. They wanted us to grow up strong and proud, yet they feared for our safety and our very lives if we challenged white people in any way or spoke up against racism and mistreatment. However, we always got along well with the Rudd family. And we have maintained communications and close friendship with the oldest son, Willard, throughout the years. Every time I have seen him in my adult years he has talked about how much he respected my parents and how much they taught him about life.

My father was a member of the National Association for the Advancement of Colored People (NAACP) and had membership buttons, but he never wore them. As a young child I saw the buttons and decided to wear one. My father was serious that I should not wear it. I did not know why and my father never gave a reason. I realized only later in life that it was fear for his family—there was no protection from the law for black people.

The KKK (Ku Klux Klan) must have been active in Gadsden County. Once when I was in middle school riding the school bus on Florida State Highway 12, we passed a place where a black family was living in several houses on their own property. I saw what appeared to be a cross that had been burned on that property over the previous weekend. This alerted me to my father's actions regarding the behavior of some white people in Gadsden County.

My paternal grandfather, Alonzo Thigpen, Sr., a mulatto, was born approximately in 1856 in Gadsden County. His father, Edwin Thigpen was of German ancestry. Edwin was born in 1826 in North Carolina and moved to Gadsden County. Alonzo Thigpen Sr.'s mother, a slave, was the sister of Brister Gunn. Brister Gunn ended up owning much property in the Sawdust Community of Gadsden County and in Quincy. My great grandmother had two sons, Alonzo Thigpen, Sr. and Henry Porter, who worked for their uncle Brister Gunn. Her name may have been Melvine because Grandpa Alonzo had a daughter whose middle name was Melvine and names were kept in the family. We were told that she is buried in a "white" graveyard in Mountplesant, a rural community in Gadsden County. I have been informed that Grandpapa also had a sister named Lucy but I know nothing about her life or her descendents.

The Family

My paternal grandmother, Emma Gilliam Thigpen, was born in 1863 in Gadsden County. She had three sisters—Laura, Carrie, and Anaka. Grandma Emma's father, Samuel Gilliam, was born in Alabama. We know nothing more about her father and nothing about her mother. However, we were told that one of her parents was Native American.

Grandpapa Alonzo and Grandma Emma Thigpen had thirteen children—five boys and eight girls. However, only three boys and five girls lived past birth: boys Johnnie Thigpen, James Thigpen, and my father Alonzo Thigpen, Jr.; and girls Laura Thigpen Jordan, Lucy Thigpen Rolax, Carrie Ardean Thigpen Gunn, Mary Melvine Thigpen Paul, and Addie Thigpen Hall. Uncle Johnnie, the oldest son, had a farm next to a farm that Grandpa Alonzo owned in the community of St. Mary.

This was a very close-knit family of brothers and sisters who looked out for each other and the children. The two closest members of the family were Carrie and my father. Aunt Carrie was sixteen years old when my father was born, while their oldest sister Laura was already married and had one son, Merrit Jordan, Sr.

Aunt Carrie married late in life. Her four daughters, Essie, Willie Mae, Adell and Ruby were like sisters to us.

Aunt Mary Melvine and her husband, Wallace "Uncle BB" Paul, had four children. When she died, her oldest two children, Quinton and Winfred came to live with my parents and Grandma Emma. Her two youngest children, Waymon and Dorothy, went to live with Aunt Addie until Uncle BB was able to make arrangements to take care of his four young children.

Aunt Addie would always bring clothes for us when she visited from Gainesville, Florida.

All of Grandpa Alonzo's and Grandma Emma's children lived in the Sawdust Community until they married and had children, except James who moved north possibly to Chicago, Illinois, or Hartford, Connecticut. It was reported that James was a gambler. It was said that after winning a significant amount of money, he was robbed and killed.

After Grandpa Alonzo died, his farm became "heir property." After Uncle Johnnie died, there were offers on Grandpa Alonzo's farm next to Johnnie's but my father and Aunt Carrie, who was managing all of the Thigpen property, would not sell it. Their reason was that "they did not want strangers living next to Johnnie's children." That property remains in the Thigpen's family today. Uncle Johnnie's son Spurgeon Thigpen sharecropped this property with Aunt Carrie. The property is located at the east end of Thigpen Road in Gadsden County. Today the property is managed by my brother James Woodrow and rented to help pay the taxes.

My maternal grandfather, George Ray, was born in Donaldsonville, Georgia. I have no additional information related to him. My maternal grandmother, Emma Brown Ray, was born in Gadsden County, Florida, probably around 1885. Her father, Great-Grandpa Allen Brown, was a school teacher and owned a large farm, 205 acres. Allen Brown had a brother named Silas Brown and many of the descendants of those two brothers still live in Gadsden County. Grandma Emma's mother, Betty Goodsen Brown, had four sisters, Adaline "Aunt Minnow" Anderson, Amanda Armstead, Jane Isaac, and Rebecca Whitfield. My mother's middle name was Adaline but she shortened it to "Line."

Grandpapa George and Grandma Emma Ray had three children—two girls and one boy: my mother Emma Line Ray Thigpen, Ezella Ray, and Allen "Uncle Buddy" Ray. Grandpa George and Grandma Emma separated when their children were very young. After Grandma Emma died in 1918, my mother and her siblings were raised by their grandparents, Allen Brown and Betty Goodsen Brown.

Great-Grandpa Allen and Great-Grandma Betty Brown had eight children, including a set of twins. The children were Emma, George, twins Albert and Elbert, Charlie, Benjamin, Eddie, and Jesse "Sam." My grandmother Emma was the oldest and Sam was the youngest.

George and his wife Janney had two houses on Experiment Station Road, which is now Martin Luther King, Jr. Boulevard in Quincy. Great-Grandma Betty lived in one of those houses. It had only two rooms: a bedroom with living area in the front and a kitchen area in the back of the house with no running water. A green outdoor toilet was at the end of the back yard. It may have been a custom to paint the outdoor toilets green in those days. Visitors did not enter through the front door and bedroom. Instead, they entered from the yard around the right side of the house and in the back door into the kitchen and dining area.

The first time that I remember visiting Great-Grandma Betty was in the early 1940s with my mother, and we entered the house through the back door. I remember my mother calling her "Mama." My first thought was, "Why is my Mama calling this little old white woman "Mama"? After all, blacks entered a white person's house through the back door. Great-Grandma Betty had light skin, blue eyes, and gray hair. At that time, she was in her mid to late seventies. She had a granddaughter, Julia, who lived with her. Julia was the daughter of Great-Grandma Betty's son Albert.

Great-Grandpa Allen also had a daughter Mary by another woman. I first met Mary's daughter, cousin Carrie Black, after I had graduated from college while shopping in Randy's Convenience Store in Quincy.

The only grandparent I knew was Grandma Emma Gilliam Thigpen and the only great-grandparent I knew was Great-Grandma Betty Goodsen Brown. We called Grandma Emma "Grandma" and Great-Grandma Betty "Grandma Betty."

Grandma Emma lived with us and got what was called "old age pension," a part of the Social Security Act, each month. She would go to town (Quincy) monthly to purchase things she needed. One month she would take Amos with her and the next month it would be my turn. I loved this because she would give me a quarter to buy a lot of candy and other things. A bar of candy cost a nickel and you could get a Tootsie Roll for a penny. Grandma taught us how to make candy out of sugar cane syrup and peanuts. She was also the only one who drank coffee in the family and let the children have sips.

We loved Grandma. She had only a few teeth in her mouth. In those days, people did not have dental care; when they had a toothache, the dentist would remove the troubling tooth. As a young child, my baby brother James Woodrow said, "Grandma, when I grow up I am going to buy you some teeth." Grandma later moved into the house with Aunt Carrie. Grandma died in the summer of 1948 at age eighty five, and James Woodrow had not grown up. He was only five years old.

My mother and father had seven children. In order of birth, they are: Leatrice, Mildred, Gladys, Amos, Lewis (me), Isabel, and James Woodrow. Leatrice is the oldest and James Woodrow is the youngest. Mildred passed away on June 1, 1984. All of the children are separated by more than two years in age. Leatrice is nine years older than me and I am about four and a half years older than James Woodrow. All of us attended college and three of my siblings earned master's degrees. I earned both the master's and Ph.D. degrees.

Leatrice worked in bookkeeping in the office of the AFRO American Life Insurance Company in Quincy and Tallahassee. She attended a community college in Tallahassee later to enhance her accounting skills. She subsequently worked at Citizens Bank in Quincy which, after mergers, ended up as Bank of America, until she retired in 1991 after twenty-one years. After retirement, she worked part time as a Deputy Clerk in the Quincy Courthouse until age eighty-seven, when she was no longer able to work.

Mildred entered Florida A&M College (FAMC) in 1948. During her enrollment it became Florida A&M University (FAMU). She earned the Bachelor of Science in Mathematics and Science and began teaching science to middle school students at Stevens School when I was a junior in high school. She later earned the Master of Science in Mathematics and Science at FAMU. She taught at four high schools in Gadsden County (Stevens, Carter Parramore, Greensboro, and Shanks) until she passed away.

Gladys earned the Bachelor of Science and Master of Science degrees in Mathematics and Social Studies at FAMU. Her first position after earning the Bachelor of Science degree was teaching history in Blountstown, Florida. She taught social science and mathematics at St. Johns Middle School and Quincy Junior High School in Gadsden County after leaving Blountstown. She later taught mathematics at Shanks High School in Gadsden County after the schools were integrated. She retired from teaching in Gadsden County.

Amos studied Building Construction for about two and one half years, the closest program to Architecture that was offered at FAMU, on the GI Bill for Korean War Veterans.

I was a pre-engineering student from 1959 to 1961 during Amos's enrollment. I left FAMU because I realized that I was wasting my time taking repetitive mathematics courses that I would not have to take in an engineering program. Amos left FAMU after I did. My sister Mildred told me that she believed that Amos left for the same reasons. Amos moved to California and became a successful building contractor.

Isabel enrolled at FAMU in 1959 to study business. She attended only one year. Isabel took a job at the Florida State Hospital in Chattahoochee. She later accepted a teaching assistant position at Carter Parramore High School in Quincy. The office of the County Superintendent of Schools in Gadsden County offered her a position as an accounts clerk in the food service department. Isabel retired from that accounting position.

James Woodrow earned a Bachelor of Arts from FAMU. He taught art in Jacksonville, Quincy, and Ft. Lauderdale, respectively. While teaching in Ft. Lauderdale, he earned a Master of Education in Educational Administration and Supervision at Florida Atlantic University in Boca Raton. After earning the master's degree, he became an Assistant Principal in Broward County and retired from that position. He now spends his time painting and gardening in Gadsden County. He is a member of the Art Association in Gadsden County. He exhibits his art at the gallery in Quincy.

I must say that all of my siblings have been adept in mathematics and science and successful in life.

Chapter 2

My Early Years

My Birth

I was born on the Thigpen family farm in the rural Sawdust Community of Gadsden County, Florida, at the peak of the Great Depression in 1938 in the United States. Family and neighbors called the Great Depression "HOOVER TIMES" after President Herbert Hoover (1929-1933). Sawdust is about ten miles southwest of the town of Quincy, which is the county seat. Gadsden County is on the northern border of Florida, across the line from Georgia.

My mother said that I was born on a certain day in early September 1938 and I used that date until I applied for a Social Security card in 1954. However, my birth certificate showed that I was born in late August 1938. I believe the discrepancy is due to a communication and reporting error between the midwife, Mrs. Syneda Madry Gilliam, who delivered me at home, and the doctor who reported my birth to the State of Florida. It was the responsibility of the doctor to report births delivered by midwives. I was informed that I was the first baby that Mrs. Gilliam delivered. My mother named me "Lewis" and did not allow nicknames in her family.

I am the fifth of seven children born to Alonzo Thigpen, Jr. and Emma Adaline Ray Thigpen. Both my mother and father were thirty-one years old when I was born. They were a poor farm family and did not have or keep records or pictures of their children's activities.

At the time of my birth, Franklin Delano Roosevelt was president of the United States and Adolph Hitler had seized total power in Germany by elevating himself to Führer, or absolute leader, of the German nation and its people. I spent my early childhood during World War II.

Early Childhood

We lived on the family farm in Sawdust. Our house was roughly in the middle of the farm. No one lived closer than one eighth to one quarter of a mile to our house. It was built by our grandfather Alonzo Thigpen, Sr. and our grandmother Emma Gilliam Thigpen. My father was born in the house and all of his children were born there too. Grandma Emma was living in the house when I was born. My grandfather had passed away many years before I was born.

An illustration of the house is included in this book. It was drawn by my younger brother, James Woodrow, based on what I told him from my memory.

The front porch is on the left side, and the back porch is on the right side. On the front porch were two doors. The door to the left was to the kitchen, with a wood burning stove and ice box, and the dining area. This was the only way to get into or out of the kitchen and dining area.

The second door on the front porch led to the main room. It was a large room with a bed, living room area, and large fireplace. It had three doors: one from the front porch, one to the back porch, and one to the second bedroom.

The second bedroom, right behind the kitchen/dining room (but no door between them), was also large, with two beds. It had two doors. One door led from the main room. The other door led to a third bedroom.

The back porch had two doors: one from the main room and one to the third bedroom. To get to the third bedroom, you could enter either from the second bedroom or from the back porch.

In those days, many houses in Sawdust required you to enter the kitchen from a porch or through a hallway that opened to the outside. There was no electricity, no running water, and no indoor toilets. Kerosene lamps were used for light. If you had to use the toilet at night, there were bed pans (called chambers) under the bed; they were emptied and cleaned the next morning.

The front of our house faced north. There was a well with a hand-powered pump about fifteen to twenty yards in front of the kitchen. A green outdoor toilet was about twenty yards to the east and back of the house. The barn was about fifteen yards north of the well. A corn crib and stable for the mules were north of the barn. The corn crib and mule stable were later rebuilt about fifteen yards west and south of the original location. There were two large oak trees in the front yard and one large oak tree in the back yard. The smokehouse, about ten yards east of the kitchen, was used to cure meat. Sunflowers grew near the smokehouse. There was a coffee tree about halfway between the kitchen and the smokehouse. There was a fence on the west side of our house. On the east side of the fence was a grapefruit tree and on the west side of the fence was an orange tree.

We lived in that house until in the early 1950s, when my father built a new house next to the road that passed our farm. Unlike the old house, this house had three bedrooms, living room, dining room, kitchen, and space for a bathroom. However, it did not have running water and a bathroom until I remodeled it in the early 1970's.

Our nearest neighbors when we lived in the old house were Aunt Carrie Thigpen Gunn's family; Aunt Addie Thigpen Hall's family; Willie Campbell and his family; and Lucius Edie, his wife Mabel Edie, and Mabel's niece Lula Mae Paul. Aunt Carrie and Aunt Addie had houses on the Thigpen family farm; Willie Campbell owned a farm across the road from the Thigpen family farm on the north side; and Lucius, Mabel Edie, and Lula Mae Paul lived on the white man's farm which was next to the Thigpen family farm on the south side. I was informed by someone in the family, probably Aunt Carrie that the Fergusons, a black family, had once owned the white man's farm but lost it due to unpaid taxes. After the Edie family built a house in another area of Sawdust and moved, that house was occupied by Elbert Doyle and his wife Lillie Mae Jeffrey Doyle, the elementary school teacher.

Aunt Addie, her husband David "Esau" Hall, and their sons Lennon and Donald "Pat" moved to Gainesville in 1940. That left their house empty. Professor George Washington Farmer, the principal at Sawdust School, moved in and lived there until he retired in 1948 and moved to the Rudd farm for a short time. He later moved to High Bridge. Professor Farmer's wife was named Daisy. She had two children, Isaiah and Dora, who lived with them for a short time. She had three other children who lived in the High Bridge neighborhood in Gadsden County.

The housing pattern showed that blacks were a close-knit community with several adult households living on or near "the family farm." People with professional status such as teachers lived next to farmers or laborers. Over the years, people came to know their neighbors.

I was five years old when I entered school. Two of our nearest neighbors, Professor George Washington Farmer and Mrs. Lillie Mae Doyle, were the educators in the community—at the Sawdust School. Professor Farmer, the principal, was a very important person in the community and was well known throughout his life. Mrs. Doyle taught first through fourth grades. She was my first teacher. Professor Farmer taught grades five through nine.

Sawdust School had just one main room, with folding doors that made it two classrooms. There was a small cloakroom on each end of the school house to store wood, coats, and other things to carry out instructions. The cloakroom was also used as a punishment room by Professor Farmer, where students were placed in detention or given a few slaps with a one-yard wood ruler or told, "Mr., smell this stick." A wood burning stove was located in each of the classrooms for heat. On the east side, about five yards from the classroom building, there was a kitchen. A well with a hand-powered pitcher pump was next to the kitchen. The boys and girls toilets were on the north side of the school grounds, and about fifty yards back of the school building. Playgrounds were on the north, south, and west sides of the school grounds.

The road ran east to west. There was a wire fence on the south, east, and west of the school grounds. The north side was bordered by Cypress Pond. On the south side, next to the road, were bleachers where people could sit, i.e., an outdoor auditorium. People could enter the grounds from the southwest without walking around to the gate on the northeast or climbing over the fence.

During non-school hours, the school house and its grounds were used as a Community Center. Examples included social events such as plays, dances and a fish fry on Saturday nights, and community gatherings and cook-outs on the 20th of May. *The 20th of May in 1865 was the day that Confederate forces in Florida formally surrendered in Tallahassee, and the slaves were freed under President Abraham Lincoln's Emancipation*

Proclamation. *The Proclamation had been issued on January 1, 1863—it did not take effect in Florida until over two years later!*

The school house did not have electricity. For most events at night, Kerosene lamps were used to light the building. However, for Saturday night dances and fish fries, Overhoultz, who owned a record shop in Quincy, strung electric lines with lights. He had a generator in the trunk of his car to power the system. Overhoultz also placed speakers in the building and played records from the turntable in his car. He was probably one of the earliest disc jockeys ("DJ's"). There was a cover charge at the door of the School-House-Turned-Dance-Hall to help pay the DJ.

Mullet fish sandwiches were sold outside at the kitchen. Mullets were very inexpensive—I remember when they were a nickel per pound. People loved those sandwiches.

Gladys, Ruby, Amos, and I would attend the Saturday night dances and fish fries without permission from our parents. Aunt Carrie thought that her daughter Ruby was at our house and my parents thought we were at Aunt Carrie's house. I was probably six or seven years old. Early Sunday morning, after a Saturday night dance, Gladys, Ruby, Amos, and I would go to the school house to search for coins that people might have dropped. Sometimes we would find a quarter but mostly dimes, nickels, and pennies.

Amos tells a story about a time when our cousin Aunt Addie's youngest son—Donald ("Pat")—took us to gather wood for cooking and heating in an area on our farm next to the property on the south side of our farm. Amos says that I was two years old. The white man who owned the property but did not live there released his dogs and they ran after us. Pat picked me up and he and Amos ran and protected ourselves behind a fallen tree. The man took the wood that Pat and Amos had collected and left. The only thing that I recall about that time period in my life is when I was at Aunt Addie's house standing on the northeast side of her front porch in a long home-made shirt that looked like a gown. I probably remember this because I did not like wearing that outfit.

My sister Gladys tells a story about me and a fear of roosters. The chickens were allowed to roam the yard and the roosters would chase me. She and our cousin Ruby Gunn said that if we were having dinner and they wanted my share of the meat, they would tell me that it was chicken, knowing I would not eat something that I was afraid of and did not like. We called chickens roosters, hens, and pullets in those days.

I had a boil (called a "rison" by some Southerners) on my neck. My parents and others would look at it. One day they said that it was "coming to a head." I was afraid that I was going to have two heads. They never explained what they meant by that figure of speech. My fear lasted for a few days, constantly thinking I would grow another head.

Other vivid recollections of those years pertain to the day my baby brother James Woodrow was born, activities at the sugar mill on the farm, a cow giving birth to a calf, unusual things grown on the farm, and Mrs. Daisy Farmer's ghost stories.

On the day James Woodrow was born, I was four years old. My mother gave my oldest brother Amos an egg to take to school to buy candy from Mayo Flournoy's Rolling Store. It came on Thursday of each week. Amos wanted a dime instead of taking the egg. After Amos left, Mrs. Syneda Gilliam, the midwife, came to our house carrying an attaché case. After Mrs. Gilliam left the house, my mother asked if I wanted to see a little boy. She was lying in the bed and removed the cover from the baby. I was expecting to see a little boy large enough to play with me but I vividly remember seeing only the shiny head. I thought Mrs. Gilliam had brought the baby in the attaché case.

One day, my sister Gladys, first cousin Ruby Gunn, brother Amos, and I were at Aunt Carrie's house. Gladys and Ruby knew that Aunt Carrie's cow was going to give birth to a calf. We hid behind a tree to watch the birth. Standing up, the cow dropped the calf to the ground, turned around, and licked the after-birth off the calf. I had heard adults talk about cows dropping calves but here I saw it. In less than a couple of minutes, the calf stood and walked, trembling.

There were non-traditional plants grown on the farm. I remember a mortar and pestle near the well and pump to husk rice that grew in the wet area of the farm. It flooded during storms. About five yards east of the house, there was a coffee tree. However, there were no coffee beans on the tree during any time that I remember. Farther out was the smokehouse, and there were sunflower plants that grew voluntarily—we did not have to plant the sunflower seeds each year. The plants grew from seeds that had fallen from plants that grew the previous year. On the west side of the house were a grapefruit tree and an orange tree.

I vividly remember our longtime, neighborly relationship with Professor George Washington Farmer and family. His wife was Mrs. Daisy Farmer. Her son Isaiah and daughter Dora lived with them a couple of years. Amos and I would follow Isaiah hunting in the woods for squirrels or birds. He had a 0.22 caliber single shot rifle while Amos and I had only sling shots.

Late in the evening, Gladys, Ruby, Amos, and I would visit Mrs. Farmer, sit on the porch, and listen to her ghost and other scary stories. Isaiah and Dora had moved from Sawdust back to High Bridge in Gadsden County.

The ghost story that I recall was about a ghost with eyes as big as a tea cup. She also told a scary story about a man and a black panther. When the man saw the panther, he played dead, so the panther left and did not bother him. In my imagination, I pictured the location where the man played dead. It was on the path from our house about halfway to Mrs. Farmer's house. After hearing the stories about her ghost, panther, or whatever, we had to go home in the dark and were afraid of seeing them. Yet we continued to visit her and listen to her scary stories.

One time I went with Grandma to meet Mayo Flournoy's Rolling Store. He was a white man. We walked about one eighth of a mile to meet it. Grandma made her purchases and was two or three pennies short. She had bought things from him for many years, but he would not give her credit for just two or three pennies until the next week. Flournoy said, "No, Annie, I just can't do it." White people during that time called older black women "Annie" and older black men "Uncle." I will never forget that incident. It made me terribly sad to see that Grandma was very disappointed and had to put back an item she wanted for our family.

We had a sugar mill on our farm. In the winter, the sugar cane was ground. The mill had a machine to mash the juice out of the sugar cane. It was powered by mules that moved in a continuous circle all day. The cane juice was cooked into syrup in an evaporator heated by wood. Neighbors gathered around the mill at night to socialize. One night, neighbors Demp and Abel Dudley brought their dog "Smokey." They had taught Smokey to smoke cigarettes. In his mouth, Smokey actually held a lighted cigarette that was smoking.

Later, my father later joined Willie Campbell in a business partnership. They purchased a two-cycle engine to power a cane grinding mill that squeezed the juice from the sugar cane. Now for the first time, mules were no longer needed to power the mill.

The whole operation was located on Willie Campbell's farm. A structure was built to house the evaporator where the cane juice was cooked into syrup. The building had walls and a roof so that rainy weather would not prevent cooking the cane juice into syrup. The building was similar to the one that had been on our farm prior to the merger. This building also had many shelves for storage of cans of syrup, during operations that were for personal use.

The front of the building was open but the rest was closed except for a door in the back on the right side to roll out the barrels after they were filled with syrup. Wood was used as the fuel to cook the cane juice into syrup. Outside was a grinding mill connected to the two-cycle engine by a wide belt to supply power to the mill to squeeze the juice from the cane stalks. A large vat was elevated above the height of the evaporator inside the building to allow gravity to supply the pressure force to push the juice through underground pipes from the cane grinding mill outside up to the evaporator inside the building. There was a valve to open and close to allow the correct amount of juice into the evaporator for cooking.

I believe Willie Campbell ("Mr. Willie") and my father had one of the most efficient cane grinding mills in the county. During the summer, they grew large acres of sugar cane for money crops that would generate income through the winter and they needed efficient operations that neither could afford alone. They also ground cane and made syrup for neighbors with small patches of cane who wanted it for personal use. Mr. Willie cooked the cane juice into syrup and he made the best and longest lasting cane syrup in Sawdust. Cane syrup cooked by other people in Sawdust spoiled in several months while Mr. Willie's syrup didn't spoil. His syrup remained thick or would only turn into sugar crystals.

The cane grinding was done in the winter. Mr. Willie cooked the juice into syrup, his son Jack fed the mill to squeeze the juice out of the cane, and my father hauled the cane to the mill. After Jack moved to Detroit, I did not see him again until the early 1970s. Mr. Willie's youngest son Jesse took over the job of feeding the mill. One time Jesse got one of his fingers caught between the rollers and lost that finger. Mr. Willie's oldest son hauled the mash away from the mill when their cane was being ground and squeezed. Amos and I had the responsibility of hauling the cane mash away when our cane was being ground.

The major sugar cane grinding took place between the Thanksgiving and the New Year's holidays. Our cane was always ground when we were out of school during the holidays. I did not like this job and I came to dislike the holidays.

During this time, the United States had entered World War II. All commodities needed to support the war effort were rationed, including gasoline, sugar, coffee, black pepper, etc. There were ration stamps for everyone in the family including children. Sugar, gasoline, coffee, and black pepper were very rare commodities. Since my father and mother did not drink coffee, they traded coffee stamps with white farmers who had large farms for things such as gasoline or black pepper. We also got black pepper from a cousin who worked on a farm whose owner was also involved in meat processing. After the war ended, my mother kept the unused ration books for the rest of her life.

How do rationing and the trading of ration stamps relate to grinding cane and making syrup?

Prior to the rationing, my father sold his syrup in 42-gallon wooden barrels to the Fletcher Company in Greensboro, Florida—the "Company Store" as depicted in country singer Tennessee Ernie Ford's song *"I owe my soul to the company store."* However, without ration stamps, moonshiners could not purchase the sugar for their operations. They probably offered as much as one dollar and fifty cents per gallon in cans for syrup, more than twice what Mr. Willie and my father were getting from the Fletcher Company per gallon in 42-gallon barrels. My father and Mr. Willie replaced the 42-gallon barrels with one gallon cans. They already had a holding unit for the syrup after it came out of the evaporator. The holding unit was made from one-half to three-quarters of a 42-gallon wooden barrel, with a valve to fill a one-gallon can. This changed my duties at the sugar mill. I now had to fill the one gallon cans with hot syrup. Amos had to haul the cane mash alone. Previously, Mr. Willie filled barrels alone.

During the time when moonshiners were paying as much as one dollar and fifty cents per gallon for syrup, a man working on a farm earned only one dollar and fifty cents to three dollars per day.

We kept syrup in one-gallon cans for personal use for the coming year. They were stored on shelves in the building at the mill, an unclosed building. One year, my family's syrup was on the first shelves on the right. We also made and stored syrup for two other families: A. D. Paul and Claudia "Mr. Naud" Madry. Their cans were on shelves following our syrup, from right to left, respectively.

One night after the cooking was shutdown, many cans of syrup were stolen. The stolen syrup was selectively taken from all who had cans on the shelves. Some of my family's storage was taken, some of Mr. Naud's syrup was taken, and all of A. D. Paul's syrup was taken. The thief/thieves knew whose syrup they were taking. Otherwise, why not take all of our family's syrup since it was at the front of the building?

The sugar mill was a place for men to socialize during the evening. Some walked as many as three miles one way while Mr. Willie was cooking the last juice of the day. There could have been conversations regarding the cans on the shelves. The thief/thieves knew exactly whose syrup they were taking. They knew that my father had seven children, a wife, and his mother to take care of. These same people thought that A. D. Paul was well off; they took all of his syrup. Otherwise, it could be speculated that the theft was an inside job. Whoever stole the syrup had a close connection with moonshiners and re-selling it to members of the community.

The names of two people surfaced but their names were never discussed in public because there was no proof.

My father drove his wagon to Quincy in the spring to plow garden plots for people. In the fall, he would drive to Quincy to peddle during the harvesting. I went with him on the wagon one spring and he plowed lots for gardens. I had to be very young at this time because I was not attending school. Two places that I remember were at Mellon Jackson's on Crawford Street and one place was near Grandma Betty's house on Experiment Station Road, which is now Martin Luther King Jr. Boulevard. Mellon Jackson had a small store in the front of his house and I sat outside while my father was plowing, looking at bananas but unable to purchase one. The bananas cost ten cents each.

My father and Naud Madry peddled products in Quincy that were harvested on the farm. Other than Willie Campbell, Naud Madry was the man that my father worked with closely. He considered these two men to be his friends. Both of them were old enough to be his father. Naud Madry had a pickup truck but he did not drive, and my father always drove Mr. Naud's vehicles. We would be riding on the back of that truck, and Ogie, the grandson of Naud Madry, would always let the open air blow his hat off. Ogie would say, "My hat done lost," and we had to stop and backup so he could get it. He never removed his hat when riding on the back of the pickup truck. I recall that we frequently got a flat tire that had to be repaired. The tires had inner tubes and people carried patches and a hand powered air pump to repair a tire on the spot.

In the other story I recall from this period, there were commodities at the Sawdust School before I attended school. The items included fruits, canned beans, and other food-related things. My brother Amos told me a story about Ogie and apples. There was a barrel of apples and Ogie took one without permission from Professor Farmer. Students sit on a stage in the school yard (likely the bleachers). Professor Farmer would stand in front of the stage and make announcements. Professor Farmer went home for lunch, which took about an hour, but punished Ogie by saying that he must eat the whole barrel of apples. After Professor left, all of the students asked Ogie to give them each an apple to help him with his punishment, but Ogie would not do so. He said, "Professor told me to eat all of these apples and that's what I am going to do." Ogie did not eat the barrel of apples but would not give other students any of them.

Naud Madry purchased a used van from a company that exterminated termites. The van was kept at our old house in Sawdust. We called the van "The Termite" because it had "Termite Control" written on the side. We went fishing in The Termite and my father hauled tobacco in it to barns to be cured. Eventually, too old to be repaired, The Termite perished in the back yard of our old house.

If Naud Madry did not have a pickup truck or van, my father would drive our mules and wagon nine miles to Quincy to peddle their farm products. He had Kerosene lanterns to light up the wagon because he never got back home before it was dark. There was a canvas in case it rained. I remember Amos and I went with my father and Naud Madry peddling on the wagon and we made yard brooms out of gallberry bushes to sell. I was in either the seventh or eighth grade. We asked fifteen cents for the brooms but probably sold some for ten cents or less through bartering—we did not want to bring them back home. People used the brooms to sweep their yards. They did not have grass lawns. There were some houses where we stopped and my father and Naud Madry went inside. I did not realize it at that time, but later I believed that those customers sold moonshine and they went in to get a drink. There was one woman, Ms Beady, who was a beautician and also, I believe, sold moonshine. She was a good customer of my father. Every year, he would butcher a hog for sale to her and take it to her home in Quincy.

My father had cars but he never owned a pickup until long after he had quit peddling.

During the time when World War II was at its peak, I remember searching the woods alone for junk to sell to the junk man. The junk man visited on a regular basis to purchase metal that was no longer used on the farm, such as broken plows and other metals. The closest that I came to the war activity was when I was five or six years old. Amos and I were working in the field. The propeller-powered U.S. fighter planes from Ft. Walton, Panama City, or Pensacola flew over our farm at near tree top level, probably on training exercises. We would dive into the furrows. This was scary for young boys.

I also remember a quartet of black soldiers who were invited to sing at Union Chapel AME Church in Sawdust on Sunday evenings. One of their songs was, "What a Time My Lord, What a Time." The words included: *"It was in nineteen hundred forty one the Second World War had just begun Hitler from Berlin stretched out his paw and brought a new nation into the war, what a time my Lord, what a time, Great God Almighty, what a time."*

The soldiers were stationed in Panama City and traveled in a two-and-one-half-ton truck (deuce and a half) with a canvas cover over the bed for protection from weather. The congregation raised money at these events to help support the soldiers' activities off base.

During this time period, I wore overalls and was barefoot most of the time. I probably had only one pair of shoes: brogans. The soil was so hot that it would burn your feet during the summer. Amos and I jumped from one grass spot to another.

The Twentieth of May Celebration is an event I recall fondly. All black families met at the Sawdust School grounds to celebrate the day when blacks received word that they were freed from slavery. It is similar to "Juneteenth" in Texas, which most people are aware of. The black people in Texas received word of their freedom on June 19, 1865—one month after blacks in Florida. The Twentieth of May celebration was a great cookout day. Everyone in the black community brought their favorite foods to cook and share. The children played together, ate homemade ice cream, and drank Kool-Aid to their hearts' content.

Amos now lives in Los Angeles with his family. He is the only one in our family who still celebrates the Twentieth of May. He barbecues goat when he can find it.

My family never celebrated birthdays. However, I remember that on my fifth birthday we walked three miles to Greensboro, Florida, had ice cream and cookies, and then walked three miles back home. The trip included my mother and father, Aunt Carrie, Gladys, Amos, Ruby, and me. My parents and Aunt Carrie purchased things at the Fletcher Company Store in Greensboro.

I remember that my sister Gladys taught me how to write my name and count as we sat around the fireplace at night. She would use charcoal to write my name and I then would write it myself. Around the fireplace was wallpaper, a combination of newspapers and advertisements. One advertisement was for Chef Boyardee Spaghetti with Meat Sauce. Thus, I learned to read not from books but from wallpaper. My sister Mildred later taught me the multiplication tables.

On winter nights, we also used the fireplace to roast peanuts and cook eggs and sweet potatoes in the ashes. We would cover the peanuts or sweet potatoes with hot ashes and charcoal and let them cook. To cook eggs, we would wrap them in a wet rag and cover them with hot ashes and charcoal. They were like boiled eggs.

At an early age, I believed in Santa Claus. He was used by adults to control young children's behavior. They would say, "If you are not good, Santa Claus is going to get you" or "Santa Claus is not going to bring you anything for Christmas." This put fear into kids about Santa. I was certainly afraid at an early age. There were Christmas programs including plays related to Jesus Christ's birth. These were held at Union Chapel AME

Church on Christmas Eve or a day or two earlier, and Santa presented gifts to children after their plays and recitations. Santa was played by Aunt Lucy's husband, Uncle Henry Rolax, in the typical Santa uniform. I did not know that he was Santa. As the children's names were called, they walked up to Santa to receive their Christmas gift. Some children would not go because of their fear of Santa. When my name was called, I was so afraid. However, I walked slowly up to get my gift and ran back to my seat.

At home on Christmas Eve, young children were required to go to bed early. This would allow the family and older children to sort out the Christmas gifts. The children who believed in Santa would place a shoe box under their bed; Santa would put their gifts in the appropriate box. The gifts were fruit, candy, a simple toy, socks, and clothing. We were all happy to receive these gifts.

I quit believing in Santa when I awakened early one night and my sister Mildred was filling the shoe boxes with gifts that he was supposed to deliver.

Chapter 3

School Years

Elementary and Middle School

I attended Sawdust School from the first grade through sixth grade. I started first grade at age five. My sister Gladys, brother Amos, first-cousin Ruby Gunn, and first-cousins Juanita Ray and her brother Wallace "Bro" Ray were all attending Sawdust School at that time. Juanita and "Bro" were my mother's brother Allen "Buddy" Ray's children. They lived with us for about a year after Uncle Buddy and his wife Aunt Teresa "Tee" separated.

Meanwhile, my two oldest sisters Leatrice and Mildred were attending Stevens High School about ten miles away in Quincy. They boarded in Quincy as there were no school buses to take black children to high school from any rural area in Gadsden County. Professor George Washington Farmer promoted Mildred to the same class as my sister Leatrice. Hence, they attended high school at the same time and graduated together. During their high school years, they worked to help support themselves. Leatrice worked at the AFRO American Life Insurance Company and Mildred rolled cigars at one of the factories in Quincy.

Because of the lack of adequate infrastructure, Stevens High could not support the number of black students attending. Stevens was forced to develop two sets of classes for its students. One set was assigned classes in the morning and another set in the afternoon. Leatrice and Mildred attended the morning session, which allowed them to work during the afternoon and evenings. The teachers had double duty, teaching the same courses in the morning as they did in the afternoon.

Sawdust School was located across Providence Road next to our farm. We walked to school along the road and sometimes took a short cut across our field unless my father had planted a sugar cane field blocking our path. He rotated crops on the farm in different years. For example, he would plant corn in a certain field for two or three years, then plant sugar cane there the next year. When sugar cane was there, no one wanted to walk across the field if they had other options.

Maintenance of the school grounds was the responsibility of the children, including gathering wood for heat during the winter, janitorial work, and sweeping the yard of trash and burning it.

During my last years at Sawdust School, the County School Superintendent, Mr. "Sneaky Pete" Williams, a white man, began to show up at the schoolhouse. He was called "Sneaky Pete" because he would hide his car away from the school grounds and walk to the school to try to find something bad about the operations. I must say that after Sneaky Pete began to visit the school, wood for heating was provided by the County. Several years later, the Sawdust School building was moved to Greensboro and merged with the Salem Elementary School for black students. One weekend, I watched the moving company's preparation of our school for relocation.

I remember very little about the classes or curriculum during my years at the Sawdust School. My favorite subjects were whatever was being taught: probably reading, writing, and arithmetic— "the three R's" —in first through third grades plus history and maybe some civics in the sixth grade. The way the classrooms were set up worked great for me. I had the opportunity to learn what was being taught in four classes in the same room. I had a good memory; it was easy to learn things taught in each class. I skipped the fourth and fifth grades.

When I was in the second grade, President Franklin D. Roosevelt died. One day, our Principal, Professor Farmer, came from his classroom (grades five through nine) to our classroom (grades one through four). He wrote about ten names on the blackboard. He then began to ask different students, "Which of the men listed on the blackboard is the President of the United States?" None of them chose the correct name. When it was my turn, I chose Harry S. Truman, who had been Vice President for only about three months. I was six years old at that time. I believe my answer impressed Professor Farmer about my knowledge of current events. He had a subscription to *Time Magazine* and I read it when we were visiting with his wife Ms. Daisy at their house.

In Professor Farmer's classroom, I participated in the exercises assigned to the sixth grade. One time I solved a math problem on the blackboard and Samuel Gilliam said, "Your answer is wrong." I said that I didn't care because I knew my solution was correct. Samuel told Professor Farmer that I said that I didn't care. Professor sent me to the cloakroom for punishment. Samuel had had a similar experience when he told Deanna—a student in Professor Farmer's classroom for grades five through nine—that he did not care. Older students were jealous of my academic abilities; this was a chance for one of them to get me in trouble. I went to the cloakroom that morning and remained through the lunch period. In the afternoon, my sister Gladys, who was in the ninth grade, observed how long I had remained in the cloak room. She got angry with Professor Farmer and said, "You better let that boy out of the cloak room." He let me out without any comment to Gladys. We never told our parents.

I remember an incident when I entered the fifth grade in Professor Farmer's classroom. Amos was in the sixth grade. Students in the sixth grade were to purchase workbooks for some of their classes. Professor Farmer asked Amos about purchasing one. The workbook cost fifty cents—a lot of money in those days. Amos said that he was not going to buy it. Our cousin Alice Jordan had promised to give Amos her workbook. Professor Farmer punished Amos in the classroom without further questions. As I write this memoir, I am not sure whether Professor was getting a percentage of the sales for those workbooks. My parents were never informed about this incident either.

For children in my family during my early years, the curriculum for learning included more than taking formal classes at school. It included survival techniques. The family members and others taught us knowledge to survive with limited means in a rural community under Jim Crow. I learned from parents, grandparents, brothers, sisters, aunts, uncles, cousins, neighbors, and *Time* and *Popular Science* magazines. The lessons included planting, growing and harvesting farm crops, butchering pigs, home remedies for human and animals including castrating pigs, making wagons and popguns, making fishing lines, making outdoor clay stoves, slingshots, making traps to catch rabbits and birds, muddying ponds to catch fish, and catching fish in a large burlap sack in the ditch that prevented flooding on the farm.

As an engineer and scientist, I believe that it is important to provide details on activities in the non-academic curriculum during my early years in school. The three R's and non-academic curriculum provided me with knowledge to survive. Some details related to the things that I learned outside of the classroom follow.

I believe that I got along well with others in school. However, there were times when I believed that others, including Professor Farmer, treated Amos and me unfairly. For example, Amos gave our cousin Wallace "Bro" Ray a pocket knife for peeling sugar cane. It was routine for all boys to have knives to peel cane to chew. Pocket knives were also used for small tasks on the farm or around the house. Months after Amos gave Bro the knife, Bro got into a confrontation with an older student at Sawdust School. At the time, Bro happened to have the knife Amos had given him months earlier. To protect himself, Bro took out the knife. Other students told Professor that Amos gave Bro the knife. Professor Farmer did not ask the students about <u>when</u> Amos had given it to Bro. Professor Farmer merely assumed that Amos gave it to Bro specifically to confront the older student. He punished my brother on incomplete knowledge in front of everyone. This shaped my thoughts about how some adults can jump to conclusions that have negative impact on others. We did not tell our parents about the incident.

I had incidents with students at Sawdust School too. One student, whom I shall call "Big Guy," was on his bicycle riding fast toward the fence around the school grounds. When he approached the fence, his brakes did not work. When the bicycle hit the fence, he was flipped over the fence. He was not hurt but all of the students who observed the incident laughed. He ran around the fence, through the gate, and attacked me—I was the youngest boy there. He was at least three years older than I was. I bit him on his hand. He jerked and broke out one of my teeth. I feared that I had lost the tooth permanently. Fortunately it was a youth tooth that would grow back. Once I bit him he left me alone.

One Sunday morning, Amos and I were at the unpaved road that passes our property. The dirt road had "ruts" because car tracks were worn into it. As I was standing in one of the ruts, Big Guy was riding his bike. Clearly he intended to run over me if I did not move out of the rut, out of his way. When he got near me, I stepped out of the rut and he passed by. His first-cousin was riding behind. I stepped back into the rut. When his cousin tried to run over me, I stepped out of the rut again, grabbed his handlebars, and flipped him. Perhaps I was channeling my future knowledge of engineering? They ran home and came back with the cousin's younger brother to fight my younger brother. Well, my brother scored—and that was the end of that.

One evening, an event was going to take place at Sawdust School. Prior to the event, my cousin Charles and I had an altercation with the same two cousins in front of Aunt Carrie's house. I had Big Guy's cousin down and he said, "I know you have a knife. I dare you to take it out of your pocket." I took the knife out of my pocket. He then said "I dare you to open the blade." *When I was growing up, ignoring a dare was a sign of being weak or a coward.* So I opened the blade. While I had his cousin down, Big Guy jumped on me and got scratched by the knife. That was enough for them to leave. We knew that they would go home and get others to come after Charles and me, so we decided to wait and go with the older people to the event at Sawdust School.

Big Guy and his cousin tried everything to best us. If they could not beat us at every game, they tried to get their dogs to beat our dogs. One time they brought their dogs on our farm to attack our dog. We had a bull terrier named Glad. When they sent their dogs to attack him, Glad sent both of their dogs on a run. Glad had already hunted and chased black bear and panther in Liberty and Franklin Counties in Florida; two "sooner" mixed-breed dogs were no match for him. This was the last time that I had confrontations with those two guys.

Big Guy and his cousin told their parents about all confrontations that they had with others.

The father of Big Guy's cousin was a man I shall call "BEA." He transported moonshine and sold it at his house. He had threatened me by saying that he was gathering support from people in the community to send me to reform school, a penal institution for teenagers, because of incidents with his son and nephew. But those boys were two-and-a-half to

School Years

three years older than me, and I was less than eight years old at the time. Obviously BEA did not gather support.

In August 1948, when I was only nine years old, Amos and I were scheduled to transfer to school in Quincy. Earlier in the summer, BEA said to me, "Them boys in town ain't going to take the stuff that you have being doing here in Sawdust. They are going to kick your tail." I was afraid throughout the summer of what was going to happen to me during the next school term, but I never told my father or mother what BEA said.

Well, Big Guy and his cousin succeeded in one way—because BEA had caused me to worry about my safety in the upcoming school year.

I must say that I was able to take care of myself at school in Quincy. The boys in Quincy were no more aggressive than those in Sawdust. I had learned how to handle aggressive boys in Sawdust: fight back.

In later years, I learned that Big Guy and his cousin were my distant cousins, one on my father's side and the other on my mother's side. In fact, we became good friends when I was in middle school.

I learned about farming from my father. Planting, growing, and harvesting farm crops included a lot of physical labor and intensive work. I learned those things from watching my father and helping him plant, cultivate, and harvest the crops. This included how to prepare the fields for planting, what fertilizers to use for different crops, how to till the soil during growing season, and how and when to harvest the crop. The field had to be prepared for planting in late winter. The *Farmers' Almanac* was used to find the best time to plant different crops.

The first step was "breaking the field." This meant turning old vegetation from the previous year underground. My father used either a turning plow or harrow with discs. He divided the farm into approximately rectangular areas and chose which ones to break ground with the turning plow and which ones with the harrow. The turning plow was a large plow that shoveled soil to the right and was pulled by two mules. My father began on the outside of a designated area and plowed around the area until he completed the middle. He had to walk behind and hold the plow. This was physically intensive. On the other hand, the harrow, which had rows of circular discs, was pulled by two mules and he could ride. The harrow was used only in areas for planting oats, for turning in manure and mixing it into the ground after it had been spread across the field, and for breaking up thick clumpy soil on "new ground" that had been cleared of trees, bushes, roots and shrubs—ground that had not been planted before.

The next step was to plant the crops. This included three operations: making the rows to plant seeds with a middle buster plow; spreading fertilizer with a distributer; and planting the seeds with a seed planter. The middle buster was a plow that shoveled soil to the right and left as it was being pulled through the soil. The fertilizer distributer had knobs on the wheel that caused the distributer to vibrate and spread fertilizer based on the setting. The planter had gears driven by the wheel to allow the seeds to be planted at the desired distance apart. The planter also had internal plates for picking up seeds. The plates could be changed based on the size of the seeds being planted.

I learned which fertilizers to use for each crop. For most crops, we used 3-8-5, the percentage of nitrogen, phosphorus and potassium (N-P-K) in each bag of fertilizer; the remainder was filler materials. We used N-P-K values 4-10-6 and 5-10-5 for crops such as tobacco and cotton. After the planting, we turned the soil with plows made for specific purposes, such as for mixing more fertilizer into the soil, and for breaking up packed or crusted soil. We used a mule-drawn cultivator to plow the fields for controlling weeds and for banking more soil as needed against the growing plants. We could ride on the cultivator.

I learned how to butcher the hogs raised on the farm as well as animals that we hunted or trapped. The butchering of hogs took place during the winter when there were no flies, gnats, or mosquitoes. Colder weather also helped to cool the meat and keep it from spoiling. Butchering hogs was labor intensive; one man could not do it alone. Hogs weighing 120 pounds or more had to be lifted and hung on a beam attached to six-foot-tall poles in the ground. Relatives and neighbors helped each other during the butchering. Aunt Addie's husband, Uncle Esau, came from Gainesville each year to help my father. When adult relatives came to visit, the children gave up their beds and slept on the floor, on a home-made bed called a "pallet."

Slaughtering and butchering hogs began early in the morning and lasted until late in the night. First the hogs were slaughtered and blood drained from their bodies. When I was able to fire a 0.22 caliber rifle accurately, I helped my father butcher the hogs. We took the wagon over the field to slaughter the hogs. I shot the hog in the head above the eyes and my father stabbed it to drain the blood. We loaded the hog and continued the process until we had slaughtered all we wanted to butcher that day. The hogs were taken to near our house for butchering.

The blood was one product that was wasted—we never made blood pudding or blood sausage. After the hogs were slaughtered, they were placed in hot water in a large diameter cast iron pot for preparation to remove the hair. Fresh clippings from pine trees were used to test the temperature of the water. Once the water was hot enough, the hog was placed into the hot water and turned over several times while checking how easy it was to remove the hair. The hog was then removed from the hot bath and everyone began to remove the hair from the body. A variety of tools were used—hands; knives; Mason jar rings that held the lids; and a special tool made for removing hair from a hog. I used my fingers on both hands.

Once the hair was removed, a knife was used to slit the foot, exposing the strong muscle. The men then used a wooden homemade oak bar about an inch-and-a-half in diameter and one and one-half to two-feet long, sharpened on each end, to slide between the muscle and feet. The hog was lifted and hung on the beam by the oak bar. The process was repeated until the hair was removed from all hogs slaughtered that day.

Meanwhile, the first hog hanging on the beam was being butchered by my father. He did all of the butchering. First, he placed a corn cob up the anus into the rectum of the hog to prevent waste from the large intestines getting on the meat. Once its intestines and organs were removed, the hog was placed on a table and the body was cut into the appropriate sections: hams, shoulders, bellies or middling meat, backbones or pork chops, feet, heads, etc. Then the women trimmed the fat and other meat from the major cuts to make lard as well as sausage. The children who were old enough—Gladys and Ruby—washed the intestines to be used for sausage casings and chitterlings. A hole was dug in the ground in the field to bury the waste from the intestines. I watched them washing the intestines in the field, and I must say that they probably buried as many intestines in that hole as they washed, and our parents probably knew that. Cleaning the chitterlings in the field and burying the waste there took the smell away from near the house where the main butchering was taking place.

The major cuts of meat were taken to the cold storage to salt cure for forty days. The fat was cooked in large cast iron wash pots in the yard, heated by a wood fire. It was called a wash pot probably because it had other uses. It was used every week to heat water to soak and wash clothes. It was used to make soap using lard or tallow from cows and lye. The lye soap was used to wash work clothes. The wash pot was also used to fry fish and to cook perlau, a dish made with rice and meats such as chicken or squirrel. Every black family in the Sawdust Community had at least one wash pot and we had two. These pots were well seasoned inside and black on the outside from years of use—thus no rust.

The lard was strained through the cloth of clean flour sacks into new lard cans and would be used for cooking food during the coming year. The cracklings and pork skins from cooking the fat were stored in used lard cans to be eaten later and to make crackling bread.

We ate brains and eggs for breakfast during the hog butchering. The next morning after butchering, the sausage meat was ground by a small hand grinding machine, seasoned and stuffed into the casings made from the small intestines that had been prepared by scraping the fat from them. The machine had an attachment to stuff the casings for the sausages. The sausages were hung in the smoke house to cure. Heads, feet and tails were cooked to make hog head cheese. Some of the pig feet were used to make pickled pig feet. My mother also used her pressure cooker to preserve ("can") in Mason jars much of the meat that would spoil if not frozen.

Neighbors and relatives were given generous portions of meat called messes. A mess was an undetermined unit of measurement. They would be given a mess of pig feet or other parts which included tenderloin, organs (livers, brains, hearts, sweet breads, and lungs), backbones, etc, that did not go to the cold storage. The cold storage or ice plant was a privately owned facility in Quincy where farmers paid to have their meat cured for a period of time, forty days.

Hog butchering was a two-to-three-day operation and nothing was wasted except blood. There was a saying: **We use everything from the rooter to the tooter.** Next I discuss home remedies that I learned on the farm.

We had home remedies for both animals and human. For farm animal care, a veterinarian was only used to vaccinate the hogs against known outbreaks of diseases each year. Home remedies were used to prevent infections during the castration of pigs. After their testicles were removed, used motor oil was applied to the cut area to prevent infection. For other animals such as mules and dogs, we used home remedies to take care of symptoms. The mules at times would break out of their stable, eat too much green stuff growing on the farm, and get sick. My father used a mixture of Kerosene and salt and forced the mules to swallow it. It worked.

At times our dogs came down with distemper (a viral disease). I learned to treat it with tar drawn from fatwood, called "lighter'd" (wood from the heartwood of pine trees). I took a gallon can and filled it with chips from the lighter'd, dug a hole in the ground, placed another smaller can down into the hole to catch the tar, and placed the chip-filled gallon can upside-down at ground level over the hole. Then I piled damp soil around the gallon can and built a fire around it. When this process was completed, the chips in the gallon can were charcoal and the smaller can in the ground contained the tar from the lighter'd. The tar was rubbed on the dog's head to cure him. It worked.

Home remedies for humans included remedies for cuts, insect stings, colds, croup, constipation, infections, and poison ivy. For small cuts, spider webs were used to stop the bleeding. It may be that the pressure that was used to hold the spider web was strong enough alone to stop the bleeding. For ant bites and insect stings, Grandma dipped Railroad Mills Snuff from a small "bladder," a thin-skinned holder that she carried in her purse, and rubbed the freshly dipped snuff on the insect bite. *Dipping snuff—placing a small amount of powdered tobacco between the teeth and lower lip—was a somewhat common habit, especially among women. Men used chewing tobacco.*

For coughs, croup or other respiratory illnesses, we were treated with Vicks salve, cough syrup, cough drops, or camphor. The Vicks salve or camphor was rubbed on the chest prior to going to bed. We also drank sassafras tea, made from the roots of the sassafras bush that grew wild through the region, and sweetened with molasses made on the farm.

For intestinal problems such as constipation, prune juice, mineral oil or castor oil was used. The castor oil was the most unpleasant thing I have ever tasted; it was mixed with orange juice to mitigate the taste. It still tasted terrible. Every time I drank plain orange juice, I thought of that castor oil and could taste it.

Tobacco poultices were used to treat infections and boils, to relieve inflammation or pain, to draw the poison from a bee sting, and to hasten the flow of pus from an infected area. The poultice was made with cured tobacco leaves that were contained in a thin cloth holder. The poultice was heated and moistened with hot water and applied to the infected area. The poultice was reheated after a few hours or when it dried out.

The treatment for poison ivy was a paste made from gunpowder and milk. I was very allergic to poison ivy so I learned how to make my own treatment. I would open shotgun shells for gunpowder and mix it with milk, make the paste, and apply it to the affected area of my body. It worked as well as treatments developed today by drug companies. *Amos said that I was so allergic to poison ivy that if someone said the words poison ivy I would break out with the symptoms.* Psychologically, my brother's statement may be true.

Other home remedies included corn shuck tea to treat chicken pox, sardines to treat mumps, and hog hoof tea to treat measles. For hiccups we were told to hold your breath and drink water. Aloe Vera—the "medicine plant"—is one home remedy that I use for burns and cuts today.

I also learned to make my own toys and other things to survive with limited resources. I learned to make wagons, popguns, slingshots, baseballs, and traps to catch birds and rabbits from my third-cousin Jesse Campbell.

To make the wagon, we used materials found on the farm such as iron rods, boards, and pine trees. Young children could ride in the wagons that I built.

I made popguns from elderberry bushes and a board that was carved to make the staff for propelling the china berry used for the shot. The elderberry bush had a cork-like filling in its center that could be removed to leave a circular hole similar to a rifle barrel. We cut a section of elderberry about a foot and a half long for the gun barrel and removed the filling. Then a wooden board was trimmed into a cylindrical shaft the size of the hole in the elderberry gun barrel and a handle was built onto this for propelling the china berry. The shaft was made so that it could push a china berry only about two or three inches from the end of the barrel. The first china berry stayed in the barrel. The second china berry, when placed in the barrel and pushed by the shaft, compressed the air to a pressure sufficient to force the first china berry to accelerate out of the barrel, similar to a gas powered gun. When the first china berry exited the barrel, the air reached sonic speed and you would hear a pop, thus "popgun." Bamboo was also used for popgun barrels as it also has a hollow interior.

The first thing in making a slingshot was to find a perfect Y-shaped staff from trees or bushes grown on the farm. It could take hours of searching to find an acceptable staff. Once the staff was found, the bark was removed and the two sides of the Y were cut to allow you to tie wide rubber bands to each side of the Y. The rubber bands provided the energy to propel the projectors, which were small rocks. The holder for the projectile that was attached to the other ends of the two rubber bands was made of leather from the tongue of an old worn-out shoe. The wide rubber band was cut from worn-out inner tubes of car tires; all tires had rubber inner tubes during the 1940s.

I was taught how to make two kinds of traps to catch birds: a wooden trap and a trap made out of chicken wire. The wooden trap was also used to catch rabbits. The wooden trap was about fourteen inches wide, about eighteen inches long, and about a foot high. Thin boards approximately one inch wide by one half inch deep were used to build a rectangular box (the trap) from bottom to top to the desired height. First, two boards were placed lengthwise. Next, boards the width of the trap were nailed to the end of the lengthwise boards to make a rectangle. The process continued until a rectangular box was built to the desired height. Thin boards then covered the top of the box (trap). To use the wooden trap to catch rabbits, a piece of tin the size of the open bottom of the wooden trap was attached to the back of the bottom of the trap to prevent the rabbits from digging their way out after the trap was sprung. The trigger to spring the trap was a three-piece mechanism—a kickstand to hold the front above the ground, a flipper over the kickstand on which the front of the trap rested, and a long trigger that held the bait. A sweet potato was used as bait to catch a rabbit. Shelled corn placed on the long trigger was used as bait to catch birds in my wooden trap.

The trap made from chicken wire was about two feet long, about one and one half feet wide, and about eight to ten inches high. The sides, front and back and top were all chicken wire. There was an opening in the middle of the front of the trap with a chute that led about eight inches into the trap. Shelled dry corn was used as bait. This trap was used to catch quail. Once the birds entered the trap through the chute, they would not leave through the open chute because they would try to leave through a corner in the trap. We would catch a half dozen or more quail at one time in this trap.

Amos and I made our own fishing lines with number-eight black thread used for sewing. We took a length twice the length of the line that we wanted and held the thread tight, and then twisted the line in opposite directions. Then we brought the two ends of the thread together and I climbed to the top of the roof on the porch and held the line to allow it to twist into a strong fishing line.

At an early age, I read a lot of things in my favorite magazine *Popular Science* that encouraged my interest in science and engineering. I learned to make clay stoves from reading *Popular Science*. Basically, Amos and I made pottery without a kiln. The clay was formed around wood into the design that we wanted, including a stove that had eyes on the top as well as a chimney. The wood was then burned and the clay hardened—and I had my clay stove. Amos and I built it away from the house at the old sugar mill. Now that it was ready, we made a small fire on the ground and placed the clave stove over it; the eyes became heated and smoke came out of the chimney. We tested it by boiling peanuts in a metal can. However, we were not allowed to harvest peanuts until my father said that they were ready. With our clay stove, Amos and I could gather peanuts whenever we decided to, and cook them away from our house.

From my cousin Jesse Campbell, I learned to make my own baseball when I was seven or eight years old. All farmers in Sawdust who were involved in growing shade tobacco had special thread for sewing cheese cloth over the tobacco fields, looping and stringing tobacco. I would find a pebble or rock about an inch or more in diameter, stringing or looping tobacco thread, a tobacco stringing needle, and leather tongues from worn out shoes or brogans. I used these materials to make the ball.

The most challenging part of making a baseball was finding a pebble or rock with a nearly spherical shape. I searched in the area on our farm that had rocks and pebbles and in the area at the crossing on Juniper Creek about one-half mile southeast behind our property where Amos and I fished. The crossing had rocks eroded by the flowing water in the creek. Once a satisfactory pebble or rock was found, the process of making the baseball began.

Having assembled all materials, I sewed a leather cover tightly around the pebble to anchor my wrapping (winding) thread.

I cut a long length of thread to be used for stitching to hold the layers of wound thread in place.

I threaded the needle with the thread from the roll of tobacco stringing thread. To make sure that there was enough thread for all wrappings of thread to make the ball without having to cut and re-tie the wrapping thread, I did not cut the thread from the roll of stringing tobacco thread.

I sewed the wrapping thread to the leather cover around the pebble as an anchor to hold the thread on the roll of tobacco thread, tied the thread to the leather anchor, and removed the needle.

I threaded the needle with the long length of thread for stitching to prevent unraveling.

I wrapped a layer of wrapping thread tightly around the rock and stitched it in many places to hold that layer and continue wrapping layers around the previous layer of thread, stitching after each layer to hold the wrapping thread tightly to prevent unraveling.

Each stitch was tied to hold the thread in place. The wrapping was done in a winding manner to assure a spherical outcome of each layer.

This process continued until I had a baseball of the size that I wanted. Numerous stitches were made until I was satisfied that the thread would hold together without unraveling when my homemade baseball was used. The leather shoe tongues were cut into strips that could be sewn tightly around the ball. My ball was finished and ready for testing and use.

We also made homemade bats from oak wood or boards found on the farm. I used my pocket knife for carving the wood.

Professor Farmer participated in many of the games that boys played at Sawdust School, including baseball. He knew that I had a homemade ball and wanted me to bring it to school, or he would ask me to go home to get it. Some of those boys were fourteen to sixteen years old. I was probably seven or eight years old at most at that time. One time Professor asked me to go home during the lunch period to get my ball, but I was not allowed to play when I returned. After that, I did not bring it to school because I would not be allowed to play with my own ball. I believe that Professor was frustrated with me because I never brought it to the school again.

In writing this section, I am reminded of the importance of games and play in the lives of children. These games brought enjoyment, the thrill of winning, the downer of losing. They were a normalcy in our childhood in Sawdust as we learned to navigate life in the Jim Crow South. I thought of how I learned to enjoy life with very limited means—design and build things we were unable to purchase and repair things that we could not afford to pay someone else to do. I had a curiosity about how things worked when I was growing up. I even learned to repair the New Departure Coaster Brakes on my Western Flyer bicycle.

In so much of what I did in play, just as in working on the farm, I see that I had talent, or what one might call a "natural bent" for engineering. I had a curiosity about how things worked, and as I have described, I enjoyed making things: sling shots, fishing lines, bird traps, baseballs, gourd bird nests, and treatment for poison ivy, poultices, and a tar solution to cure distemper in out dogs.

Looking back, I have no doubt that the skills and hands-on experience I acquired growing up on the farm—including through play, skills such as leadership, team work, and ways of learning—served me well in the earning of three engineering degrees and in my long career of more than forty years in the engineering field.

My non-academic curriculum taught me numerous things including non-traditional ways to catch fish, paying attention to details, and having patience. Discussions follow.

There were several ponds that contained fish in my community in Sawdust. Amos and I would go fishing with Mr. Willie Campbell. As the water in those ponds got to low levels, Mr. Willie would say it was time to muddy that pond. Those participating in muddying were Mr. Willie and the young children in our family. We would go into that pond with sticks and whatever we could use to muddy the water. The fish would come to the surface and we would catch them by hand. We probably caught a washtub full of fish. Mr. Willie must have studied the weather patterns because within the next day or two, it would rain which brought the water in the ponds to levels that would sustain the remaining fish in that pond.

We also fished in a ditch that used to prevent flooding. A large ditch that I call the main ditch was dug to prevent flooding from the Cypress Pond of four major properties during major thunder storms or hurricanes. The Cypress Pond was always full of water throughout the year during the 1940s and 1950s. The properties that were subjected to flooding were Mr. Willie's farm, the Sawdust School grounds, the Thigpen family farm, and the Strom farm adjacent to the east side of the Thigpen family farm.

There were two small ponds on our farm that overflowed during major storms. Ditches were dug to drain water during a storm to prevent flooding. The water flowed from the first pond through a ditch into the second pond. The water from the second pond flowed through a second ditch to a wooded area on our farm where the ditch ended. The water then flowed into the southern end of the main ditch between two waterfalls near the Strom farm. All of this water entered a pond in a wooded area on the Strom place that we occasionally would muddy. The overflowing water from the pond would end up in Juniper Creek.

Cypress Pond was not the source of Juniper Creek. As is the case with all flooding, water flows from high ground to lower levels and in this case it was Juniper Creek. The main ditch had two waterfalls— a vertical stream of water that falls over the edge of a steep place. The first waterfall had a vertical drop of four to six feet and the second waterfall had a vertical drop of two to three feet.

I learned about catching fish in a large burlap sack in the main ditch from my first cousin Willie Mae Gunn and my oldest sister Leatrice. We walked to the ditch one Sunday afternoon and Willie Mae said that we should get a burlap sack to catch fish. One of us would stand in the sack with his or her feet spread apart to hold down the bottom of the opening to the sack; his or her hands would hold the top of the opening to allow fish to enter. Others would get in the water some distance from the opening of the sack and use their feet and sticks to drive the fish into the sack. Catching fish in the ditch in a sack was fun; everyone wanted to hold the sack.

On one occasion, Ruby, Gladys, Amos, and I were fishing below the lower waterfall and it was my turn to hold the sack. Everyone else got into the water, and used sticks and their feet to drive fish into the sack. We pulled the sack out of the water and held it open to see what we had caught. Sure, we had caught fish but a snake was also in the sack. We dropped the sack and the four of us climbed up a tie-dye tree and watched our sack until the snake crawled out. Then we took our fish and went home.

Several questions about those ditches and ditch fishing still reside in my mind as I write this autobiography. These questions concern the starting point—the location of the original water source for the fish that we caught.

Where did those fish come from to end up in the ditch?

Did they come from Cypress Pond?

Did they travel upstream from the pond at the southern end of the ditch?

Did they come from the second pond on our farm behind the sugar mill?

It is difficult to say that the fish came from the Cypress Pond because we never saw or caught fish north of the first waterfall. Mr. Willie placed a wire fish trap in a culvert under the road to allow water to flow from Cypress Pond through the main ditch and there were never any fish in that trap. If the fish came from the pond at the southern end of the ditch, they would have to swim upstream where most of the fish were caught in our sacks.

Mr. Willie said that the fish could have come from the lower pond at the end of the ditch. They would have traveled upstream like salmon and scaled waterfalls. This means that they continued to the upper waterfalls which they could not overcome. As I look back on this, I might have been the only kid who was curious about the source. It was a mystery that I <u>needed</u> to solve, perhaps as a precursor to my pursuit of engineering. Other than my father, I considered Mr. Willie and his youngest son, Jesse Campbell, to be mentors regarding what I needed to know about life on the farm. Jesse was an all-around Handy Man.

On some Sundays, my cousin Charles, my brother Amos, and I would go fishing on Juniper Creek. However, we never took fish home because our parents did not allow fishing on Sunday. One Sunday we were at Juniper Creek back of Harris Harden's house where there was a small pond. I stepped in quicksand next to the pond and could not get out. Charles came to help me and also got stuck. There was no panic because we probably got stuck in mud or some other difficult situation before this incident and were successful with team work. Amos then went and got a piece of wood (or a tree limb) and passed it to us and pulled us out of the quicksand. I learned to be careful and observe the surroundings in sandy areas near water; it could be quicksand.

Our chickens ran around the yard during the daytime. Hawks would swoop down and take the chickens. Mr. Willie told me about small birds called martins that chased chicken hawks. He taught me how to build nests for the birds using dried thick skin melons that we called gourds. I cut down a tall skinny pine tree for a tall pole and nailed a board at the top to hang my two gourds with the nests for the martins. I dug a hole with our post-hole digger to place the pole with the nests high in the air. I asked Amos to help me place the pole in the hole, but he said that he had something else to do.

I had very short patience at that time and tried to complete the job myself. I almost got the bottom of the pole planted but it was too heavy. The pole fell and broke my gourds with the bird nests inside. My first thought was Amos should have helped me plant the pole. I found no more gourds on the farm for bird nests and my project ended. I learned not expect significant accomplishments immediately. Take responsibility for my own actions—I should have waited for help to plant the pole.

Mr. Willie would play practical jokes on you if you allowed him to do it. The first one he tried on me was a Snipe Hunt. In this prank, he gave me an impossible task. We would go hunting for a bird at night and he would give me a pillow case to catch the snipe "bird." I was supposed to go into the woods with him, and he and others would drive the bird to me to catch in the pillow case. Well, I knew that birds roosted at night and this would be stupid and a wasted effort on my part. I did not join him in any Snipe Hunt. I think the hunt was a way to test young boys on their ability to think for themselves and become ready to join the group of older people.

However, there was another practical joke by Mr. Willie that I fell for. During the winter, hundreds to thousands of robins feasted on our farm and other farms in the area. We ate birds of many species including robins. Mr. Willie said that, to catch a robin, all you had to do was sprinkle salt on its tail. That sounded to be a simple task with so many robins feeding on our farm. I wasted much of my mother's salt throwing at them and knew that some had landed on those tails. Then I analyzed what the problem was. If I got close enough to sprinkle salt on the bird's tail, I could catch it by hand. I never told Mr. Willie about his successful prank.

LESSONS: Pay attention to details and analyze the situation or problem. Thanks to Mr. Willie, I have carried these lessons throughout my life.

I attended Sawdust School for four years and completed the sixth grade. I entered the seventh grade at Stevens School in Quincy in the fall of 1948. Stevens was an all-black school.

In 1949, after I completed the seventh grade at Stevens School, black students in the seventh and eighth grades in all rural communities in Gadsden County were transferred to Stevens School.

Stevens School was approximately ten miles away from our farm in Sawdust. When starting my first year at Stevens in seventh grade, there were no buses to take us to school. My father would take Ruby, Gladys, Amos, and me in the morning and we would have to wait at the house of Lucius and Lizzy Jenkins after school until my father could come to take us home after he finished his farm work. Lucius Jenkins was the person who delivered ice to our house every other day from an ice plant in Quincy.

A school bus passed our farm carrying white children to the school in Greensboro, three miles away from our farm, with only two or three kids on it every day. We were not allowed to attend that school. The schools were not integrated in Gadsden County until 1970 following a riot by blacks fighting for equal rights including employment.

The county had built an addition to Stevens School that was not completed when the school year began in 1948, when I started there. There was no heating system nor were any desks in these new classrooms. We had to sit on boards that were supported by concrete blocks. Later the heating ducts were completed, desks were placed in the classrooms, and the county provided one bus to transport students from Sawdust and Greensboro. The same bus had to drop off students from Sawdust and Greensboro and then go to East Quincy to pickup students to take to Stevens School. The reverse happened in the evening. We had to wait until the bus took the students from East Quincy home, and then come back to take the students from Sawdust and Greensboro home. Thus we had to leave home very early in the morning and arrived home late in the evening compared to other students.

School Years

There were not enough seats on the bus for everyone, so some students ran to get in line when they saw the bus coming and others stood in line and waited about a half hour to get a seat. I was ten years old, the youngest student riding the bus, but I did not have to worry. Amanda Rolax, a senior in high school, was the bus driver's daughter and always sat in the seat behind her father, Pierce "Mr. Sonboy" Rolax. Amanda would save the seat for me next to her and no one challenged her.

Amanda was a truly good friend. Years later—eleven years after that first year of the school bus rides to Stevens—she influenced me to attend college instead of returning to active duty in the Army from the Army Reserves in 1959. I had already signed up to go back to active duty when I talked to her. As a result, I sent an application to attend college at Florida A&M University instead.

The curriculum when I entered Stevens School in the seventh grade included mathematics, health, geography, home economics, and probably English. My registration showed that I had completed the fifth and sixth grade in the same year. The mathematics teacher, Ms. Pittman, questioned my ability to succeed. I thought to myself: I will show her who will be the most successful student in this class—and I was indeed the best student in her class! I attended the other classes without any comments regarding my ability. My cousin Samuel Gilliam and my brother Amos had the same courses and schedule.

In the middle of our first week at Stevens, Samuel said that he was not going to take home economics and went to the Agriculture Building. Mr. McPherson allowed him to join his agriculture class. The following Friday, Amos left the home economics class and Mr. McPherson allowed him into his class too. The next Monday, I thought, "I am not going to stay here in home economics class by myself" and went to the Agriculture Building to join them. However, Mr. McPherson said that he had no room for another student and that I should check with Professor LaSalle D. Leffall, Sr. Professor Leffall accepted me into his classroom in the seventh grade. Why did the three of us leave the home economics class? Because we had been taught that sewing, cooking and taking care of housework was women's work. We would not have any part of it!

Led by Samuel, we were the first students to take any action on that subject at Stevens. There were other times when we followed and listened to him too. However, Samuel dropped out of school after the seventh grade and moved to his grandfather Harry Gilliam's house. I believe he moved there because he had problems getting along with his stepfather. Later, as a young teenager, Samuel moved to Tallahassee. I never saw him in Sawdust again, but I did see him in Tallahassee a few times.

My sister Gladys left Sawdust School and attended Stevens High in 1948, the same year as I did. She was in the tenth grade and her curriculum included a course in biology. She had an assignment to identify and name the bones in a frog. This meant that a frog had to be prepared to show all of its bones to identify and discuss. Gladys discussed her assignment with Amos and me. We decided to carefully boil a frog and strip the meat from it. This would show all of the bones and she could identify and discuss them. Amos and I caught a live toad frog, boiled it, and carefully removed the meat to show only the bones. We gave the skeleton to Gladys for her project.

I remained a student in Professor Leffall's agriculture class for a few years. His classroom was more of a shop than an ordinary classroom like others at Stevens School. This room had all types of boards and equipment to do construction projects and the shop had a large pot belly wood burning stove to heat the room in the winter.

When I was in the eighth grade, we built a wall around the large playground on the north side of the school buildings. Each agriculture class participated in building the wall during their one-hour class period. Prior to the wall, all major sports such as football and basketball were open to the public. The wall allowed the school to charge admission for these events.

Additional projects in which I participated included taking shrubs from wooded areas and planting them around the school buildings, growing a garden on the property where St. James AME Church is now located. We also raised chickens for the Father-Son Banquet. Amos and I worked on the preparation of the chickens for the banquet but the two of us and our father never attended one because we did not have transportation at night to get to Stevens School.

Black students taking courses in agriculture became members of the New Farmers of America (NFA). This shows the emphasis on farming for youth at that time. Many of the NFA members were also members of the 4-H Club that emphasized farming under different leadership.

Soon after I entered Stevens in the seventh grade, I earned a reputation as the most clever, "smartest boy" in the class. I was a target of many students because of my intellect.

The eighth grade was my most challenging year in school. I was eleven years old. The challenges were due in part to jealously from other students—especially because there were sixteen-year-old students in the eighth grade.

One day I was in Professor Leffall's Shop classroom alone when one older student, whom I did not know, came into the shop. He said, "You think you are so smart," and pushed me. The back of my right hand hit the hot wood burning stove that heated the room. I walked back to one of the tables that had short pieces of pine boards with knots. The boards were about one-inch-by-one-inch in cross-section and about three feet long. I picked up one and hit him across the face hard enough to break the board at one of the knots. He left the room and never confronted me again. The burn mark is still on the back of my hand more than seventy years later.

At other times, a group of students would tell lies about me. The teachers believed them and I was punished.

One time a student said that someone had stolen his paper; my friend was blamed. The students said that my friend would steal paper and I kept it for him. My friend was a great marble shooter and I kept marbles for him that he won during the games.

My friend and I found out who took the paper and reported it to the Professor. The culprit confessed that he had taken the paper that was left under a desk after the change of that classroom for the next course (we changed classrooms for each course hourly). However, my friend and I had to suffer the punishment along with the culprit sentenced by the Principal. The punishment was scrubbing walls each day at lunch time for a week on the elementary side of Stevens School.

The students, some whom I thought I had a good relationship with, had lied and enjoyed the fact that I was punished. They had fun embellishing my punishment and telling jokes about me and the Sawdust Community.

Why did I keep marbles for my friend?

Students played "shot" marbles for keeps during the lunch hour. You kept all marbles that you won in this game. It was called "First to Go You" which meant that you got the first shot if someone accepted your challenge. Others were allowed to enter the game and all who entered placed their marbles in the pit (a hole dug in the ground). You could shoot with anything that you preferred including the toy (large shooting marble) that came in the pack of marbles you purchased, or you could use small and large steel ball bearings. There were students who were very good shooting marbles with the toy that they chose.

My friend used a large steel ball bearing and was a winner in most of the games. He asked me to keep his winnings after each game. Several of these games took place during the lunch period. I believe that the students who lied were also trying to punish my friend for winning their marbles.

Another incident where students lied occurred in Mr. Montgomery's class. He was our eighth grade science teacher and also the football coach at Stevens. He later became the football coach at Florida A&M University.

There were students talking in class when he was lecturing. He turned from the blackboard and asked who was talking. Some of them pointed to me and my distant cousin Charles Holt. Although I was not interrupting the lecture, I was punished. Mr. Montgomery sent a student to borrow Ms. Jiles' paddle. Ms. Jiles, the health teacher, had a beautiful paddle carved out of pine wood and stained. Yes, corporal punishment was allowed in those days.

I was the first to be punished. I held out my right hand, Mr. Montgomery hit me, and the paddle split. There was no punishment for Charles because the paddle had split. The male students had won against me once more with their lies. They had so much fun about the fact that the paddle had split on my hand. Actually, the paddle did not hurt my hand.

There were numerous other incidents where I was the target of students conspiring to get me in trouble in the eighth grade.

Another classroom incident during the fall of 1949 also gave the students fun. Professor Leffall asked me personal questions related to the number of animals on our farm. However, his questions had no relationship to the number of animals on our farm and failed to elicit correct information.

At that time, I had only one hog that I was going to sell to buy myself a bicycle for Christmas. Aunt Carrie Gunn had given Amos and me one pig each from a litter of pigs. I had a female and Amos had a male and I swapped with Amos under the condition that he would give me a pig from each litter born from the female. Professor Leffall asked, "How many chickens do you have?" and I replied, "None." He asked, "How many cows do you have?" Again, I replied, "None." He asked, "How many hogs do you have?" and I said, "One." Professor Leffall then said, "You have a farm and no chickens, no cows, and only one hog." All of the students laughed. However, the way I saw it, I did not own a farm. My father was the farmer who owned the animals. One Sunday after that, Mr. McPherson brought a group of agriculture students from our class on a wide-bed truck to our farm and they saw all of our farm animals. I always wonder if the students thought that I was lying to Professor Leffall.

I now believe that Professor Leffall thought highly of our farm and was trying to showcase our farm because I had given him many things that we grew. He would say, "Thigpen, bring me some taters (sweet potatoes)" or "Bring me some frog legs," etc. I never took him frog legs although bull frogs were plentiful in Sawdust in Cypress Pond. I did not know how to prepare frog legs and no one in Sawdust, that I knew, prepared and ate frog legs. Professor Leffall's questions showed that adults must be specific when they ask questions of young children because the children are going to be literal and answer directly.

The other reason for my eighth grade being so challenging was that, in the spring of 1950, my father was in the hospital in Donaldsonville, Georgia. Amos and I had to stay out of school for more than a week to work on the farm. We had to work on our own farm as well as one that we sharecropped.

There was a hospital in Quincy but it may not have accepted blacks at that time. My mother went to Donaldsonville, Georgia, with my father and stayed there during the time my father was convalescing from the removal of a kidney.

My mother never smoked but when she returned from Donaldsonville, she was smoking Lucky Strike cigarettes. She later quit smoking after she got back home. My mother met a cousin on her father's side for the first time, Hazel Ray Rambeau, who worked at the hospital. They had no more contact until 2006 when Hazel's grandson contacted my mother while he was visiting in Quincy. I believe Hazel had six children, and I met some of the family at my mother's funeral in September 2006. My sister Isabel and the Rays still remain in contact with each other.

Our cousin Robert Rolax, a World War II Veteran who served in Germany, supervised the work on the farm while my father was away. He told Amos and me what to do each day and then left to do his own farm work. We had to plow the fields and, because we were so young, Amos held the plow and I held the lines to drive the mules that pulled the plow. We worked the farm six days one week.

When I returned to school, I felt lost in the science class. To make matters worse, we had an exam and I made a C, the lowest grade that I had ever made in a science class. However, being absent for a straight week did not affect my grades in other classes because I could memorize poems or short passages after reading them a few times. We had an assignment to memorize Lincoln's "Gettysburg Address." I was able to memorize it one Sunday night at Aunt Carrie's house where we stayed while my parents were in Donaldsonville.

There were two interesting things in the eighth grade related to my history and geography classes.

My history teacher, Ms. Johnson, was from Jacksonville, Florida. She talked about current issues and topics which she believed successful black people considered important. Ms. Johnson said that they drove Cadillac cars and wore suits and ties. She required boys to wear ties to her classroom. Stevens School did not require ties.

I remember the night that Amos and I learned how to tie a man's tie. After Ms. Johnson's class, we would remove our tie. One time she scolded Elijah, a classmate, because he had not combed his hair. Elijah responded immediately with "Shucks, Ms. Johnson, that's Northern Straw, good hair." The next year, Ms. Johnson was not on the faculty because either (a) she found a position elsewhere or (b) many students had complained, their parents got involved, and her appointment was not renewed.

I excelled in the geography class from Mr. Gibbs. Later, in the spring semester of 1950, he was teaching a class to graduating seniors. He must have been discussing geography around the world and was disappointed with their performance. He sent someone to my classroom to bring me to his senior class to answer questions that they could not answer. He obviously had great confidence in my ability. When I entered his classroom, Mr. Gibbs asked me to go to the blackboard, draw a map of the world, and name and show the locations of capitals of countries. That was no problem for me. I answered all questions about world geography that they asked me during that class, and I did not think there was anything all that important about this exercise. However, I soon realized that the exercise was a very important wake-up call to the graduating seniors. I did not let Mr. Gibbs down in his confidence in me.

Clubs and Organizations

Black students taking courses in agriculture became members of the New Farmers of America (NFA). The NFA was created in the mid-1930s to serve young black agricultural students in segregated schools in southern states. Similar to the National Future Farmers of America (FFA) for white agricultural students, the NFA provided young black men with activities to enhance their abilities in leadership and agricultural endeavors. The NFA promoted the acquisition and use of knowledge and skills in farming, improving home and surroundings, developing leadership skills, cooperating with and providing service to others, demonstrating improvement in scholarship, and finding and developing their own talents. Our NFA advisors were the agriculture teachers at Stevens School.

I was also a member of the 4-H Club. This was a youth organization sponsored by the U.S. Department of Agriculture to instruct rural young people in improved farming and farm-homemaking practices. The goals were to improve H̲ead, H̲eart, H̲ands, and H̲ealth. My 4-H Club advisor was the black County Agent, Mr. Russell Stevens. County Agents visited farms all over the county to discuss improvements in farming methods and techniques to gain higher yields. Prior to Mr. Stevens, the County Agent who visited our farm was Mr. Fischer, a white man. Mr. Fischer was found dead in his car; the word was that he committed suicide. Many blacks did not believe that he killed himself. The black farmers in Sawdust liked Mr. Fischer's help in their farming efforts and were sad to hear of his death.

As a part of the 4-H program, a black lady named Ms. Bouie worked for the county and visited black women to discuss improved homemaking practices and home economics. The 4-H Club also supported a week-long summer camp for boys at Lake Doe in the Ocala, Florida area. I attended the summer camp one year when I was in the eighth or ninth grade. The 210-mile trip to summer camp at Lake Doe was the first time that I had been more than forty-two miles from home. Prior to Camp Lake Doe, my longest travel from home was a field trip in seventh grade to the Florida Caverns in Mariana, Florida. On the way back home from Lake Doe, we visited Silver Springs State Park and took one of the renowned glass bottom boat tours to view life underwater.

The NFA and the 4-H Club encouraged contests among members of the local chapter. Competitions that I participated in included growing the largest number of bushels of corn per acre and competitions at the county fair.

In my first year in high school, I was a member of the Spanish Club. The goal was to teach Spanish to interested students. The club lasted for only the last six weeks of the spring semester because our advisor did not return to Stevens in the fall semester.

In my senior year, Amos and I joined the School Boy Patrols. There were no security personnel on the campus to monitor events on campus or maintain order on school buses. These were tasks of the School Boy Patrols.

Chores at Home

Throughout my elementary and high school years, we had numerous chores on the farm after school. The chores depended on the time of the year. They included gathering wood for cooking and heating, feeding the animals; year-round, hoeing the vegetables and other plants, dusting tobacco during the growing season, covering up sugar cane, and hauling cane mash during the Thanksgiving and Christmas holidays. The chores that I disliked most were covering up cane to protect it from frost and hauling the cane mash from the sugar cane mill.

We also had to shuck and shell corn to take to the mill in Greensboro to grind into corn meal, a staple food on the farm. Ruby, Gladys, Amos, and I had that task. I remember when we were shucking and shelling corn, there was a buck barrel, which held an alcoholic beverage made from that winter's cane skimming. Every farm that made syrup had a buck barrel in their corn crib for drinking. As a young boy in elementary school, I took a drink of the buck and decided to entertain Ruby, Gladys, and Amos while they were shucking and shelling corn with the Corn Sheller attached to a wooden barrel. I had practiced alone in the field what I heard from the preacher giving his sermons. I got on top of the corn in the crib and gave my sermon while they worked. They laughed and did all of the work while I preached.

My father would take a bushel of shelled corn to Sheppard's mill in Greensboro. The miller would take a share of the corn to pay for grinding the corn into meal. Yet, we would return with a bushel of meal, despite the share given in payment. I was curious. I did not understand density at that time. The meal had a density much less than the shelled corn. Therefore the meal occupied more volume than the corn it replaced.

Gladys and Ruby also milked the cows by hand. I watched them but never learned how to milk. My mother skimmed the cream from the milk and made butter in her stone butter churn. The churn had a stone lid with a hole in the middle to insert a wooden paddle to churn the cream into butter. My mother used buttermilk to make biscuits and we also drank buttermilk.

When we were not doing chores, Amos and I tried to be entrepreneurs. Amos sold an African American newspaper, the *Pittsburgh Courier,* and I sold seeds from Lancaster County Seed Company in Pennsylvania.

Selling vegetable, flower, and garden seeds was costly because no one wanted to pay. They always wanted to purchase the seeds on credit. I had to make many trips to collect money, until I would just give up. I had to use my commission to pay for the seeds. At an early age, I became discouraged from attempting other business ventures.

Meanwhile, Amos was successful in selling the *Pittsburgh Courier.* His customers thought that the comic strip "Sonny Boy" would give them the number for the weekly Bolita (Cuban) game, a lottery popular among the Hispanic, Italian, and Black working class in Florida. One time the number 52 was thrown in the lottery. The people later saw a comment in the Sonny Boy comic strip that said "two eggs with fifty two." This encouraged believers that they could get the number from Sonny Boy. People used magnifying glasses to search for the Bolita number in the Sonny Boy strip.

There were other superstitions regarding Bolita as well. Some people thought that they could dream the number that was going to "fall" and they played based on their dreams. Some thought that they could get the number from the devil by sprinkling whiskey on the ground near the edge of a graveyard and listening for the devil to speak the number. Others thought that spiritualists could give them the number. Those spiritualists expected pay for their consultations. One time, Uncle Esau brought a psychic from Gainesville to Sawdust to consult on the game.

Bolita paid seven dollars for a dime bet, seventy dollars for a dollar bet, etc. if you had the right number. You had to pick the winning number from one to one hundred. Thus, for a fair game, the odds of winning were one in one hundred. However, the game could easily be unfair because numbers were sold by runners prior to the Saturday night when the numbers were thrown, i.e., when the lottery occurred. So there was opportunity for the game to be unfairly tilted—there could be fewer than one hundred numbered balls placed in the bag, or certain numbered balls, especially those with the largest bets, could be heavier, so that those numbers with the largest bets could fall to the bottom, and not get thrown.

Amos obviously developed entrepreneurial skills. In the early 1960s, after he moved to Los Angeles, he became a successful small business owner. Instead of entrepreneurship, I devoted my time to science and education—my best talents.

Games and Events

Some of the games we played in my elementary school years through middle school were baseball, stick ball, hopscotch, marbles, dominoes, stick frog, goosey-goosey gander, touch football, nubbin with spinning tops, and whist (cards).

Stick Ball is a form of baseball that used a broom handle for a bat. The stick ball, or "monkey ball," allowed fielders to throw the ball at base runners, eliminating the need to tag the runner or a base to get a runner out.

Hopscotch, Marbles, Stick Frog, and Dominoes are well-known games are described on the world-wide-web. Hopscotch and dominoes were played by both boys and girls. Stick frog was played to see who could get a pocket knife to stick into the ground or piece of wood.

Goosey-Goosey Gander is not the nursery rhyme. It was always played on the Sawdust School grounds. It is a game that boys played about a fox on a sandbar in a river chased by male geese. It involved two teams of equal numbers. The teams lined up facing each other, separated by fifteen to twenty yards. A member from Team #1 would stand halfway between the two teams to be (a) captured by Team #2 or (b) protected by his team.

A call was then made by Team #1: *"Goosey-goosey gander, fox in the Mander (river)."*

Team #2 would respond: *"How many have you got?"*

Team #1 would reply: *"More than you can handle."*

"HANDLE" was the key word for each team to run to protect or capture the person halfway between each team.

If Team #2 captured the person in the middle, then that person would become part of their team.

In the next half-cycle, Team #2 would place a person halfway between the two teams and make the call.

This cycle continued until the allotted time for the game ended—when the bell rang to end the lunch recess.

The winner was the team with the most members at the end. Speed was the most important attribute because the person who could run fastest was able to capture a person from the other team or protect the person on his team.

Jimmy Shaw was the fastest runner in Sawdust—his team won most of the games. When my father wanted to catch a hog running loose in the field, he would get Jimmy to do it. Jimmy could have excelled in track and field if he had had the opportunity on a college level. However, he never completed middle school.

There is a story about Jimmy catching a rabbit. He would chase a rabbit and pat him on the side to see if he was fat enough to eat. If it was too lean he would just pass that one and continue to catch another. Jimmy was also a great rapper. A group of us boys including my brother Amos, Cousin Charles Rolax, Cousin Jimmy Shaw, Cousin Samuel Gilliam, me, and others would get together in the woods or at a creek or fishpond for rap sessions. We all tried to rap. One of my favorites was Jimmy's story about the "Signifying Monkey" belittling a lion regarding his title as the King of the Jungle. It seemed to me that Jimmy would rap for nearly a quarter of an hour. Yes, we had rappers in our community way back when I was growing up. Rapping is in our African American heritage. However, I never learned to rap.

Living in the Sawdust Community, I had never heard of football. I learned about it when, at nine years old, I went to Stevens School in Quincy in the seventh grade. The boys my age or a couple of years older played touch football. We used small orange juice cans for the ball. I loved this game. However, I quit playing because "Zip," a much older guy, probably fifteen or sixteen years old, would break into our game. I am not sure whether he was a student at Stevens. He purposely tried to hurt you. When he was carrying the ball we would get out of his path and let him score. After he scored, no one on the opposing team wanted to touch the ball because they knew that he was going to try to hurt them. He took all of the fun out of the game so we quit playing when he came onto the field.

Another game I played in the seventh or eighth grade was Nubbin. It was played with a wooden spinning top. The objective was to split your opponent's spinning top in the ring, while it was spinning, with your own top.

The Whist Card Game, Checkers, and Baseball are games that I also played as a young child. Ruby, Gladys, Amos, and I learned to play the standard whist card game from Professor Farmer. Later, I learned to play bid whist from soldiers who returned from the Korean War.

We played checkers with a board made from cardboard box. We used bottle caps for pieces. One player's pieces had the bottle caps turned up and the other player had the pieces turned down.

We attended baseball games on Saturday afternoons. Every neighborhood in Gadsden County had an all-black baseball team. There were three or more teams within five or six miles from where our Sawdust team played. Our ball diamond was in a pasture on a farm adjacent to our farm on the west side.

During this time we did not have electricity. Hence, we listened to a radio connected to a large battery. The non-rechargeable battery was larger than the radio. When the battery lost its charge, you had to replace it. The radio was our media for news, music, and entertainment.

The family listened to the "Beulah" and "Amos and Andy" shows. My favorite program was the "Lone Ranger and Tonto," a western that aired at 6:00pm on Monday, Wednesday, and Friday. I made sure that my chores were completed by then. The Lone Ranger program was sponsored by Merita Breads. Everyone listened to the Joe Louis fights on the radio.

Several families would get together to listen. Joe Louis was a hero of black people in our neighborhood and surely around the nation.

My cousin Ruby, my sister Gladys, my brother Amos, and I would stay up late on Saturday nights to listen to rhythm and blues songs. This program was sponsored by Randy's Record Shop in Gallatin, Tennessee. We were able to get the radio signal only late on a Saturday night. The local radio station in Quincy did not play rhythm and blues or black gospel songs.

My father obtained a used Gramophone from a white family whose farm he sharecropped. It was incorporated into a cabinet with a top to cover the gramophone and space to store records at the bottom. This gramophone was driven by a spring. A crank allowed you to wind up the spring to power the turntable; electricity or batteries were not needed. The gramophone played plastic records that could be purchased at the local record shop in Quincy. It produced sounds that could be heard for nearly a quarter of a mile. We could now purchase records and listen to rhythm and blues and gospel without staying up late on Saturday nights. Before Talquin Electric Corporation provided electricity in Sawdust, I believe that we may have been the only black family in the community that had a record player.

Mrs. Ola Clark built a structure with two rooms. She was a beautician and decided to have her shop next to her house in Sawdust. The smaller room contained her beauty shop. The larger area became a juke joint with a counter, chairs, tables, juke box, and the works. My father called this place the Cypress Inn because of its proximity to the Cypress Pond. The name my father gave it was accepted. From then on, everyone called it the Cypress Inn.

The Cypress Inn was more than a beauty salon and juke joint; it was a place to socialize and enjoy activities in Sawdust within walking distance from home. Of course they sold beer and "a little something else," but we were allowed to go to the Cypress Inn when we were children. The Cypress Inn was a place to meet new people from different age groups in the community. Entertainment included dancing, boxing, playing bid whist, and watching movies. My favorites were bid whist and the movies.

Every spring, there was a Bid Whist Tournament at the Cypress Inn to raise money for the March of Dimes charity. In bid whist, there were four players consisting of two teams of two; each player sat opposite their partner. For tournament play, you chose your own partner. There were several tables for players. If there were more players than tables available, the remaining players waited in the queue until a table became available when a team lost its game. The losing team had to leave the table—we called it "Rise and Fly."

Each two-person team initially paid a dime to sit at a table to play. If your team was the winner at your table, you remained there without having to pay for the next game. Another team paid a dime to challenge you. There were several games at different tables at the same time. Whenever a team sat at a table, they had to pay a dime even if they had lost the game at that table or another table. If you lost a game at any table, you had to wait in line for other teams that had been waiting to play, and then pay to continue to play at an available table. This continued until the tournament was over. The winner of the tournament was the team that won the most games. The prize was not an inscribed plaque or a certificate—it was a home baked pie. My cousin Charles and I always teamed up to play and won the pie every year. We shared the pie with my brother and another cousin on our way home that night. When we got home, there was no record of who won because we had eaten the pie, i.e., certificate!

During my years in high school, movies were introduced at the Cypress Inn. The movies were shown by Parker. I do not remember his first name, but he worked at a movie theater in Quincy as a camera operator. During good weather, Parker showed the movies outside of the Cypress Inn building. During bad weather, he showed them inside the building. It cost fifteen to twenty five cents for admission. He showed a full movie plus clips to keep you coming the next week. Unlike a regular movie theater, Parker had only one projector—the movie had to be interrupted while he changed the reel. Theaters in Quincy had more than one projector and they were synchronized. At the Cypress Inn, when one reel was completed, Parker would say, "The show continues when we change the reel." I enjoyed those movies.

High School

At age eleven, I completed the eighth grade at Stevens and entered high school, also at Stevens.

I liked school and all subjects and excelled in most classes. My favorite subjects were science and mathematics. I believe that those two areas of study helped develop my critical thinking. They taught me how to analyze a problem and arrive at a reasonable solution in any area of study, especially in English composition. Typical days in high school included five academic courses plus a sixth period. The sixth period was a free period for electives such as activities in clubs.

My most memorable teachers were Mr. Norris, my chemistry teacher who later became a medical doctor (M.D.); Mrs. Ruby Gilliam Francis, my English teacher who challenged me with sentence structure; Mrs. Eva Simms Butler, my civics teacher and senior advisor; Mr. Raymond Grant and Ms. Marilyn Wiggins, mathematics teachers; and Mrs. Hazel King, English and literature teacher.

Honors and awards I received include an award-winning paper that was entered in competition at the county fair by Mrs. King. My title was "Life in the Country Has Changed Significantly in the Last Several Years." This paper discussed changes that had taken place in rural areas in the county. It related to Rolling Stores which brought grocery and other needs, the installation of electricity, paving of roads, etc., after World War II. Installation of electricity and paving of roads took place in the late 1940s and early 1950s in Sawdust.

I graduated from Stevens High School as Salutatorian of my class in 1954. Mrs. Butler was my senior advisor in the preparation of my commencement address.

I credit Mr. Norris with shaping my interest in engineering. His chemistry class was the only course in which I obtained significant laboratory experience since the eighth grade, when we built a wall around the Stevens School playground.

PART II
Teen Years after High School

Chapter 4

Farm and Construction Work

The summer after I completed high school in 1954, I worked on the farm picking shade tobacco. I also worked as a migrant worker. After the shade tobacco harvesting was completed in Gadsden County, a neighbor informed us that the tobacco companies were planning a trip to take workers to Windsor, Connecticut, near Hartford, Connecticut. My oldest brother, two cousins, a man we called "Heavy" who lived in Sawdust, and I prepared for the trip in one day. Others in the group came from all over Gadsden County, including several members of my graduating class at Stevens from Quincy and the St. Johns Community.

A charter bus took us to Windsor. We lived in barracks. There was a kitchen and dining area in the complex. Heavy was much older than the rest of us and was assigned to work in the kitchen instead of in the tobacco shades. Heavy's assignment made sense to me. However, one young guy in our group misplaced his money and falsely accused "Heavy" of taking it, probably because he worked in the barracks during the day. This was another example of false accusations that I witnessed during my early life.

We ate breakfast and dinner in the barracks. Lunches were prepared to take to the fields. I learned to eat eggs that were either sunny side up or over-easy with the yoke running. I would put ketchup, salt and pepper on the eggs and eat them; I had no other choice. I had never eaten eggs with a running yoke before, but I had to eat. The work in Connecticut was cut short by a storm that destroyed the tobacco in the shades and we returned home.

Thus, my first trip north of the Mason-Dixon Line was much shorter than expected, and I was disappointed to be returning home so soon. Still it had been an adventure—living away from home for the first time and not with family members, but in a barracks—definitely a different kind of community from Sawdust. Here, I lived with non-family members and experienced new sights and new foods. I surprised myself by adapting to eating eggs that were not scrambled or boiled!

The work was hard, but we found time to relax and have fun. However, I had one memorable experience that was not fun. In fact, it was quite painful, but I will always remember the kind and thoughtful action of the farm supervisor.

I had had toothaches before but this one hit hard with terrible pain, and I had a swollen jaw. The farm superintendent, a white man, drove me to a dentist in Hartford. On the way, the pickup truck had a flat tire. Observing my excruciating pain, he ignored the flat tire and continued driving to the dentist, who removed my tooth. Then he changed the tire. At that time and throughout my three years in the U.S. Army, I never had dental cleanings or cavities filled until I obtained my Ph.D. Whenever I went to a dentist with a problem, the problem teeth were always removed by the dentist. When I was on active duty, the U.S. Army did not support dental health care. I wear dentures today because of the lack of dental care at an early age.

On reflection, I think the Connecticut trip sparked my life-long passion for travel, and, in a way, launched ***my journey around the world in eighty years***.

For the rest of the year after returning home from Connecticut, I worked with my father on our farm. My brother Amos volunteered to be called by the local draft board into the Army as did some other male classmates in the class of 1954 at Stevens High School. Some classmates volunteered for the Air Force and the Navy.

I was too young to enter military service. And I was unable to attend college because my parents had no resources to send me to one. I had a sister, Gladys, attending college at FAMU. Many black farmers would send their daughters to college, if possible, to become teachers. They wanted their sons to work on the farm and later manage the farm.

One might ask, "You graduated salutatorian of your class; why didn't you apply for a scholarship before you completed high school?" Well, we did not have a high school counselor to advise us of scholarship opportunities. I had no alternative except to work on the farm, either our farm or the farms of others.

Even though I had dreams of a different future for myself, it was not difficult to fall into a daily routine, to become absorbed in working. After all, it was a life I knew, and I couldn't imagine not working. I would take "pick-up" jobs and look for extra things to do on our own farm.

I saw the need to dig up fatwood stumps from our fields that had been breaking our plows during planting and cultivation. So I took the initiative to do it in my spare time. A neighbor saw me digging stumps and must have asked my father if he had assigned this work. My father must have replied that it was on my own initiative. I later heard that the neighbor complimented what I was doing on my own to improve the family farm.

For almost one and one-third years after my high school graduation, I had numerous jobs as a common laborer on road construction, building construction, and as a farm worker. Projects included the paving of a road in Havana, Florida, by Doyle Pope Construction Company; farm work on the Blount Farm in Sawdust; and construction of the Perry-Page Building on the Florida A&M University campus in Tallahassee.

Jobs in farm work or construction were unsatisfactory to me. As soon as I was old enough, I volunteered to serve in the U. S. Army.

Chapter 5

Life in the U.S. Army

On September 2, 1955, I was sworn into the Army in Jacksonville, Florida. For processing, the other inductees and I traveled to Fort Jackson, South Carolina, near Columbia. I recall a black corporal (E-4) whose last name was Sergeant, so he was "Corporal Sergeant." And I remember signs everywhere that read "Do not enter."

The top song of the day was "Maybelline" by Charles Edward Anderson Berry ("Chuck Berry"). This was the beginning of rock and roll music.

We were given a choice to serve in Alaska or West Germany. I chose the 3rd Armored Division that was redeploying to West Germany. The 3rd Armored Division was first activated in 1941 and active in the European Theater of World War II.

Fort Knox, Kentucky

After processing at Fort Jackson, we took buses to Fort Knox, Kentucky, for Basic Training. We arrived late at night and were shown to our sleeping quarters.

I was assigned to the Second Platoon C Company, Seventh Tank Battalion. My platoon sergeant, a Master Sergeant (E-7), was clearly an "Uncle Tom"—a black man exceedingly obedient or servile to white people. He played up to white soldiers and was in no way favorable to blacks. He even put down blues music and made fun of me playing it on the harmonica on my free time in the barracks. Other sergeants in the Second Platoon were: Sergeant First Class Hayes (E-6), a Black man; and

Sergeant First Class Cordova (E-6), a Hispanic. No other platoons in C Company had Black or Hispanic Non-Commissioned Officers (NCOs) except Master Sergeant Eddie L. Johnson (E-7), a black man in the First Platoon.

There was only one Black enlisted soldier in each platoon in C Company 7th Tank Battalion. C Company had three line platoons plus headquarters platoon. All four platoons were housed in one building.

Enlisted men in Headquarters and First Platoon lived in one large room at the end of a long hallway. Enlisted men in Second and Third Platoons were in another large room at the other end of the long hallway.

The large rooms were divided into cubicles. Each cubicle had two sets of bunk beds to accommodate four people.

Along the long hallway were private rooms for unmarried NCOs.

When I arrived at Fort Knox, the majority of the enlisted men in the Company had already completed six weeks of basic training. In preparing all of the Company to move (Gyroscope) with the Division to Germany on schedule, late arrivals had to go through a special four weeks of basic training exercises. We were led by the Junior Sergeant in the Third Platoon in C Company. As all of us enlisted men (black and white) observed, he was not very intelligent, and he was a racist. Behind his back, all enlisted men under his charge called him "Dumb Dumb." He always assigned the few black soldiers to cleaning and after-hour details.

The First Sergeant (E-7) of Company C was one of the most racist people I have ever met. He was very small in size compared to others and this probably added to his demeanor. This Company had sergeants who were prejudiced against all black soldiers and college-educated white soldiers. Here are some incidents to illustrate my point.

Just prior to Christmas, Baker, a black soldier, was accused of stealing a 0.45 caliber pistol. All soldiers in the Company were assigned weapons and had to perform guard duty on the post. This time Batts, a college-educated white soldier, had guard duty. He checked out a 0.45 caliber pistol from the arms room and performed his tour of guard duty. As always when one completed the guard duty, the first thing was to take a shower after returning to the barracks. Batts placed the pistol into his wall locker and took a shower. Preparing to go home for Christmas, he forgot to clean and return the weapon to the arms room before he left for the holidays.

When the weapon was reported missing, Baker, the black soldier, was accused of theft because it was assigned to him—but without his knowledge. He was always being accused of something and punished. Later, the records were checked and showed that Batts, the white soldier, had checked out the weapon. His wall locker was opened and the weapon was there. The white soldier served fifteen days of company punishment when he returned from the Christmas holidays.

Other cases of prejudice and racism involved me directly. The first case happened the night after a payday. We were paid in cash and locked our money in our wall lockers. The wall lockers had combination locks that we purchased. I went on guard duty that day. Every soldier on guard duty would spend two hours serving on his post and four hours off throughout the night. Thus, there were three two-hour shifts on the guard posts. Each shift spent two hours on their guard post and four hours traveling to/from the guard post and sleeping. The next morning, on my way from the guard house to the cafeteria for breakfast, I met a white soldier in my platoon. He told me that someone had stolen his money the past night.

At the next C Company assembly, the First Sergeant called out three names—Baker, Batts, and Thigpen (me)—to fall out of the assembly and report to the Orderly Room, Office of the First Sergeant and Company Commander. The Company assemblies always took place outside the building that we lived in and the Orderly Room was inside the building. We were ordered to be interviewed by someone from the Civil Investigating Department (CID).

I was the first to be interviewed. The investigator informed me of the alleged theft and said that he was interviewing "some people" who were in the barracks the night of the incident. I asked him who told him that I was in the barracks that night. He said that it was the sergeant in charge of quarters. I knew that the sergeant was a white racist from Arkansas. I said that I was on guard duty—he should check the records and the sergeant's lies. I also said that the victim informed me about the theft when I met him on my way from the guard house to the cafeteria (mess hall) for breakfast. That was the end of my interview. I do not know what took place in the interviews with the other two soldiers. However, no money had been stolen. The "victim" found his money in his locked wall locker; it was locked with his personal combination lock. He was not punished.

When we were on bivouac (temporary camp where each soldier had a shelter half to provide cover from rain, sleet or snow), two soldiers had accidents because of their own negligence—but I was blamed. One of them was in my platoon and the other was in Headquarters platoon.

I had been assigned by my Platoon Sergeant to serve as Company runner for the Second Platoon and Headquarters Platoon. My responsibility was to take messages to the platoon leaders from the company headquarters. I slept in the Headquarters tent to be available at any moment to carry messages to the platoons.

The First Sergeant sent me with a message that the platoons needed only one guard to patrol the area that night. When I delivered the message to my Platoon Sergeant, he asked me to return to Headquarters and get a clarification. He wanted to know if we needed one guard on each tank or only one guard patrolling the whole platoon area. The reply from the First Sergeant was that one guard for the whole platoon area would be sufficient. I reported this back to my Platoon Sergeant and returned to the Headquarters tent.

The platoons had already been given permission to build fires for that night. A soldier in my platoon was sitting by the fire, went to sleep, fell into the fire, and got minor burns. The other soldier in Headquarters Platoon got soaked from the rain. Both white soldiers were the guards for their respective platoons, yet they were not blamed for dereliction of duty.

Those two incidents were blamed on me by my Platoon Sergeant and the C Company First Sergeant. Their justification was that I communicated an incorrect message regarding the posting of guards. These racists, including my black "Uncle Tom" Platoon Sergeant and the white First Sergeant, knew that they had to blame someone—who better to blame than a black soldier? Yes, my Platoon Sergeant was prejudiced toward all blacks. In the Headquarters tent that night, a white lieutenant tried to talk to me but I did not converse with him. I answered questions or statements with only, "Yes sir" or "No sir." He finally asked me if I liked to talk and I said, "No sir." Why would a 17-year-old want to talk with anyone after he has been blamed for stupid accidents of others that he had no part in? However, I do not think that the lieutenant knew anything about the accusations.

I received no punishment for the incident because there was no factual case against me. However, this incident could have been used against me in hidden ways regarding positions in the future. For example, although the Communications Officer (and he was black) requested it, I was not approved for a position on the Communications Committee for the voyage on the ship to Germany.

I had a couple of incidents with white soldiers at Fort Knox. The first incident occurred with a soldier in the Third Platoon. His bunk was directly across the room from mine. I walked over one night and asked him for a light for my cigarette. He gave me a light and said, "Get your goddamn ass out of my area." I probably said, "Go to hell" or something like that, and a scuffle began. He said, "Let's go outside and fight." I said that I was not going outside the barracks to fight anyone. More than two years later, when we were in Germany, he informed me that one of his fingers was broken in our scuffle at Fort Knox.

The second incident occurred one Saturday afternoon. I was the only one in my barracks when two white soldiers came into the barracks. One of them lived in the same barracks as I did. The other one, "Red" from Mississippi, was in the First Platoon which resided in the other end of the building. Referring to me, Red said, "Let's kick his ASS." I backed into my bunk area in front of my wall locker where I had an entrenching tool, a small folded shovel on a short handle, on the top. Without looking, I could get it to protect myself. I said, "Okay, you SOBs, come on and kick my ass." When I showed no fear, Red said, "Ha ha. We were just joking." I do not know what could have happened to me if I had shown fear with no one else around to tell the story. Before we left Fort Knox for West Germany, Red was kicked out of the Army due to his behavior. The other soldier and I ended up being good friends in Germany. We traveled and socialized together over there.

My time at Fort Knox was a great learning experience about prejudices in our country's Army. It did not matter that you were a black soldier assigned to protect our country—you experienced prejudice. I got along with most of the white soldiers in our company and considered them as friends. One time, my friend, a white soldier from Pennsylvania, and I went to Louisville, Kentucky, on a pass, dressed in military uniform. This was my first time off the base. We went to a drugstore to get a milkshake and sat at the counter. The server told me that she could not serve me. I responded that I did not want to be served to anyone; I just wanted a milkshake. Well, I did not get my milkshake. My friend and I walked out. This may have been one of the earliest non-eventful sit-ins by a black at a drug store counter in the U.S. We went to a movie theater to see "To Hell and Back" starring Audie Murphy, a World War II hero. Both of us wanted to see it. However, I knew from the experience at the drug store that we would not be allowed to sit together, and did not want another humiliating experience. Being from Pennsylvania, my friend might not have understood prejudice against black people at a movie theater. I told him that he should go see the movie and I would see him back at base.

Kentucky was a neutral state during the U.S. Civil War. Yet, examine the activities of Senator Mitch McConnell from Kentucky, starting in January 2009 immediately after the inauguration of President Barack Obama. McConnell met with other Republicans that evening to set a goal to destroy President Obama and ensure that he would be a one-term President. But it did not work!

The next trip that I took off base was with two black soldiers. We went to Cincinnati, Ohio, and saw a movie, "The Man with the Golden Arm" staring Frank Sinatra. That night, we went to a night club to see a performance by Riley B. King ("BB King"). This was one of the 342 gigs that BB (Blues Boy) King performed in 1956. I was only 17 years old so I had borrowed the driver's license of an older friend, a white soldier (licenses did not have photos at that time). I wore civilian clothes because, had I been in military uniform, my military identification would have shown my photo and age. With my borrowed identification, we had no problems entering the club and ordering beer.

During the Easter holiday in 1956, and prior to deploying to Germany, I traveled back home on leave. Of course I went to the Cypress Inn, a juke joint. My cousins Charles and Daniel were there. They were sipping moonshine. Although I had never tried it or any hard liquor before, I tried to drink with them. Well, I sipped the moonshine and then tried to dance as others were dancing. The last thing that I remembered was Little Richard's (Richard Penniman) song "Slipping and Sliding." I dropped the cup with the moonshine and threw up on my military uniform. My first cousin Ruby, who was married to one of the owners of the Cypress Inn, took me in to stay at their house that night. The next morning they took my Olive Drab (OD) Ike Jacket, shirt, and tie to the cleaners. I walked across Mr. Willie's field to my parents' house in my t-shirt and pants. I swore that I would never drink moonshine again. However, fifty years later, I did try it and found it to be a satisfactory drink.

Prior to the Third Armored Division's Gyroscope to Germany in 1956, there were replacements of officers and NCOs in our Company. Officers were replaced on a regular basis because the Army did not want them to become too familiar with the men they commanded. Our C Company Commander, who was a First Lieutenant and war hero who won the Silver Star, was replaced by another First Lieutenant. Several sergeants including the current First Sergeant were also replaced. We acquired a black second lieutenant in the Battalion, in charge of communications for the trip to Germany. He found out about my intellect and informed me that he was recommending me to serve on his Communications Committee. I was proud that he recommended me and agreed to serve if approved. However, I was not approved by the powers-that-be, and did not serve on his Communications Committee. I think the people in charge did not want a committee with a black lieutenant in charge and a black enlisted man on the same committee. This could also have been part of a hidden agenda by my Platoon Sergeant and the First Sergeant of C Company to punish me for the incidents of two careless soldiers' negligence and minor injury as described earlier. After all, the Sergeants were the ones who made recommendations to the Officers regarding the elevation of an enlisted soldier's status.

Travel to Germany

In May 1956, I traveled from Fort Knox, Kentucky, to Fort Dix, New Jersey, on my way to Germany. However, my Battalion had been scheduled to leave Fort Knox earlier. As I recall, it would have been prior to the Kentucky Derby (which took place in Louisville on May 5). From Fort Dix, we would board the U.S.N.S. General William O. Darby. But the Darby had hit an iceberg. The date of the Kentucky Derby is important to me in providing a window for when we actually left Fort Knox for Germany.

After the Kentucky Derby, we took a Troop Train from Fort Knox to Fort Dix and boarded the U.S.N.S. General Alexander M. Patch. Nine days later, we arrived at the Port of Bremerhaven in Germany. From the port, we took an eleven-or twelve-hour trip on a Troop Train to Ayers Kaserne in Kirch-Göns, where we were to be stationed.

As noted previously, the officer assigned to communications on the U.S.N.S. General Alexander M. Patch during our trip to Germany recommended me to serve on his communications committee. However, his recommendation was not approved, probably because we were both black.

Instead of serving in communications and helping prepare a daily news brief, I was assigned to duties as a night cook on the Patch. Ten soldiers in my company had the same duty. Our responsibilities were to prepare items for breakfast and lunch such as frying eggs, peeling and cutting onions, cutting tomatoes, and peeling and cutting potatoes. Other teams of soldiers prepared additional items on the breakfast and lunch menus. We were supervised by a Ship Cook. We went on duty every other night, beginning after midnight, and worked until breakfast was served. All members of my group (Detail) worked on the preparation for lunch and breakfast except onions. A soldier on our Detail was much older than the rest of us, and we called him "Papa." He was assigned to the onions while the rest of us were frying eggs. Each morning, 2400 eggs were fried—enough for 1200 people on the ship, not all prepared by my Detail. We prepared breakfast for our C Company, about 100 people. Some of us cracked the eggs and placed two each in a bowl to be fried. Others fried the eggs and placed them on a warming tray to be served. Three soldiers took care of the warming trays.

In the beginning, I was one of those who cracked eggs and placed two in the bowls. However, the soldier who was frying was so slow and unorganized that I traded places with him. I had three small frying pans, each one holding two eggs. I wrapped a small wet towel around my right hand to prevent the hot oil from burning my hands when I flipped the eggs over in the pan. I flipped them over in the air and caught them without breaking the yoke. The previous guy was trying to use a spatula to flip the eggs. My ingenuity taught the others how to fry eggs. One soldier on our Detail did not follow my leadership, probably because I am African American. On the other hand, perhaps he was adverse to be assigned to the Detail and had no interest in its efficiency.

After duty as night cooks, we were not allowed to return to our bunks to sleep. We had to participate in all activities for that day including physical and other training exercises. The bunk beds were like canvas hammocks, stacked two or three levels high with only enough room to slide into. After all, we were on a ship with limited space. On the night that I worked as a cook, I went to bed early because I had to get up around 2:00am. Since I worked every other night, I went to bed at regular hours on my night off.

Ayers Kaserne in Kirch-Göns, Germany

After we settled into the barracks at Ayers Kaserne, there was much work to be done to prepare our Company, Battalion and Combat Command A, for combat readiness.

I was a member of C Company, 7th Tank Battalion, Combat Command A (CCA), 3rd Armored Division, Fifth Corp, 7th Army. The insignia of the 7th Army had seven steps on each side; we called it seven steps to hell. In late 1957 or early 1958, the name of 7th Tank Battalion was changed to 2nd Medium Tank Battalion 1st Calvary. Ayers Kaserne had been occupied by the 22nd Infantry Regiment, 4th Infantry Division prior to our arrival and was not prepared for a combat command in an armored division.

There were no tank pads within the confines of the Kaserne when we arrived in 1956. The tanks were located outside the fenced-in part. We had new M-48 tanks that had just been shipped to Germany and coated with cosmoline to inhibit rust from salty mist during the overseas travel. All of the cosmoline had to be removed to get the tanks combat ready. New concrete tank pads were constructed within the confines of the Kaserne. In short order, CCA became combat ready.

While our tanks were located outside, local Germans would visit our work area selling things that they knew we would buy. As entrepreneurs, they took advantage of opportunities. I remember them selling cognac candy and food items. I had never seen candy filled with liquor. Our soldiers bought the candy. Other items included coffee, donuts, candy, etc.

Our training was continuous and included physical fitness training (PT) and combat training exercises. We did PT every morning except

Sunday, and we had physical fitness exams. PT consisted of twelve different exercises with twelve repetitions each—the daily dozens. We also had two-mile and/or four-mile cross-country runs that were timed.

One of the PT exercises was called "Organized Grab Ass." We formed teams and could do anything as long as the game was organized. Touch football was one of those exercises. I never realized that touch football could be so brutal or vindictive until I played this game. On the first play, when the two teams lined up against each other, a white soldier opposing me punched me in the face. After that, I sought revenge. Winning the football game was not on my mind—only to get even with him. From then on, he ran from me on every play.

I was still a young seventeen-year-old and did not realize that "do anything" in a touch football game meant exactly that—you could purposely hurt someone. Due to my previous experience in touch football, I thought that "do anything" meant that you could choose any organized game or exercise.

Our combat training included small arms qualifications at our base (Ayers Kaserne). Combat maneuvers in the local area required travel through small towns or villages. We used the autobahn to get there. Major exercises were carried out at distant destinations—Grafenwohr and Wildflecken. We loaded our tanks on flat rail cars and traveled by train to get there. At a British Kaserne near Belsen, Germany, we went through qualifications to test our skills in firing tank weapons—our main tank gun. I received a medal as an Expert Tank Gunner.

Wherever we were training off base, we had to bivouac for a week or more during inclement, "terrible" weather: rain, mud, cold, ice, and snow. At night while sleeping, you had to protect yourself from moving tanks and other moving vehicles. One time when we were on maneuvers, an infantry soldier sleeping in an open area was run over by a tank. The lesson learned was not to sleep in open spaces. Instead, pitch your tent in a wooded area near a large tree or a large vehicle. We always slept within a couple of feet from our tank. We never used our shelter halves to pitch tents. Two shelter halves attached together formed a pup (small) tent. Instead, we used the rectangular shaped tarpaulin that covered our tanks in the motor pool. One end of the tarpaulin was tied to the side of the tank at two places, and the other end was tied either to two trees or to two stakes in the ground. This formed a rectangular shelter similar to a carport.

While at the British Kaserne, we visited the Bergen-Belsen concentration camp. This was one of the camps that the Nazis used in World War II for forced labor and extermination of Jews. It was horrific to see graves that contained 5,000 people. I believe that the marker read "Here Lie 5,000 Jews Killed by those Murderous Nazis" and I may have seen another grave with a similar marker. I can still picture those grave sites in my mind more than sixty years later. That sight blocked everything else at that location from my mind and memory.

Our tanks had V-12 Chrysler air-cooled engines that averaged three to five miles per gallon of gasoline. A small auxiliary engine heated the main engine compartment prior to starting. On training exercises, we used a lot of gasoline and had to fill the gas tank on our tank often. This was one of the most physically challenging exercises—we had to refuel from five-gallon cans and walk twenty-five to fifty yards to the fuel truck in mud or snow.

In the simulated combat, referees decided which soldiers were the battlefield victims. A hospital was set up in a tent to take care of the "wounded." On one of those exercises, I got the little finger on my right hand smashed helping the loader open the main gun breach to load another blank 90mm round. When firing blanks, the gunner would turn around in his seat to help the loader open the breach. The loader would place his foot on the handle and the gunner would place his hand on the handle to help. I was the gunner.

In my incident, the loader's foot slipped off the handle and the handle returned to the lock position with my finger caught in it. The blanks produced smoke from burning its contents but there was no pressure to open the breach. If a live round were fired, there would be enough back pressure between the round leaving the gun and breach to open it automatically; no assistance would be needed from the gunner.

When I went to the medical tent, I had to wait until all of the simulated wounded were taken care of before the doctors attended to my actual smashed finger.

There were times when we had Alerts on base at Ayers Kaserne and had to prepare our tanks for combat on short order. We never knew whether

Life in the U.S. Army

the Alerts were real or simulated combat. The Alerts always took place early in the morning when we were in bed. I remember one Alert in winter. We were ordered to move out. The engines on a majority of our tanks failed and we were unable to leave the motor pool. The problem was that the air used to mix with the gasoline to create a gas for combustion in the cylinder was cold and moist, thus creating a hydrostatic lock (raw gasoline on the piston), so the engines shut off.

The air cleaner was installed inside the turret of the tank so that warm dry air was available to mix with gasoline to form a combustible gas mixture. However, the heaters inside the turret of our tanks did not work because we needed to replace igniters in the heaters. Our tank crews did most of the maintenance each day. For months, we continuously reported the need for igniters and were always told that the part was not in stock. The igniters were never ordered to replace the defective ones. We believed that those in charge of procurement did not care if we had to ride inside the turret of a cold tank. I do not believe that they understood that the inside of a warm turret was needed for the tank engines to function in cold wet weather.

When the Division Commander, a General, learned why the mission failed, there must have been "hell to pay." Some personnel in charge of procurement and others down the chain of command were probably replaced. Within a week, we received the new igniters. This exercise showed the importance of Alerts to maintain readiness for war.

Our major task at Ayers Kaserne was maintenance on our tanks at the motor pool. Maintenance included repairing and painting fenders that were bent during maneuvers, cleaning the guns to keep them in working order, replacing blocks on the tank track, checking the engine, and other operations to assure that the vehicle was ready for combat at any time.

The Army replaced officers on a regular basis. New enlisted men replaced those who were returning home. We played games on all newcomers—officers and enlisted men—at the motor pool. For example, we told a new officer that Little Joe would not work on their tank. "Little Joe" was the name that we called the auxiliary engine used to warm the main engine compartment before we tried to start the main engine in cold weather. The new lieutenant, who we thought knew nothing about tanks, said, "Send him to see me and I will put his ass to work." We had fun. However, I believe the lieutenant turned the joke on us. He knew that the Tank Crew could not send the auxiliary engine to him and he never followed up.

Whenever a new enlisted soldier came on board, the Tank Crew would tell him that they had misplaced or lost the key to the hydrostatic lock. Then they sent him to borrow one from another tank crew. Hydrostatic lock occurs when raw, non-vaporized gasoline falls onto the pistons of the engine—it is not a physical lock that requires a key. The pistons freeze and the engine shuts off. This soldier would go from one Tank Crew to another, asking to borrow their key to the hydrostatic lock. Each crew said that they had misplaced their key and sent him to another tank. This went on until a crew would finally explain the meaning of hydrostatic lock and tell him that he was the victim of a practical joke.

Practical jokes also took place in the barracks. Two that I recall were "hot foot and short sheet."

When a soldier was sleeping on his bed fully clothed, someone would take a match and stick it into his shoe at or near the toe. The ignitable end would go into the crack between the leather on the top of the shoe and the sole of the shoe. Then the other end of the match would be lit. When the fire reached the ignitable part, the person would wake up from the flash of heat on his foot.

In short-sheeting, the top sheet on your bed was folded in half. When you got into bed you would pull the top back, but when you stretched out you would split the top sheet. I was short-sheeted once at Fort Knox, Kentucky, but the prank did not work. Our bed sheets were replaced with clean sheets once every week. We would strip the dirty sheets from our beds on the scheduled morning and fold our mattresses on the bed in an orderly way. When you returned to the barracks that evening, clean sheets were lying on the bed springs. When I returned that evening, my bed was already made up. I quickly realized that no one had ever made up my bed before. As I pulled back the top sheet, I saw that it was folded in half. I looked around at other soldiers and they stared at me in disappointment.

International Crises: While I was stationed in Germany, there were two international crises—the Suez Canal Crisis in 1956 and the Lebanon Crisis in 1958. If military action was required by American forces in Germany, we would be deployed.

The Suez Canal Crisis related to Egyptian resentment of European efforts—England and France—to perpetuate colonial domination in the region. I read the *Army Times* newspaper to keep up with news around the world. Well, no United States soldiers were sent to combat during that crisis. Instead, President Dwight D. Eisenhower's Administration worked diligently through many international organizations to negotiate diplomatic settlements of the disputes between Egypt, England, and France.

The Lebanon Crisis in 1958 was different. I believe it related to political and religious tensions between Christians and Muslims and the unsettled issues in 1956 regarding the Suez Canal Crisis and Egypt's dominance in the Middle East under its President Gamal Abdel Nasser. The United States sent military forces to Lebanon in July 1958, less than two months before I was supposed to return home from active duty. We had trained with a tank company that was sent to Lebanon. That company was not a part of my battalion and was not stationed at Ayers Kaserne. Some soldiers in my battalion had their active duty status extended for a short time before they could return home. However, no one in my battalion participated in the U.S. military intervention in Lebanon.

The Local Tailor, Barber and Kitchen Police: We hired a local barber to get regular haircuts. We also had a local tailor to do the sewing and repairs that we had to take care of. Both were German nationals, and had space in the day room in our barracks. Our tailor would also produce suits "made to order" at a reasonable price. I had two suits made. Other soldiers had suits made by him as well. Thus, when we traveled off base, we wore "Tailor Made Suits."

With success in hiring the barber and tailor, we decided to try to go further in hiring German nationals. As enlisted men who were not NCOs, different groups of us were assigned to duties as "kitchen police" (KP) to work in the Mess Hall (cafeteria). Every day when we were on base, we had to wash dishes, pots and pans, scrub floors, clean tables, and serve meals to officers. But no enlisted man in the 7th Tank Battalion liked KP duty. So we decided to petition to hire local Germans to do it. We were informed that signing a petition could be considered a court-martial offense. However, we signed it knowing that the majority of the enlisted men could not or would not be subjected to court-martial. Our request was approved without question.

The cost for our barber, tailor, and workers in the Mess Hall was no more than four dollars per month for each enlisted soldier in my company. It may have been less than that but I can't remember. The funds were taken from our pay each month.

Passes: There were several types of passes and leaves by which soldiers could go off the Base. These included midnight passes, overnight passes, one-day passes, three-day passes and the allocated 15-day-per-year leave (vacation). During my time at Ayers Kaserne, only fifteen percent of the soldiers could be away on passes or leaves simultaneously. That meant that only three soldiers in my platoon could be away at any time. Leaves took priority over passes.

There were many recreational activities on Base. The Service Club provided games and musical instruments that could be checked out. In the day room in our barracks, I learned to shoot pool and play ping pong. In the Enlisted Men's Club, we could buy drinks and participate in activities such as bingo. The bowling alley had a television and newspapers. You could purchase beer in the building that had the bowling alley.

Still, many soldiers wanted to leave the Base and go to local towns such as Butzbach, Giessen, or Frankfurt where they could meet and socialize with women. I and several others in my platoon wanted to get a midnight, overnight or one-day pass to go to town. But we were ignored by the sergeant in charge of authorizing passes in our platoon. He was approving passes only for the same soldiers. I had no animosity toward him, but I believed that he had gotten too familiar or friendly with the few soldiers whom he always approved for passes. Over a period of time, I kept a record of who was authorized for passes. When I had enough data to show that the same soldiers were the only ones getting passes, I took it to my Tank Commander who reported it to the First Sergeant. As a result, the sergeant was transferred to another platoon. Paying attention to details and providing data to support your grievances matter.

It had been almost ten years since President Harry S. Truman issued Executive Order 9981 on July 26, 1948, abolishing racial discrimination in the United States Armed Forces. Yet, I still faced racism and subtle discrimination in the Army. The following two examples pertain to a

Life in the U.S. Army

deserved promotion and continuous detail duty assigned by bigoted NCOs for most of my time in Germany.

The case of the deserved promotion began one day when I was on guard duty. After our two-hour shift, we slept in the guard house. When I returned to our barracks the next day, my Tank Commander told me that he would be returning home to the U.S. He added that he had recommended David for the position as the new Tank Commander and that David had been appointed to the position. As Tank Gunner, I was second in command and should have been considered for the position. In fact, I had been considering a career in the Army and tried to learn as much as possible regarding the operations of tanks and what it took to be a leader in a Tank Company.

David was the gunner on another tank. My Tank Commander told me that he had told the powers in charge that he thought I did not want the position. But nobody in my chain of command interviewed me! I had never told anyone that I did not want to be a Tank Commander. I believe that the NCOs conspired to assure that I was on guard duty when they chose a new Tank Commander.

The officers respected me and my abilities. There were times on the firing range when a problem occurred in the turret of a tank and the officer in charge would send for me to check out and solve it.

I got along well with the enlisted men as well. Enlisted white soldiers respected my abilities and came to me for assistance in mathematics. One soldier who was preparing to get a license when he returned home to become a plumber, I believe, asked me for help with the mathematics part of the examination. Other soldiers who had not completed high school were working to get the General Educational Development "GED" Certificate of High School Equivalency. The University of Maryland had a program to allow soldiers get a GED at Ayers Kaserne. Those soldiers came to me for assistance.

There were tasks called "Details" that soldiers were assigned to complete. They included cleaning the Bachelors Officers Quarters ("BOQ"), working on the firing range, policing the Base, working in other Mess Halls, etc. No soldier wanted those duties. I was always assigned by a few sergeants to more Details than other soldiers. I made an appointment to see First Sergeant Johnson to complain. In the Army you were required to carry out the assignment first and complain later. He told me that I was in for a promotion and it was best for me not to file a complaint at that time. I respected him. He was interested in education and continuously educated himself through reading. In fact he had a set of encyclopedias in his room. I got the promotion and became an NCO several months before my active duty status would end on September 2, 1958.

Return to the Land of the Big PX and Round Door Knobs

I left Germany to return to the United States after serving more than two years and eleven months of my three-year active duty military obligation. Two years, three months, and nine days of my obligation were served in Germany.

During my travels as a soldier in Europe, I learned a lot about life, human behavior, and the treatment of others. Most importantly, I saw and experienced that blacks were treated with more respect in Europe than in the United States. For example, I was invited and accepted a room (bed and breakfast) in a family home in Amsterdam, Holland, in 1958. By comparison, I was unable to rent an apartment in Livermore, California, in 1975 because I am a black man. In many places during my travels in Europe during the late 1950s, I could enjoy music played by black musicians—the beginning of Rock And Roll music. I enjoyed my travels in Europe. However, I was ready to return home and visit family members after more than two years.

At Ayers Kaserne, the Post Exchange (PX) was a store where toiletries, radios, cameras—i.e., the works—could be purchased. Doors on the buildings on Base and in the towns had handles instead of round knobs as in the U.S. By comparison, there were large department stores in the U.S. (Big PXs) such as Macys, Sears, Montgomery Ward, and others. Thus, "Land of the Big PX and Round Door Knobs" was used to describe the United States.

Prior to my leaving for the States, the First Sergeant interviewed me regarding re-enlistment. The Army gave a bonus of six hundred dollars for a six-year re-enlistment. I informed him that I was considering college after my return home, and he wished me success. He later became Sergeant

Major of the 2nd Medium Tank Battalion, First Cavalry before I left Germany.

I traveled back to the U.S. on the U.S.N.S. Alexander M. Patch. I arrived in New York and took a train to Fort Jackson, South Carolina, where I processed out of the Army. Interestingly, Corporal Sergeant was still a corporal almost three years after I processed into the Army as a private. While my papers were processed, I was put in charge of meaningless details. When I received my papers and pay, I left Fort Jackson, took a Greyhound bus that evening, and arrived in Quincy the middle of the next day. This was in August 1958 and I was still only nineteen years old.

As I walked from the bus station to Adams Street to find a ride to my parents' house in Sawdust, I saw my first-cousin who had her young baby with her. She asked me to stay with the baby until she finished shopping and then we could go to Sawdust. As I was sitting in the car in my military uniform, a former classmate, Alvin Bell, who graduated from high school with me in 1954, came by. He asked me whose baby it was and I told him that it was my cousin's. I did not realize it at the time, but later I figured that he thought I was caring for my own baby. He observed the insignia on my uniform but did not ask any questions about my military experience. Decades later, during his speech at our 50-Year High School Class Reunion in 2004, he mentioned my military accomplishment and the fact that I had earned the Ph. D. degree.

I arrived home in Sawdust with a little more than two hundred dollars. Two days after I got home, my white soldier friend from Quincy came to Sawdust to visit. Each of us had served for a little less than three years in the Army. He had talked to my cousin who was a taxi driver in Quincy, and got directions to my parents' house. We went back to Quincy and he introduced me to his father. A short time later, he obtained a job at a furniture store in Quincy. One time he came to my parents' house at night to deliver furniture to my cousin's house, and I went with him to deliver it.

If you were a white soldier returning home, you could get a job above other applicants. Black soldiers returning home in the Jim Crow South were treated with indignity, same as they were treated before they served in the U.S. Army. I was one of those humiliated when I returned home in 1958.

PART III
Young Adult

Chapter 6

My First Year after Active Duty in the Army

I returned home in August 1958 after more than two years in Germany. During my first week I met James, an early childhood friend, on Adams Street in Quincy. His brother was living in Miami, and James suggested that we go there. We stayed at his brother's place a couple of nights. One afternoon, the three of us went to a bar and sat at a table. The waitress came to take our order. His brother and I ordered beer while James ordered a Coca-Cola. The waitress asked him for an ID. Since we were both nineteen years old, I asked if she wanted my ID, but she did not request it.

We left downtown Miami and went to North Miami Beach. James stayed at his cousin's house there and I rented a room at someone's house in the neighborhood. During the 1950s and 1960s, black people rented out rooms in their houses. We stayed in Miami about a week and returned to Quincy.

Before we took the Greyhound bus for home, we both purchased 0.22 caliber pistols. After returning to Quincy, James went into the Army to fulfill his six-month military active duty obligation.

I was still trying to find myself after returning from Germany. I felt lost. Even what some might call small things made me feel displaced. For example, I did not have any idea of what things cost in the U.S. at that time, even a bar of candy. I would hand money to the salesperson and receive my change.

I babysat my sister's two-year-old daughter for a while. I looked for work but only farm work was available. I worked with my father on the farm. My father had a pickup truck to carry people to pick cotton on a farm in Calhoun County, Florida. The truck had a homemade shelter over the rear and benches for seats like a homemade camper. My father received a percentage per pound for each pound of cotton that his crew picked. I also tried my hand picking cotton as one of his crew members. However, I could pick nowhere near as much cotton as his seasoned crew.

I kept thinking, "I joined the Army to get away from farm work. Now after three years in the military, that is still the only work I can find."

I returned to Miami to look for work. As they say, "The grass is always greener on the other side of the fence." I stayed the first two days in Liberty City at my brother-in-law's sister's house. I did not want to impose on her generosity so I decided to go to North Miami Beach where I had stayed in August 1958. I got a room and began looking for work. There was a store where people hung out during the day. When someone wanted a person to do a task for only that day or less, they would stop by the store to get someone. I got a few short term jobs by hanging out there.

After some time, I landed a job as a dishwasher at a Jewish-Italian restaurant. I had a weird working schedule—one day I worked from 11:00am to 8:00pm and the next day I worked from 5:00pm until 2:00am. The cycle was repeated every two days. The schedule worked okay because I had plenty time to look for another job on the day that I worked the evening shift. I read the classified ads in the newspaper. There were ads for common laborers on construction projects. I followed up but was told that their company did not hire blacks. I also followed up on ads from department stores, filled out applications, and in some cases took an exam on educational skills such as math and writing. Those applications received no response.

My primary job at the restaurant was washing dishes. When the restaurant was very busy, I had other tasks. I had to make pizzas and prepare coleslaw and side orders of pickles among other things. I remember once when I dropped a pickle on the floor. I picked it up and threw it in the trash. The boss saw me and said, "Do not throw the pickles in the trash—it is money in the bank." When you eat in a restaurant, you do not know what the food has been through and how it is when it arrives at your table.

My First Year after Active Duty in the Army

While I was working on the temporary job at the restaurant, there was an older black man whom I relieved as a dishwasher. He seemed to be happy with his job washing dishes. I got along well with the waitresses, all white. They knew that I smoked and would buy cigarettes for me. We ate our meals at the restaurant as workers. On Thanksgiving Day, the manager said that we could not have a turkey dinner. But if there was turkey left after the customers finished, then we could have it. I decided that would be my last day working at the restaurant. I did not return at 5:00pm on the next day (Friday). When I went to get my pay the next week, the manager asked why I had not come back to work. I told him that I did not like the way we were treated on Thanksgiving. I returned to Sawdust.

Early in 1959, I got a job working in the woods cutting pulpwood with Cleve, John Emery, Jim, and Arcella. They worked by the piece and I was paid by the hour—which was not good for me. They never worked on Mondays and left early on Fridays, which limited how much I could earn in a week.

Cleve owned the truck and had the contract and drove the truck.

Jim and Arcella loaded the heavy wood on the truck. They worked hard and continuously each day.

John Emery cut the wood. He had a saw with a large circular blade powered by a gasoline engine mounted on wheels that could rotate horizontally to cut and fell the tree. The saw could rotate vertically to cut the tree into pulpwood to be loaded onto the truck. John was excellent at his job.

My job was to use an axe to cut limbs from the trees felled by John Emery, and to mark the lengths along the fallen tree where he was to saw.

We had to take lunch to work with us in the woods. After a few days, I learned that my lunch should be something that would not spoil. We did not have coolers. So I carried crackers, canned meat and fish, peanut butter, saltines, cheese, and the like. The woods were full of snakes and other pests, mostly yellow jackets. I quit the pulpwood job when I began to see snakes. Cleve offered me more money per hour but I did not return.

In 1959, a gas pipeline pumping station was being built in the Sawdust Community (St. Mary). I got a job as a laborer there. Other blacks on the job were Raymond Milton and Frank Clark. Frank, a small guy, cleaned inside the engines because of his size. I worked with a white laborer, did a lot of sandblasting, and checked on underground power lines for safety matters.

After the project ended, I happened to meet the superintendent at an intersection on the highway. He asked me to come back to help with the finishing touches. I went home, changed to work clothes, and drove to the pumping station. By the way, this station was in a series to pump gas from Texas to South Florida. I worked seven days a week so I did not have time to spend my money. When the project was completed, I bought a blue 1951 Oldsmobile car. The first place I drove it was to Lake Talquin to fish with Amos and my cousin Charles. We loved to go fishing.

I was obligated to spend three years in Active Reserves. Although President Truman had integrated the Army by Executive Order in 1948, my Reserve unit in Tallahassee was still segregated in 1958 and remained segregated throughout my three-year obligation. We had white officers. In 1959 it appeared that I could find only farm work or common labor jobs in construction. I was disgusted with civilian life and signed up to return to active duty in the Army.

I requested to return to active duty during a specific time frame but had not received any information.

One day I was driving my cousin Ruby Gunn's car, taking her, my sister Gladys, and Amanda Rolax shopping in Tallahassee. Amanda and I talked about my plans for the future. She stated that I should go to college. I had no money for college but I sent an application to Florida A&M University anyway.

One night when I arrived home, I had received a letter from the Army regarding my request to return to active duty. The letter stated that I should be in Jacksonville, Florida, the next morning. That was impossible, so I wrote a letter stating why I would not appear. I said that I did not think my request was considered, and I had applied to college. However, I still did not know how I was going to make it to college with no money. Tuition at Florida A&M University (FAMU) was seventy five dollars per semester, plus you needed money for room and board. I had taken the college entrance exam for Florida when I was a senior in high school. However, African Americans were not allowed to attend majority institutions in Florida. If I could save seventy five dollars for tuition, I could probably get at least a job washing dishes to cover room and board. I had plenty experience washing dishes.

By registration time at FAMU, I had the money for registration but had not received an acceptance letter. I went to the Registrar's Office anyway to register for the semester. The man at the office was very friendly and knew me from the picture on my application. I was able to register for the fall semester in 1959.

Chapter 7

Undergraduate Student at FAMU

Prior to entering college, I was serving in the U.S. Army Active Reserves. As an NCO, I had to give lectures on different topics related to activities needed for members of my unit. The lectures had to be prepared and submitted in writing per a required template for the record. In other words, I was teaching before I entered college. I knew that my lectures in the Army Reserves would not prepare me for a professional career and I had to get a college degree to advance my status from menial jobs.

I had graduated from high school five years earlier, in May 1954. I enrolled into a Pre-Engineering Program at Florida A&M University (FAMU) in Tallahassee in the fall of 1959. Mr. Blake was the director. There were five new students whom I knew well. Only two of us, John Owens and I, ultimately earned a bachelor's degree in engineering. Another one of us may have earned an engineering degree in the years after John.

On my first day, the first class that I attended was chemistry. Mr. Rivers, the instructor, gave a placement exam in mathematics. I earned a score of 62 out of 68 (91.1%)—one of the top scores. My second class that day was English and we had to write a paper. I wrote about my favorite baseball player, Willie Mays, and scored a B. Then I thought to myself, "College is really going to be tough; exams on the first day." I later learned that no one earned an A from my English instructor.

I worked as a dishwasher at Morrison's Cafeteria on the campus of Florida State University (FSU) four hours each night except one night per week when I attended my Army Reserve Unit obligations. I was not able to attend a FAMU football game past half-time because I had to work on Saturdays.

The first place where I lived in Tallahassee was a "dump" near the railroad station. Later, Willie Adams, who was in my squad in the Army Reserves, suggested that I become his roommate. We became roommates and shared cooking breakfast.

One of my best instructors in my first semester was my chemistry teacher. He was very serious about assuring that his students got the best instruction, and even had problem sessions on week nights to help us understand the lessons. He also had a problem session on Saturday mornings. I was unable to attend the night sessions because I worked to support myself.

The week before the first chemistry exam, there were still things that I needed to understand. I attended the Saturday morning session before Monday's exam. I prepared questions in advance to clear up my understanding. At the session, I asked my questions and, if the instructor's answer did not clear up my understanding, I would rephrase it for clarification. On Monday, I got an A. I had no more difficulties with chemistry. In fact, students came to me for tutoring. I tutored for free and it helped me to stay alert in chemistry.

I earned five A's and one B during my first semester. The B came from my English course. Because of my performance, I was invited to join a group of faculty and other honor students in my second semester to discuss works in literature, one night per week. I was unable to participate because I had to work to support myself. However, I did attend one meeting where we discussed The Prince by Machiavelli. The Prince was considered one of the first works on modern political philosophy in which truth was more than any abstract ideal.

In the beginning of my second semester, Mr. Blake, my advisor, recommended me for a drafting position with the ROTC Program. I did not get that position. It went to a classmate because he was a student in the ROTC. This position would have allowed me to participate in the honors program and eliminate working as a dishwasher at Morrison's Cafeteria at FSU. I blame myself because I did not tell the interviewer that I was an NCO in the Army Reserves. I thought that your ability to perform in the position description was the most important thing. I never thought about relating my experience in the Army and the Army Reserves.

I did not know the importance of politics in obtaining a job.

I shall recount memories of three courses during my second semester: English composition, chemistry, and trigonometry. Faculty members got reputations about how they treated students in their classes.

When I told my roommate who my English instructor was, he said that she had a bad reputation and I should not have registered for her class. I replied that I did not pick instructors, only class times that fit my needs.

The teacher gave us an assignment to do a layout of the university library. I spent much time on that project and did a scale drawing of the floor plan in ink on a large cardboard sheet of the type used for engineering drawings. When the instructor saw my work, she said, "This is great." Then she saw my name and said, "Oh, you are an engineering student." She never returned my poster and probably used it as an example to grade other students.

At midterm, she told me that she did not give me a deficiency grade because I was an honor student. But I had not earned a grade below C on any assignments in English, and I did not deserve a deficiency grade. She was setting me up to give me a C in that course. Unfortunately, I received a C for the semester. My roommate was right about her reputation. I did not fight or complain about my grade.

My chemistry course was Qualitative Analysis. It included classroom lectures and laboratory experiments. For these experiments, students were given a sample of an unknown substance or substances that had to be identified. The instructor required us to take our exams in ink.

He returned our papers of the first examination and discussed the solutions. He marked the solution to one of my problems as incorrect and I ended up with a B on that exam. At the end of the class period, I explained that my solution was correct based on the answers he had presented. He agreed that it was correct, but said that my solution was not clear to him at the time that he graded my paper. He did not give me credit for my correct solution and did not change my grade to A.

For laboratory experiments, neither my instructor nor his teaching assistant pointed out critical details in identifying unknown substances or elements. In one experiment, all students including me who had a certain element in their unknown sample received a zero. I tested for one element and got no precipitate for it. Then I tested for the next element in that sample and received a precipitate, which told me that the second element was present. But we had not been taught about the time scale for chemical reactions. The first element was precipitating during my test for the second element.

The Chemistry Department at FAMU had a reputation of being the toughest at the University. As our final experiment, we had a General Unknown to analyze which could contain any or all of the substances or elements that we had tested for the whole semester. The word was that no student had analyzed the General Unknown correctly. I decided that I would be the first. We had enough samples to do more than one analysis and we were allowed to use the laboratory on nights and weekends. I did about three independent analyses to see if I got the same results. If at least two of the three analyses gave the same results, I would report those results. I was the first to solve the General Unknown and I got an A out of the course.

Trigonometry, along with algebra, helped me on the farms in Sawdust. Several black farmers grew bright (cigarette) tobacco and were allotted a specific number of acres by the State of Florida. If the farmer planted too much, he had to plow it up or pay a penalty and lose money. If a farmer grew less than his allotted acres, he lost money. It was important that each farmer planted the number of acres allotted. They said, "You are an engineering student. We want you to lay out our plots for tobacco so that we get all the acres we are allotted." They would show me the area on their farms where they wanted to plant tobacco. I made a triangle that had the bottom of the legs one yard apart to make measurements. I could rotate the triangle and count off the yards. I took my triangle, pad of paper, pencil, and slide rule for computing. Using my knowledge of algebra and trigonometry, I laid out the plots. The farmers paid me only two dollars to lay out their plots, so I could not afford to hire someone to help me. The farmers were happy and bragged about my performance. NOTE: Men were paid only forty cents per hour for farm work in the Sawdust Community in 1960.

In 1960 there were student sit-ins at lunch counters all across the U.S. One Saturday night, we were walking home from work at Morrison's

Cafeteria on the campus of FSU. A carload of whites stopped and confronted us regarding demonstrations or sit-ins that had taken place that day. We were conscious of where we were; someone in our group said that there was a pile of bricks no more than half a block away. We continued to walk and the white guys drove off without pursuing the incident further. When I got to my room, I found out that my roommate Willie Adams had been arrested in the sit-in or demonstration. He was released from jail on Sunday.

After that, many of us FAMU students who worked at Morrison's at night began to carry handguns because we walked home. I carried a 0.22 caliber pistol and I do not know what the others carried. One evening, two of my co-workers got into an argument and ran back to the dressing room. We all had lockers there. I knew that they had handguns so I went to the dressing room to calm their argument. I said, "You guys stop this now! Just think what will be in the news tomorrow: 'FAMU students got into a gunfight in the cafeteria at FSU.' Think how it will affect FAMU." My words were enough to calm the situation.

There were times that I would go home to visit on weekends after work at Morrisons. One Saturday evening, I walked to the Greyhound bus station in downtown Tallahassee to take a bus to Quincy to visit my folks in Sawdust. There had been some trouble in another town and police were checking to see if any of the suspects had come to Tallahassee. The bus station was still segregated. When I went to purchase my ticket, some black women looked at me and said, "We better get away from you. You must have done something," because they saw the police. But the police never said one word to me. There was racial profiling even by blacks against blacks in 1960.

In the summer of 1960, I went to Tampa to look for work. My cousin Charles Rolax was living at Melvin Gunn's Place in Ybor City and I shared the room with Charles. His brother, J. Lloyd Milton, was rooming at Bernard Clark's house in Tampa. J. Lloyd was working at a company that bought and sold processed steel and suggested that I may be able to get a job there. I applied and got a job handling steel. This was a dirty job because you got oil over your clothes.

I got laid off from the steel job, went back to Sawdust, and found work as a laborer in road construction. We paved a road in Liberty County and

Undergraduate Student at FAMU

a road in St. John, Gadsden County. Some people in St. John said that I had quit college and gone to work on the roads. One day I was in Quincy and walking on the street across from the courthouse on the north side. I met a young woman who seemed to be a few years older than me, and was probably from St. Johns. She offered to support the continuation of my college education. This was probably the first time I had seen her in many years, and I could not remember her name. But she knew me. I told her that I appreciated her concern but could not allow her to support me. I said that I was not dropping out of college and that I had other avenues to complete my education. We had a good conversation and went our separate ways.

The year 1960 was interesting in race relations. We had sit-ins and demonstrations. Black people in some communities registered to vote. As late as 1960, my brother Amos was the first and probably only black person to register to vote in Sawdust. Amos voted in the primaries at Sawdust Store at the intersection of Florida State Highway 65 and County Highway 274 (Providence Road).

For the general election for the President of the United States between John F. Kennedy and Richard M. Nixon, Luther Clark dropped Amos off at Sawdust Store to vote. I was sitting on the front porch at our house when Luther picked up Amos. A short time later, the white bully in Sawdust drove by in his pickup truck headed toward the polling place. I thought that there may be trouble, so I got in my 1953 Ford and drove to the store.

When I arrived, white men were standing around and the bully had Amos by the collar of his shirt. Obviously the other white men had called the bully. I drove right up in front of them, Amos got in my car, and we left. Of course, I had protection in my car.

One Friday night in spring 1961, I went to the Sawdust Store to purchase some small canned food items. The bully was in the store with several black people who lived and worked on his family's farm. As I stood around waiting for my turn to be served, the bully said, "You Thigpens think you are something, voting." The black people with him looked at me as if I had done something wrong. They appeared to be angry with me.

I left the store and went home to get my revolver for protection. I told my parents that I had forgotten something. However, I went to another store farther away for my purchases. I did not want to be in a situation to do something that I would later regret.

I continued at FAMU [Florida A&M University] and registered for the second semester of the academic year 1960–1961. Prior to that second semester, I had not taken Analytic Geometry and Calculus. But I had studied the curriculum of the first two years in engineering at Howard University and knew that I was wasting time in the pre-engineering program at FAMU.

I talked to Mr. Blake, Director of the Pre-engineering Program at FAMU, and we went to see the head of the Mathematics Department. She allowed me to enroll in Analytic Geometry and Calculus.

However, when I went to the Analytic Geometry and Calculus class, the instructor asked if I had taken a course called Analysis, a combination of algebra and trigonometry. I had not taken that course and the instructor would not allow me to remain in her class. I responded that the head of the department had allowed me to enroll in it. The instructor might have been trying to protect her courses. She told the department head that I had not taken the Analysis course.

When I got to the next class period of Analytic Geometry and Calculus, the instructor told me again that I was not allowed to take that course. I informed Mr. Blake and we went to see the department head again. This time, I was not allowed to remain in the course.

I informed Mr. Blake that I was going to withdraw from the University. He did not want me to withdraw because he thought that I would not return to college. Nonetheless, I withdrew and received seventy-five percent of the tuition that I had paid. I sent an application to Howard University in Washington, D.C., for their Mechanical Engineering program housed in the School of Engineering and Architecture.

Meanwhile, I went back to Sawdust and worked on Newell Edwards's family's shade tobacco farm. His nephew, Marcus Edwards, ran the daily operations. My life was circling around farm work. I did everything from setting, looping, tying, wrapping, and priming tobacco to leading irrigation efforts. I also carried tobacco workers to the farm in the mornings, took them home for lunch and back to work, and home in the evenings. My mother worked on the Edwards farm too, so I would drop her off for lunch first.

The worst part of the job was taking the workers back to work after lunch. They always had to stop at the Sawdust Store. Sometimes I got back to the farm after 1:00 pm and was admonished for being late with the crew. I took the blame without making excuses. I did not get paid any more than any other male farm worker for the extra work. I worked there throughout the second semester in 1961.

I believed that with patience, I could reach my goal to become an engineer. Improving my employment status would take time.

Chapter 8

Undergraduate Student at Howard University

I was still serving in the active reserves in the Army and it was now time for summer camp. I believe that we had either a one or two-week training obligation. Several of us including Willie Adams carpooled in two cars to Fort Story, Virginia. After the training exercises at Fort Storey, Willie and I took the Greyhound bus to Washington, D.C. and arrived on a Saturday morning. Willie was headed to Atlantic City, New Jersey, to look for a summer job, and I was headed to Howard University for possible summer school if I were accepted. We walked from the bus station to the Howard campus.

The Administration Building was closed but there was a switchboard operator on duty that opened the door. He was a fraternity brother of Willie. We told him that I had applied to Howard but had not heard anything. He said that he knew the Assistant Director of Admissions, Mr. Brown, and would call him. Over the phone, I told Mr. Brown of my predicament and he said that he would come to the campus in half an hour to look at my records and transcripts.

Mr. Brown came to campus as promised and looked at my transcripts. He said that he knew FAMU. He told me to come back Monday morning, and he would let me enroll. I replied that I did not want to stay in D. C. over the weekend and then find out that I could not register for summer school. He assured me that I would be allowed to register. I was also given information about where I could get a room within close walking distance.

I got a room and Willie left for Atlantic City. On Monday, I was allowed to register. However, the process required me to go to the Dean of Men's office. He asked me where I was staying. I replied that I already had a room off campus. He said that if I were allowed to enroll at Howard, I would have to live in the dormitory on campus.

My Years Studying at Howard

I moved into Drew Hall and took two courses, Analytic Geometry and Economics. I studied Analytic Geometry with a mathematics student from Florida who knew my classmate Jimmy Buford from FAMU. Jimmy and I had taken classes together in the pre-engineering program at FAMU. After each class, my classmate and I would get together and work all problems at the end of the chapter. My instructor in Analytic Geometry gave pop quizzes that counted fifteen percent of the course grade. InmyEconomics class I met Jonathan P. "JP" Nelson, an electrical engineering student, and we have remained friends.

Someone told me that several southern states forbade blacks from attending white institutions of higher education in their states, but funded programs for blacks to attend schools in northern states if a black college in that southern state could not accommodate the student's desired course of study. Florida had such a program. I applied for educational support from the State of Florida to get an engineering education at Howard.

After summer school, Jimmy Buford was in town and we got together on occasions. One time we were at a club and I got up to go to the men's room. As I got out of my seat, my wallet fell out of my back pocket. As soon as I came back, the person sitting at the table next to ours got up and left. I was going to show Jimmy some pictures, so I reached for my wallet. I had lost everything–wallet, money, identification, driver's license, social security card, pictures, etc. The only money that I had left was the change from five dollars when I had paid for two beers. I had a little over four dollars left, which was in my left front pocket.

I was living in the dormitory but now had to find a job where I could eat. I found a job at the cafeteria at the Federal Aviation Administration (FAA), more than two miles from Howard. On that job I was able to eat breakfast and lunch. However, I had to work more than two weeks before getting paid. I used my four dollars and change wisely. The first week and a half, I rode the bus to work and walked back to Howard. Later I began to walk to and from work. On the weekend there was a place where, for thirty five cents, I could buy a bowl of beans with pig feet, pig tails, and the like including cornbread. I got down to my last quarter and I smoked cigarettes, which cost a quarter per pack. One Saturday, Jimmy Buford and I were sitting outside on the playground across Georgia Avenue from the campus watching sports. When we left, I checked my pocket and my quarter was not there. I went back and found it on the grass. Jimmy did not have a job at this time.

The last weekend before payday, I still had my quarter and knew it was not enough to feed me over the weekend. I bought a pack of cigarettes with the twenty-five cents. Thus I had no money left. Yet I had to survive the weekend and walk the two-plus miles to work Monday. I stayed in bed as much as possible to save energy. I did not have anything to eat from lunch on Friday until breakfast on Monday. I could have asked someone in my family back home to send me some money for food but I decided to see if I could survive alone in a big city with no money. After that pay day, I informed my supervisor at the FAA cafeteria that I was going to have to leave the job to return to school. She said that if I could work it out with my class schedule, they would have a job for me.

I received my pay for work in the cafeteria. I also received a check from the State of Florida later to help pay tuition for the fall semester. Because I had lost my identification, I went to the bank that made out the check for my work at the FAA. The bank cashed my check. I took Jimmy out that Friday night for a great dinner. We discussed our plans for the future. I told him that I was going to continue at Howard and earn a degree in mechanical engineering. Jimmy was very disappointed with the way things were going as a civilian and said that he was going to re-enter the military. He had an uncle who had sponsored his brother's college education, but Jimmy had no one to help him. I believe that he joined the Air Force this time and I never saw him again. I went to Florida for a short break.

In the fall semester of 1961, I returned to Howard and got a room off campus at Ruth and Ruby's townhouse at 13th and Lamont Street, within walking distance to the campus. I paid my tuition and registered. In my classes I met Hailey Baker, who had just returned to Howard after being away for one year. He was a veteran of the U.S. Navy. Hailey and I have remained friends since we first met.

Mr. Thomas Clancy, who taught the two courses Kinematics and Machine Tool Laboratory, had some rental property. He asked if anyone wanted a job helping him paint to get it ready to show to new renters. It paid two dollars per hour. I needed the money. Hailey and I accepted the job.

Tuition scholarships were available for students in engineering who had a grade point average (GPA) high enough to make the Dean's List. I was going to have to do well to be eligible. I paid tuition only my first semester at Howard because I made the Dean's List every semester during my study in engineering at Howard. I also applied for a National Defense Education Act (NDEA) student loan. Tuition scholarships were always late in the beginning of the second semester because it took time for decisions on who would receive them.

After my first semester at Howard, I was not sure how I was going to continue my studies. My rent was forty dollars per month and tuition was a little over one hundred dollars per semester. The tuition could be paid in three deferred payments, a big help. My sister Mildred sent me some money to make one of the deferred payments and the rent. That was enough to help me survive for the spring semester in 1962 because I got a scholarship and the NDEA student loan. Further, my first-cousin Essie Gunn Nealy sent me a homemade fruit cake several times that would last me a while. I learned to get by on one meal per day. There was a Chinese restaurant where I ate most of the time. The restaurant served an "American Dinner" each evening for about one dollar and fifty cents and I would snack off Essie's cake while studying at Ruth's and Ruby's townhouse. There were also restaurants across from the campus on Georgia Avenue and a cafeteria near where I lived that had prices I could afford.

I enrolled in summer school the summer of 1962 to take one or two courses at seven and one half per credit hour. I wanted to assure that I had established the prerequisites to give me a full load in the fall of 1962 and graduate in the second semester of 1964. I got a job on campus as a student janitor along with Aubrey Walker who was taking courses to assure his graduation in 1963. I was still living in Ruth and Ruby's townhouse. Early on a Saturday or Sunday morning, Ruth awakened me and said that my brother was outside. I put on my clothes and found James and a couple of cousins (Herschell Rolax and another cousin whose name I do not remember) there. They were headed to Ocean City, Maryland, to look for summer jobs. I spent time with them and they left for Ocean City.

I had to pawn my camera one time that summer to buy food until I got paid from my work as a student janitor at Howard.

During the fall semester 1962, Hailey Baker, Aubrey Walker, and I shared a house near the corner of Shepherd Street and New Hampshire Avenue. In the spring semester of 1963, we moved to an apartment on Girard Street near 14th Street because our landlord was moving into the house on Shepherd Street himself and we had no rental contract that would allow us to remain. We got another roommate, Roy B. Palmer, during the spring semester 1963.

The School of Engineering and Architecture had a "Jazz and Technology event" organized by the Student Council every spring. There was a concert by a famous jazz artist at Cramton Auditorium on campus and a dance at a downtown hotel. The jazz concert was open to the public by purchasing a ticket. Two artists during my junior and senior years were Nina Simone and Nancy Wilson.

The dance was available only for juniors and seniors. During spring 1963, when I was in my junior year, my two roommates Hailey and Aubrey, and another friend, Oswald, all from Florida, talked about attending the dance. We discussed who would get the prettiest date. None of us had a steady girlfriend.

There were two females, a staff member and a part time student, working in the Dean of Men's office. Hailey invited the staff member and she accepted. I purchased a new blue serge suit but did not have a date. Later on, as I was walking on campus with a classmate and friend Helen Britt, who was already dating a guy on campus, we met the history student who was working part-time in the Dean of Men's Office. Helen introduced us and I ended up inviting her to the dance. She accepted. Aubrey, Hailey, Oswald, and I all had pretty dates at the dance. My friend Geneva Austin, whom I met in January 1964, attended the Jazz and Technology events with me in spring 1964.

The year 1963 was very rewarding for me at Howard. I was honored to attend a concert at Constitution Hall in Washington. I do not remember the month. Howard University had box seats and Lewis K. Downing, Dean of Engineering and Architecture, took two of his students, Roy B. Palmer and me, to a concert by a classical guitarist or violinist. Roy was a student in Civil Engineering and I was a student in Mechanical Engineering. It was an honor and privilege to be selected. The Dean was showing appreciation for his accomplished students. *I think the performer was David Oistrakh, a violinist. But I have been unable to verify a date that he performed at Constitution Hall. It may have been a classical guitarist instead.*

In spring 1963, I had an interview on campus for a Goodyear Foundation Award. I received the one thousand dollar award. The Goodyear Award plus a small check of less than one hundred fifty dollar of support from the State of Florida and a five hundred dollar NDEA student loan provided me with enough money to last throughout the 1963–1964 academic year.

During summer 1963, I got a job to work at IBM in Poughkeepsie, New York. Travel to Poughkeepsie was the most difficult and demanding trip that I have ever taken. I left Washington on a Saturday and traveled by Greyhound Bus to New York City, where I had to transfer to a Trailways Bus. I had to wait many hours to get my luggage because of the transfer. I arrived in Poughkeepsie on Sunday evening.

The Personnel Department at IBM sent me a list of places that summer employees could get rooms. When I arrived in Poughkeepsie, I took a taxi to several of those places. None of them accepted black people. There was no way of knowing this by reading the IBM list. I believe that the people in the Personnel Department did not expect that blacks were being hired for summer jobs. I did not see any other blacks in the areas where I worked or visited at IBM.

Housing was as segregated as it was in the South.

The taxi cost money that I could not afford. I finally asked the driver to take me to a hotel. I believe that this was the only hotel in Poughkeepsie, and it was where dignitaries from around the world stayed when visiting President Franklin D. Roosevelt, whose home was in nearby Hyde Park.

I did not have enough money left to get to work and pay for living for a week. I called my sister Leatrice and discussed my situation before I checked out of the hotel and went to the job at IBM. She agreed to wire me money to the hotel. I took a taxi to the IBM facility and explained my situation regarding housing. They gave me another place where I could get a room. When I got there by taxi and saw the landlady, I thought, "Another dead run." However, she was a very light skinned woman of West Indian descent who accepted me as a tenant in her house. Leatrice sent me money and I sent her installments every week to pay her back. At IBM we were paid every week on Mondays.

My next problem was how to get to work and home each day. There was very little public transportation in Poughkeepsie and no public transportation to IBM facilities. I discussed this with workers in my group. A designer who drove close by where I was staying said that I could ride with him. I offered to pay him but he said that he would not accept money from a student in need.

My landlady also had a full-time employee at IBM renting a room in her house. I do not remember his name but his family still lived in Philadelphia. He was searching for a house to bring his family to live in. He and I would drive around the countryside in the evenings during the week days and then go out for dinner. He visited his family in Philadelphia on the weekends. Across the street from where we lived in Poughkeepsie was an apartment building that did not rent to blacks. More proof that housing was as segregated as it was in the South.

For the Fourth of July weekend, I traveled to Bronx, New York. I stayed at the apartment of two lady friends of Hailey Baker. While I was staying in the Bronx, from there, I visited my friend Hailey Baker, who lived at his father's house in Queens, New York. Hailey and I took a short trip to Coney Island.

In Poughkeepsie, there was a student from the electrical engineering department at Howard University. He also had a summer position at IBM. I suggested that we do things together on the weekends. But he showed no interest, said it was too hot outside, and was satisfied with staying in and watching television.

I went to movies, went bowling, and sometimes stopped at a bar on weekends. One Saturday, I came back to my landlady's house smoking a cigar. She said, "Mr. Thigpen, are you smoking a cigar?" I replied, "Yes, but I will go outside and finish it." She said "NO, my husband smoked cigars and I love to smell them."

I visited President Franklin D. Roosevelt's home on the Hudson River in Hyde Park. The home depicted his life. Poughkeepsie was noted for three things: IBM, Smith Brothers Cough Drops, and Vassar College. Vassar had no students on campus during the summer. I would walk across the campus on my way to one of the three movie theaters in Poughkeepsie.

At IBM, I worked on three different projects. My desk was a drafting board and I spent most of my time drawing on my first project. The next project was plotting data by hand. This was when most of the employees were on vacation. Most of them went on vacation at the same time during the summer. I had been transferred to a new group prior the vacation period. When my new group leader returned from vacation, I was assigned a new task making designs of evaporation masks for circuits on silicon wafers. I had to use an electron microscope to see them. I worked on this project on my last day at IBM to finish the task. Fellow employees stated that people usually do not work on their last day.

I had an exit interview with my supervisor regarding employment after earning the Bachelor of Science degree. I asked him what my responsibility would be, and he stated that that I would be doing similar things. I knew that I did not want to spend my time on a drafting board after I earned a degree in mechanical engineering.

On my way back to Washington, DC, I took the train from Poughkeepsie to New York City. Hailey Baker and John Owens met me at Penn Station in New York. Hailey was living at his father's house in Queens. John was living at his sister's house in Long Island. I stayed with John at his sister's house. The next day, a Saturday, John and I spent most of the day moving a woman friend of his sister to a new location. John's sister had rented a trailer and it was hitched to her car. John and I did all of the work. That evening, we went to the city to meet other friends from Howard University—Hailey Baker, Aubrey Walker, and Helen Britt. We went bowling. I met Helen's brother at his apartment in New York where she was visiting. Later, we went to Harlem to explore the sights. I had heard that you would always meet someone on 125th Street in Harlem that you know. Indeed, I met someone that I knew but I do not remember his name.

Hailey and I returned to Washington to find an apartment for the 1963–1964 academic year. A classmate informed us of a basement apartment at the house where he and his brother lived. The basement was separated from the main living space of the house and you entered it from the rear. We rented that apartment because it was very inexpensive and fit our budget. It was located on New Hampshire Avenue within walking distance to Howard. There were no connection for a phone in the basement but there was a pay phone on the street nearby. I did not give out a phone number because I did not have a phone.

I applied for a summer position at Sandia Corporation in 1964. The position required a security clearance. On my application, I listed my address but no phone number because I did not have one. One evening, my classmate's brother informed me that I had an important phone call and I went with him upstairs to answer it. The call was from Betty Bradwell whom I knew from Greensboro, Florida, when I was in high school. She was now living in Washington and working with the agency that was investigating my security clearance. She found me through the address on my security application. At a later date, we had dinner. I subsequently found out that Betty was a distant cousin on my Grandma Betty Goodsen Brown's side.

Aside from not being equipped with a phone, Hailey noted something else about that basement apartment. Huge rats had made holes in the ground nearby and tried to enter our apartment. Exterminators were called. I remember that I saw rats about twelve inches long there and at other places where we lived in Washington, DC.

During fall semester 1963, I received two special honors: a feature in the Engineering Student Magazine; and induction into Tau Beta Phi, the national engineering student honor society. I was inducted into Tau Beta Pi in December 1963.

During fall semester 1963, I was encouraged by my Department Chairman, Professor Steven S. Davis, by my Advisor Professor Darnley E. Howard, and by Professor M. Lucius Walker Jr., who taught heat transfer classes, to pursue graduate studies for the Ph.D. degree.

I applied to three universities: Stanford, Ohio State, and Illinois Institute of Technology. I was offered two fellowships in the spring of 1964 to attend graduate school in the first semester of the 1964-1965 academic year, one at Ohio State University and the other at Illinois Institute of Technology. I was accepted at Stanford University but there was no fellowship, so Stanford was out. I accepted the fellowship at Illinois Institute of Technology (IIT) for graduate study in the Mechanics Department.

Graduation at Howard

I graduated in June 1964 from Howard University with a Bachelor of Science in Mechanical Engineering, *Magna Cum Laude*. This was the last time that I had to worry about where my next meal was coming from.

My mother, my sister Mildred and her daughter Janice, my sister Leatrice's daughter Sharon, and my brother James Woodrow came to Washington to my graduation. A classmate of James Woodrow informed me that his landlady had rooms available and my mother, sister, and nieces stayed there. My brother stayed at my place. During that time, the graduation ceremonies lasted for at least a week. There was a Baccalaureate Ceremony a week before the commencement when degrees were awarded.

I introduced my family to Geneva Austin and she attended the graduation ceremonies. This was the first time that I had ever introduced my mother or any member of the family to someone whom I really liked.

We celebrated and then left for Florida. We drove to Columbia, South Carolina, and spent a day or two with our cousin. His wife had a young son who had a foul mouth with the most four-letter words that I had ever heard from a young person. We continued on to Florida and I spent a few days in Sawdust. Then I took a flight to Albuquerque, New Mexico.

Chapter 9

Summer Job at Sandia Corporation

I accepted a summer position to work at Sandia Corporation (now Sandia National Laboratories) prior to graduation from Howard University in June 1964. Sandia paid for a round trip from Washington, D.C., to Albuquerque, New Mexico. Sandia offered me six hundred thirty dollars per month, which was above the average salary for graduates of mechanical engineering programs at that time.

Getting to Albuquerque was round-about because there were no commercial jets into or out of Tallahassee or Albuquerque. To get from Tallahassee to Albuquerque, my flights were on National Airlines. We stopped in Panama City, Florida; Pensacola, Florida; Mobile, Alabama; and I changed planes in New Orleans, Louisiana. I took a jet plane to Dallas, Texas, and changed planes again. From Dallas, I took a propeller plane, stopped at Midland Airport (between Midland and Odessa in Texas), and finally arrived in Albuquerque that evening.

Eight airports in one day on one trip! I call that trip the milk run—the milk man delivered milk to many customers in the city every morning similar to the ice man in Sawdust. Probably a better name is a "puddle jumper"—you jump over one puddle and rest, jump over another puddle and rest, and continue until you jump over all puddles and reach your destination. The "puddle" was the distance between each airport, not a pond, lake, or swimming pool.

A former classmate at Howard University, JP Nelson, met me at the Albuquerque airport. The terminal was a small adobe building and you did not go inside. Your luggage was placed outside the building.

JP had duplex apartments. Another classmate from Howard University and I were going to share one that summer. However I had to wait until JP's current tenants moved so I slept on the couch in his living room until the other apartment became available.

JP liked to entertain and people came by during the week. I could not go to bed until everyone left. As a result, I would get very sleepy in the afternoon at work. I was very relieved when I was able to move and not have to sleep on his couch. I could now go to bed before midnight or later and get a good night's sleep.

I worked at the nuclear reactor site on Sandia Base, several miles from the main buildings. I did not have a car and had to take a bus to Sandia Base and then a laboratory bus to the reactor site. The problem was that, due to its schedule, the laboratory bus would get me to work late and then I would have to leave work early. Fortunately, I solved the problem. I checked out a truck at the nuclear site each evening and drove it to the main laboratory. The next morning, I drove it back to the reactor site.

At the reactor site, there were numerous scorpions and tarantula spiders. You had to be careful.

I worked on two projects that summer. The first one related to fracture mechanics, something I knew nothing about and is not part of an undergraduate curriculum today. I had no one to mentor me. I spent much time in the library trying to learn fracture mechanics. I was later assigned to design a portable hoist for one of the technicians, something I was able to accomplish. I learned that I should express my interests in the future prior to accepting a position. I left my summer job at Sandia Corporation to pursue graduate studies at Illinois Institute of Technology in Chicago, Illinois.

Chapter 10

Graduate Student at Illinois Institute of Technology

The years that I was a graduate student at Illinois Institute of Technology (IIT) in Chicago, Illinois were probably the most eventful, rewarding, and lasting experiences in my life prior to my experiences as Chair of the Department of Mechanical Engineering at Howard University. I have vivid memories of travel, living accommodations, people I met, studies, service to others, politics, degrees that I received, and problems along the way. I shall begin with my route in summer 1964 from Albuquerque to Chicago.

Travel to Chicago

My plans called for me to leave Albuquerque at least two weeks prior to the beginning of the fall semester at Illinois Institute of Technology. I had not seen my brother Amos since I entered college at Howard. He had moved to Los Angeles after I enrolled at Howard in 1961, three years earlier. Amos did not like to travel, so I planned to visit him. He and his wife Dorothy were living in a small apartment in downtown Los Angeles.

I traveled to Los Angeles by Greyhound Bus on the Saturday before Labor Day (Monday, September 7, 1964). That was the worst bus ride that I ever had. At one place we changed to another bus. We traveled probably through Death Valley. The bus did not have working air conditioning—it was hot as hell.

I arrived in Los Angeles that evening. Amos, Dorothy, and I went to San Diego the next day. We stayed at the house of Bernice "Baby Gal" Gilliam and her husband Carter Sunday night. Baby Gal's three sons by a previous marriage lived with her and Carter. The house had plenty of room.

Baby Gal was originally from the Sawdust Community. She and her family were very good friends with Amos and Dorothy.

The next day, Amos, Carter, and I went to the race track in Tijuana, Mexico, just across the border from the U.S. I believe it was Labor Day. I had gotten hiccups after I arrived in California and tried many home remedies but none worked. I was miserable at the race track. We decided to leave the track early. I got in the back of Amos's compact car, a Chevrolet Corvair, to stretch out while we were trying to cross the border and go through customs back into the U.S. It was very hot. There was only one place to cross and many cars were in line in front of us.

We left San Diego the next day for Los Angeles, where we visited my cousin Ruby Gunn and her family, and other acquaintances from Quincy. I left Los Angeles the following Sunday by plane, heading to Chicago. As soon as the airplane took off, my hiccups ended, and my trip was free of the week-long miseries suffered in California.

I arrived at O'Hare Airport in Chicago, but had not made reservations for a place to stay. I took a bus to downtown Chicago after midnight. The first stop was the Palmer House Hotel, where we arrived around 2:00am. I got a room there for fifteen dollars per night—a lot of money for an average person in 1964.

Check out time was at 11:00 am. When I went to check out, I was told that I had another night because I had checked in after midnight—my good fortune. I went to the IIT campus to find out when I could check into the graduate student dormitory. I also wanted to learn other things about IIT. The next day, I checked out of the Palmer House and moved into a YMCA in downtown Chicago for about a dollar and one half per day. I stayed there until I could move into the dormitory.

On Wednesday, September 16, 1964, while I was at the YMCA, there was a large parade on State Street. This was Mexican Independence Day. I did not know that there was a large Mexican population in Chicago.

Places Where I Lived as a Graduate Student

The first place that I lived was the graduate student dormitory at IIT. I checked into Fowler Hall after it opened for the fall semester 1964. The Resident Advisor had a meeting to discuss housekeeping details. I met Thomas Hilliard, the only other African American living in the dormitory. I asked Tom where could I get a beer and he said that we could go to Jimmie Cooper's place on 35th Street after the meeting. Subsequently, we went to Jimmy Cooper's often and I met a lot of the blacks living in the neighborhood.

In 1965, I took my second summer position at Sandia Laboratories in Albuquerque. My friend Archer S. Mitchell, Jr. and I shared a duplex apartment on Alcazar Street in Albuquerque. We had to walk a half mile or more to the grocery store because there was no bus service. Each of us had to carry two large bags of groceries back to the apartment.

I returned to Chicago in the fall for the 1965–1966 academic year. Tom Hilliard and I shared a dumpy apartment on the near North Side in Old Town Chicago. I rode the subway ("EL") to and from IIT every day. Old Town Chicago was near Lake Michigan with music venues around. Around the corner from where we lived, there was the Mother Blues Club where many blues singers performed. I saw Muddy Waters, Howling Wolf, Paul Butterfield, Corky Siegel, and Otis Rush play there. There was a cover charge. However, I became a regular customer and the people on the door let me in for free. I would purchase a beer and sip it through the show.

I lived on North Avenue in Old Town Chicago. The Old Town Ale House and Art Gallery was across the street from my apartment. There were paintings on the wall and games to play. Friends and I would spend some afternoons drinking ale and playing chess.

One Sunday evening, I was walking on North Wells Street and ran into George Madry. He was from my hometown and in my high school graduating class of 1954. George was now living in Chicago. It seemed that we were following each other—we both received degrees from Howard University in 1964.

On a different evening when I was walking on North Wells Street, another interesting event occurred. There were numerous places to eat and enjoy entertainment between Division Street and North Avenue. A man said, "Eddy Stone, Eddy Stone," to me. He thought that I was a musician named Eddy Stone, or that I could be Eddy's twin. I had heard that people have someone who looks like them all over the world. My father looked like Anwar Sadat, the Egyptian President. Hope that your look-alike has no problems to get you into trouble.

I returned to Albuquerque for my third summer to work at Sandia Corporation in 1966. I shared one of JP's duplex apartments on the corner of Pine Street and Lead Avenue with my friend Archer Mitchell, Jr. I purchased a brand new 1966 Chevrolet Chevelle 396 Super Sport car that summer. On my return trip to Chicago after the summer in Albuquerque, I was driving through Amarillo, Texas. A dump truck rear ended me at the red light at the corner of Eight and Hughes Streets. The truck had lost its brakes and the driver pulled out of the right lane and hit my car in the left lane. Still, I was able to drive my new car to Chicago and have it repaired there.

I moved into the graduate students' dormitory at IIT when I arrived, and lived there during the 1966–1967 academic year.

In summer 1967, I returned to Albuquerque to work at Sandia for my fourth consecutive year. Again, I lived in one of JP's duplexes.

When I returned to Chicago for the fall semester at IIT in 1967, I did not have a place to live. I contacted my friend Tom Hilliard who was living in Old Town Chicago. I may have stayed a couple of days at his apartment. After that, Eugene Topoleski and I got a small place in a house that was turned into an apartment at Yates and 72nd Street on the south side of Chicago. This place was intended to be an efficiency apartment. It had a bed that folded into a closet. However there were two additional beds. Eugene, Bill McCain (Eugene's former roommate at IIT), and I lived there. Bill got married and moved out in the spring semester of 1968. Eugene moved out after graduation in June 1968. Sometime during the 1967–1968 academic year, my car was stolen and sold to a used car dealer in Indiana. However, in preparation to send the car out of state, the dealer found out that it was stolen because the hidden serial plate did not match the serial plate on the door post. After it was returned to me, I had to get the wiring harness replaced.

During the summer or fall of 1968, my Chevrolet Chevelle 396 Super Sport car was stolen for the second time. This time, it was stripped from the engine through to the transmission. **That is, the engine and complete drive train including transmission had been taken.** I had bought it new just two years earlier (1966), but my insurance company paid me only their appraised value which was less than the cost of a used vehicle of the same make and model.

The owner of the building that I lived in on the South Side decided to sell. I did not have a lease and had to move out sometime after the summer or fall of 1968. I moved in with Robert Naftzger in his efficiency apartment in Lake Meadows. We shared the costs. I remained in Bob's efficiency and slept in a sleeping bag on an air mattress on the floor until he married Mary Owens in the fall of 1969. He gave up the apartment and I moved to the Lincoln Hotel in Old Town for about fifty dollars per week.

While I was staying at the Lincoln Hotel, I interviewed for jobs until I accepted a position at Sandia Corporation in Albuquerque.

In December 1969, I moved into an apartment on Palomas Avenue in Albuquerque.

Academics at Illinois Institute of Technology

I enrolled as a graduate student in the Mechanics Department at IIT in fall 1964. Professor Peter Chiarulli, Ph.D., was Chairman of the Department. He was the most effective chairman I had known during my studies. He advised all students on what courses they should take.

One time I was upset about actions in the department and discussed my concerns with Professor Chiarulli. When I left his office, I felt guilty about my negative thoughts. He was excellent in the way he related to people. When I became Chairman of the Mechanical Engineering Department at Howard University in 1988, I wanted to be as effective in relating to people as he was, and I believe that I almost accomplished that goal.

As a student at IIT, I had several experiences and challenges worthy of note. I knew of only eight black students who were full-time—the combined total for the undergraduate and graduate programs. There were only a few female students enrolled and I do not remember seeing any black female students. Local blacks in the neighborhood called IIT a white island in the middle of a black neighborhood. It was more a peninsula than an island because the Dan Ryan Expressway bordered near the campus on the west side with white neighborhoods.

The Department of Mechanics was comprised primarily of graduate students. There were no more than three high-achieving undergraduate students associated with the program. The undergraduates were enrolled in graduate courses. I taught several undergraduate courses in the Mechanics Department to help support myself. The first course I taught was during the first semester 1966–1967 prior to earning the master's degree. I taught an evening course, Statics and Dynamics, to non-traditional students. This course prepared me well to teach any undergraduate course offered by the department.

In January 1967, during the break between the first and second semester, we had the "Big Snow." It was like in a science fiction movie. I was living in the graduate student dormitory and studying for the comprehensive examination. Chicago stood still and many people on buses were stranded. IIT set up cots in the basement of our dormitory for people to get out of the weather. I admired IIT for supporting people stranded on the streets.

There was only one comprehensive examination in our department. A student's performance was based on whether he or she passed the exam at the master's level or Ph.D. level. Some questions on the examination did not relate to courses that students had taken. And in some cases, there were questions related to research that had just been published in scientific journals.

I had been admitted as a Ph.D. student, not as a master's student. I was informed that I had passed at the master's level. Then I asked for my exam paper to see how I performed. When I showed my results to my friend Ray B. Stout, he said, "Lew, it looks as if you have done as well as many of us but it may be they just do not want to acknowledge that you passed at the Ph.D. level." Later, I found out that faculty members argued in support of those whom they advised. I had no one to argue for me. It was up to me to handle my own problems wherever I went.

In January 1967, I parked my car in the parking lot on the campus, where I paid for parking. After the snow melted, I drove to Florida for a short stay in the first week of the second semester of the 1966–1967 academic year. I had already completed all courses for the Ph.D. and did not need to be on campus at that time.

Normally, I was always on campus every day. When I was not seen, the department questioned Ray Stout about my whereabouts. Ray told them about me leaving for Florida, and that he was not sure if I was going to return because of how I was treated compared to other students—I had no advocate on the faculty to support me on comprehensive exams and on other matters. Ray's words were compelling and very helpful. When I returned from Florida, I was told to talk to Steve Thau, a faculty member in the department. Steve was about my age and we talked about my situation. I had received excellent grades in his courses, and we had a meaningful discussion regarding my status as a graduate student. He assured me that, from then on, I would get support from the faculty.

After two and a half years in graduate school, I decided to write a master's thesis because my fellowship would end after the second semester in 1967. I wanted something to show after three years of graduate work. I was not required to obtain a master's degree because I had entered the Ph.D. program directly from my undergraduate degree program. I wrote my thesis, "Heat Transfer Problems in a Channel with Turbulent Flows," in spring 1967, in time to apply for the degree and graduate at the June commencement. My advisor was Professor L. N. Tao. I was awarded the Master of Science in Mechanics (Engineering Science) on June 19, 1967.

I talked to Professor Chiarulli about support for the coming academic year and he offered me a position as a Teaching Assistant (TA). My job was to teach undergraduate courses. I earned eleven hundred dollars per semester plus tuition.

After my fourth consecutive summer at Sandia in Albuquerque, I returned to IIT for the fall semester 1967 and taught one undergraduate course. Some other graduate students in the department were instructors and members of the faculty. I did the same work but, as a TA, did not receive the same recognition or pay. I had not passed the Ph.D. Comprehensive Exam.

At the beginning of the fall semester, I took the Comprehensive Exam. It consisted of a written exam followed by an oral examination.

The written examination was four hours. It was taken several days to a week prior to the oral exam. I was the only student taking the exam at that time. Previously, the written part was a one-day exam and students were taken to lunch. My exam covered the same period of time as the previous exams.

The oral exam was scheduled for two hours each on two consecutive days, for a total of four hours. I had five or six faculty members participating in my orals and I did well. Whenever I was asked a question, I would give my answer and look at my advisor. He would nod up and down in the affirmative. This was helpful to me.

Shortly before the oral examination, I had a little itching in my throat but paid no attention to it. The itch turned out to be strep throat, but I think my body decided to let me pass the exam before it showed what it meant. I went to the doctor, found out the problem, and took prescribed drugs.

The next day, Barry Bernstein, a mathematics professor, congratulated me on passing the examination. He was the only faculty member to congratulate me. Because of my strep throat, I could hardly speak to him. I could not eat even Jell-O without pain.

My roommate, Eugene Adam Topoleski, took the Masters Comprehensive Examination on the second day of my oral exam. When he returned to our apartment, he was very upset with his performance. I probably said, "Gene, you have passed the damn exam. Don't let it worry you anymore. I am now sick because of my exam."

After I passed the Ph.D. Comprehensive Examination, I began the search for a dissertation topic. My advisor of record, Professor L. N. Tao, did not have any research grants and did not suggest a research topic for me. So I took leadership by becoming my own advisor.

I planned everything to assure that I would earn the Ph.D. My plan was to do research in fluid mechanics, particularly in the area where smooth fluid (laminar) flow transitions into chaotic or unstable eddying motion (turbulence). During my search of the literature, I found a paper that had an incorrect solution. I discussed this with my advisor of record, and he approved my research area.

Having a research project to exploit was not the end of my problems. There were new things I had to learn to do the research, particularly computer programming, and I needed to be well versed in linear algebra involving matrices with complex algebra elements. I got a publication on

FORTRAN, took it home, and learned to write FORTRAN programs in one night.

I also had to contend with one other important non-research element. There were two foreign language requirements, and students could choose two out of three: German, French, and Russian. I registered for a reading course in German. My plan was to take the course and study writings in German until I felt comfortable reading and writing in that language. Then I would take the examination to satisfy that requirement.

The German reading course was one of the most interesting courses I ever had in college. Professor Richter, a native of Germany, was amusing. He always had something comical to say in the classroom. While writing this memoir, my friend Ray Stout reminded me of a story Richter told concerning when he first came to the United States.

Professor Richter's first teaching position was at a women's college in Pennsylvania. He was invited to speak at the luncheon of a nearby social club. The event was a short train ride away and the club would pay him a two dollar honorarium, a lot of money in those days. He was picked up at the train station. After the lunch, he gave his talk about Europe and his studies at Sorbonne University in Paris.

This must have been when there was great inflation in Germany. His family had given him large sacks of money for his trip to Paris.

During the question and answer period, a well-spoken gentleman asked, "To who do you attribute your language skills?" or something to that effect.

Richter was perplexed. Being extremely knowledgeable about the English language, he knew that the preposition "to" accepts only the objective form of the "who" pronoun, which is "whom." He finally responded, "Oh, do you mean *to whom* I attribute my language skills?" There were gasps from the audience.

Richter thought that he probably would not get the two dollar honorarium, since he had made such a social gaffe. He got paid the two dollars in forty nickels but no ride back to the train station. During the walk to the station, with nickels jingling in his pocket, Richter wondered when, if ever, it would be okay to bend the rules of American English.

I sat on the front row in Richter's German class. When it came time for him to discuss assignments that he had graded, he would pull up a desk, sit next to me and face the class. Sitting next to me and looking over my paper, he would say, "I would like to say something about your results but Ms Peach is in this room." She was the only woman in the class. Then he would say things like, "How did you screw this up so badly? It is your mother tongue." He never used the words "father tongue." I always wondered why he referred to German as "my mother tongue." At the time, I did not know that my name was German, though young children in Germany could pronounce it correctly when I was a soldier there. I believe that he did not use "father tongue" because Hitler talked about the father country when he was in power.

I took Professor Richter's class in the evening around 4:00 or 5:00 pm. After class, prior to a holiday, we would talk about life and backgrounds. I believe that he lived alone. We sat and talked about what we were going to do on the holiday weekend. We got along well.

I taught two courses as a teaching assistant, one per semester in the 1967–1968 academic year. I taught Fluid Mechanics in the fall semester 1967. In spring 1968, I taught a service course, Statics, for architecture students who had failed the course in fall 1967.

I remember this because I had a mailbox in the department office. I always checked my mailbox when I arrived on campus after 11:30am to go to lunch with fellow graduate students. One day, there was a note in my mailbox from Professor Kulinski requesting that I see him. I went to his office and he was not there. I had my own private office (a large storage closet) and a mailbox because I was teaching courses. When I returned from lunch I stopped into one of the offices of graduate students. Talapa was in the Mathematics Department. He had shared offices with us in the Mechanics Department prior to when I earned the Master of Science degree.

I had my back to the door and entered saying, "Talapa, you have a German name. What does this word "Grenzschicht" mean? I heard someone behind me say, "Boundary Layer." Without turning around, I replied, "BS"—reverting to my military vocabulary. Unfortunately, the person behind me was Professor Kulinski. He then said "You are trying to screw me, I am on your Dissertation Committee and I shall have the last laugh."

When I heard Kulinski's threatening words, I said "Let's go see Chiarulli." Apparently, Kulinski had written his note for me to come to his office to discuss why I had not shown up for the student problem session that morning. For some reason, he thought that I had been assigned to be his Teaching Assistant (TA) by Professor Chiarulli, Department Chairman. I was angry and upset about Kulinski's threat. After all, as a member of my committee, Kulinski could jeopardize the success of my dissertation and efforts to obtain the Ph. D. degree.

We met Professor Chiarulli in the hall. He told Kulinski that I did not show up as a TA for a problem session that morning because I had not been informed. Chiarulli asked me what I was doing and I said, "I am teaching a course for you." Discussion followed regarding whether one of Kulinski's graduate students could serve as TA for Kulinski's course. He said, "No," because his student was studying for the German examination. I told them that I was studying for the same exam.

In the end, I had to serve as TA for Kulinski's course. But it created no difficulty for me because I had taught it the previous semester. The problem could have been solved the way it ultimately was—through conversation between Chiarulli and Kulinski, with notification to me.

This situation occurred because the TA assigned to Kulinski's course completed the requirements for his degree early in the semester and left IIT to take a job in industry. At the end of the academic year, Kulinski also left IIT for a position at another university. He never served on my Dissertation Committee.

During the summer of 1968, I taught two sections of an undergraduate course in Fluid Mechanics and continued developing my computer code to study the transition of laminar (smooth fluid) flow to turbulence. There were more than two hours between the two sections of the same course, so I had to prepare and grade two different exams each week. I wanted to make sure that students in the later section did not have an advantage through communications with students in the earlier section.

Early in the 1968–1969 academic year, changes took place in the Ph.D. committee activities. A student from Turkey, advised by Professor Barry Bernstein, thought that he had completed enough work for the degree. The student was informed that he had a good start but still had more to accomplish. He pushed the issue, and the Mechanics Department gave him a dissertation defense. Yet he did not pass the dissertation defense and left the university. After that, the Mechanics Department required all Ph.D. graduate students to undergo committee reviews of their research prior to their dissertation defense.

My friend Ray Stout was the first student and I was the second to have committee reviews under the new process.

During my review, Professor Levans asked why the fluid flow looked as I had presented it. I replied that there was an adverse pressure gradient. Oddly, my answer was not understood by a majority of the committee members; they began to talk among themselves. Their discussions shook me up. If my answer was incorrect, I would have to begin my dissertation work all over again.

Then Professor Barry Bernstein said, "You are okay. Continue your presentation," but I did not hear him. Bernstein spoke up again. I heard him this time and continued my presentation. Later, Bernstein came by my office and I thanked him for his support during the presentation.

Later that spring semester in 1969, Professor Tao came to my office late on a Friday and said that Professor Markovin wanted me to give a seminar on my work. Markovin was the Principal Investigator of a large research project in the Mechanical Engineering Department. I said clearly that I was not interested. Yet, the following Monday morning, Professor Chiarulli came to my office and informed me that Professor Tao said that I was going to give a seminar the following Friday afternoon.

During that presentation, I was interrupted numerous times by Professor Levans asking questions. After I completed my presentation, Markovin said, "Levans has harassed Thigpen enough. Does anyone else have any questions?"

After the seminar, I went upstairs to my office. Tao came to me and told me to write up my dissertation. I had already written it but decided <u>not</u> to give it to him in less than two weeks.

Giving a seminar that I did not want to give was the best thing that could have happened for me at that time. Yet, my delay in giving my dissertation to Professor Tao immediately after the seminar probably cost me more than half a year in receiving my Ph.D. I could have done the dissertation defense and made the deadline for June 1969 graduation. Instead, I had to wait until September to have the defense.

During the summer, I worked on a research project that Tao acquired.

I defended my dissertation in September 1969. I was awarded the Ph.D. degree at the IIT commencement on January 23, 1970 but did not attend the ceremony. I had started my full-time position at Sandia Corporation the previous month (December 1969) and did not have the money to travel from Albuquerque to Chicago.

In later years, I regretted not going. I should have tried to borrow money to travel and to invite my parents and siblings. I was probably the only African American to receive a Ph.D. from IIT at the January 1970 commencement.

PART IV
Professional Life

Chapter 11

My Employers

My professional career includes positions at Sandia National Laboratories, Lowell Technological Institute, Lawrence Livermore National Laboratory, Howard University, and Los Alamos National Laboratory. This memoir includes my duties, responsibilities, and accomplishments at each of those organizations.

Sandia Corporation

After completing the requirements for the Ph.D. in September 1969, I went to work full-time in December at Sandia Corporation (Sandia National Laboratories) in Albuquerque, New Mexico, as a member of the Technical Staff. Sandia Corporation was managed by Bell Laboratories in New Jersey. All presidents of Sandia Corporation came from Bell Laboratories.

I worked on several projects at Sandia. All of those projects related to my research on projectile penetration in geologic materials and water entry by a projectile.

I worked with engineers who were performing full-scale experimental studies of the behavior of projectiles into geological materials. The objective was to develop empirical models and computational techniques to model that behavior.

I performed the first computations showing that earth materials could be modeled with simple constitutive equations to simulate projectile penetration into rock. That pioneering work was published in the *Journal of the Geotechnical Division of the American Society of Civil Engineering* in 1974. It led to proposals for updating coal-mining techniques using penetration mechanics and methods for obtaining dynamic engineering properties of earth materials.

The experimental work in earth penetration required aircraft to perform the experiment. Each experiment was very expensive.

My Group Leader asked me how much propellant it would take to propel a projectile of a certain dimension and weight to a given exit velocity in a recoilless gun. The gun would reduce the cost of field experiments immensely. I found no formulas in the library to answer the question. Then I searched for information on internal ballistics and found what I needed to write a computer program to answer his question and design a recoilless gun.

About a week after my Group Leader asked about the amount of propellant, I informed him that I was writing a computer code to solve the problem. He told me to forget about the problem and left my office. I informed Bob, my Project Manager, about the discussion. I said that I wanted to complete my work on developing a computer code to study internal ballistics. Bob gave me the go-ahead, and I completed the development and testing of my code. I placed all of that work in my desk drawer.

One year later, when I was in a different group and had a new Group Leader, my previous Group Leader asked me the same question about the amount of propellant. I told him that I would give him the information the next day. In those years, we used punch cards to access the computers. Most of the time, it took overnight to get results. The next day, I gave him even more information than he had requested. I gave him enough information to design a recoilless gun to meet his specifications. I was able to provide the information because I had not given up on my work in internal ballistics a year earlier.

I was also a Project Leader in the development of a high-sink-rate water entry projectile for attacking submarines from aircraft. This work included analytical, computational, and experimental studies. One Friday, my Group Leader brought the Laboratory's published newspaper to my office and asked if I had seen it. I replied, "No." The paper showed that another group that had worked with me on my project had taken credit for all of my work without acknowledging my efforts. They also published results of my full-scale experiments in a professional journal. Despite that group having cut me out of receiving credit for my work in their publication, I received credit in a larger way. From my studies in water-entry phenomena, I co-invented an Ice Penetrating Sonobuoy with three other engineers.

I assisted in developing a vehicle to study properties of marine sediments at the bottom of the sea. I took two one-week-plus trips to sea with oceanographers from Texas A&M University to test our vehicle.

On the first trip, we launched from Panama City, Florida, boarding Texas A&M's ship, the Alaminos. It was the sister ship of the Pueblo that was captured by North Korea. We spent a week in the Gulf of Mexico and disembarked in Galveston, Texas.

On the second trip, we flew from Albuquerque to Aruba to meet the Alaminos via Merida, Mexico, and spent the night in a hotel. We flew to Aruba the next day and checked into a hotel there. We spent a few days on the ship in the Caribbean Sea. After leaving the ship, we returned to Albuquerque.

My group members and I knew what experiments would enhance our efforts, but our managers wanted outside people to verify what we suggested. Woodward Clyde Associates was a consulting company in Orange County, California. One of their employees consulted with us on developing models to study the penetration of projectiles into earth materials. We would have discussions with the consultant "expert," and he would repeat our suggestions to our upper management, and they would fund us for our experiments. This relates to an expression I heard when I was very young and is true: "The grass is always greener on the other side of the fence." That is, Management saw the other side—consulting "expert's" advice—as being superior ("greener") than staff-their own side. Another time, we scheduled a trip to Woodward Clyde Associates. We were invited to arrive early on a Sunday and go sailing. My colleague, John, rented a car at the Los Angeles Airport after our arrival that Sunday morning. John sold sailboats in Albuquerque and was looking forward to the trip. I was not interested in sailing so I asked him to drop me off at my brother Amos's house.

That evening, Amos and his family took cousin Ruby Gunn and her husband and me in his camper to the Holiday Inn in Orange County where I had a reserved room.

On Monday, my group from Sandia Laboratories and I visited with the consultants. They invited us to a lecture on sailing, held at the apartment of a person whom Woodard Clyde Associates hired to give lessons that evening. The lecturer talked about his wife's sailing, his sailing trips to South America, and visiting villages of indigenous people. He had a large glass container in his apartment with what looked like a human head. I asked him about the contents. He said that the elders in a village had caught a man in another man's tepee with that husband's wife. The man's head was cut off and stuffed with hot coals to shrink it. Since the lecturer was a guest, he was given the shrunken head. This was an interesting story whether true or false.

At Sandia, we had a contract with the Civil and Structural Engineering Department at Texas A&M University to develop material models to use in computer codes for computing the response of projectiles into soil and rock. I served on the review committee.

We had the same consultant from Woodward Clyde Associates who had visited Texas A&M University with our group previously. After dinner, we went to a club. I believe the club was in Bryan, Texas. When we got there, I was told that they could not serve me because I was black. Our consultant wanted to leave immediately. The next day, some members in our group told the Dean of Engineering at Texas A&M University about the incident. The Dean responded that they should have known better than to take me to that club.

The next time we visited Texas A&M University, my office mate and I decided to visit the same club again. We informed the others at dinner that they should not go with us if they were not going to support us. Three of us went to the club this time and had no problem with the management.

I first worked at Sandia as a summer employee after I received the Bachelor of Science degree in 1964. I worked there for four consecutive summers while in graduate school. During that time, there was only one black Ph. D. employee at the Laboratory. There were very few black employees in any position, including technicians. The Laboratory hired technicians from several institutions that did not have blacks in their programs. I believe that this was to ensure that black technicians were not hired. When I was hired full-time in December 1969, the Laboratory was hiring mostly professionals with Ph.D.'s. Most blacks were being hired into

My Employers

low level positions such as janitors or mail room personnel. Only three black Ph.D.'s worked at the Laboratory at any time when I worked there. There were blacks working at the Laboratory who deserved leadership positions but were not promoted.

In 1971, we blacks requested a meeting with the president of Sandia to discuss our grievances about hiring, promotions, and other issues related to black employees. In the meeting, the president stated that the Laboratory could not find black people to fill the positions. We pointed to the practices used for finding and hiring technicians. I said that I had a list of black Ph.D.'s in engineering science alone. The president questioned me and seemed to resist our efforts to bring greater diversity into the Laboratory's workforce. We demanded a second meeting in the next two or more weeks as a follow up.

Following the first meeting, the EEOC officer, a Hispanic, asked for my list of Ph.D.'s and I sent him a copy.

Our second meeting was within the next two weeks. At this meeting, the president announced the names of one or two black employees who had been promoted to leadership positions.

Shortly after the second meeting, I was transferred to another group and two other black professionals left Sandia. I left in 1973, leaving only one black Ph. D. there.

In 1975 or 1976, a class action suit was filed against Sandia regarding salaries for blacks being less than salaries for whites. The Laboratory lost the case. I contested the small amount of money offered through the settlement, and spent it on my personal lawyer.

My work at Sandia prepared me well for positions at universities and other laboratories, and for consulting. Several universities and companies tried to recruit me while I was at Sandia. The first one was the Mechanical Engineering program at Howard University in Washington, DC. The Chairman of the Department, M. Lucius Walker, Jr., called and asked if I was interested in a faculty position. I said that I had two major research projects and was not going to leave until I brought closure to them. However, I told him that my friend Charles Watkins, Jr. was interested in a faculty position, and I would transfer the call to Charles's number. Charles accepted the position at Howard and became Chairman of the Department two years later.

While working at Sandia I had the opportunity to witness the first Hot Air Balloon Fiesta in Albuquerque. It began in the parking lot of the Coronado Center Shopping Mall and ended up with a gathering of thirteen balloons on April 8, 1972. My office was in a building on Sandia Base with no windows. Someone announced that there were balloons flying all over the area. I went outside the building to see. I believe that the majority of Sandia employees were outside watching the flight of the balloons. I thought to myself "How much is this event costing the Laboratory?" but I enjoyed the sight. The next year, Albuquerque hosted the first World Hot-Air Balloon Championships in February and the Fiesta became an international event. The Balloon Fiesta grew each year for decades, and today is the largest balloon convention in the world. It is held annually in October.

In summer 1973, I received a letter from the Chair of the Civil Engineering Department at Lowell Technological Institute (Lowell Tech) in Lowell, Massachusetts, informing me of a position available in his department. He had successfully fought to create a master's degree program in Civil Engineering at Lowell Tech and now needed to hire faculty.

At Sandia, I had brought closure to some major projects in the Aerothermodynamics Department. By invitation, I had taken a position in another department, headed by Walter Hermann. The invitation came after I had given a very successful presentation on computational earth penetration mechanics. Hermann was one of the most highly rated department managers at Sandia. His department would be the best one for me to expand my career at Sandia.

My lady friend was a social worker and had been working with Native Americans in Albuquerque. However, she left Albuquerque and returned to Chicago for a position working with children. After she moved, Albuquerque no longer had strong meaning for me. I decided to interview for the position at Lowell Tech.

During my interview at Lowell, I was impressed with the amount of space available for research laboratories. The State of Massachusetts had allocated funds for equipment. Lowell Technological Institute was originally Lowell Textile Institute; huge spaces filled with old textile machines were not in use. Further, the department chair, one faculty member, and I had a lot of experience in common in geotechnical engineering. I thought we would make a great team. The only negative was the lack of computing facilities for my needs. However, I felt that if we developed the laboratories we could get research contracts and grants. I could purchase computer time from Control Data Corporation (CDC) for my large computing needs.

I decided to accept the position if it were offered. At the end of my interview with the Provost, the Department Chair told me that I would hear from him shortly.

After my interview, I took a train to the station in Boston. I had many hours before my flight back to Albuquerque so, at the train station, I asked a taxi driver to give me a tour of the area. We toured the Old Boston area. This shows what can be done if you inquire. Then he drove me to the airport. I returned to Albuquerque that night.

Lowell Technological Institute

In fall 1973, I accepted a faculty position as assistant professor in the Civil Engineering Department at Lowell Tech—which is now the University of Massachusetts at Lowell. I taught both undergraduate and graduate courses. The graduate courses were in the evening and at night. I would get out of class at 10:00pm, just in time to stop at the McDonalds restaurant on my way home before it closed at 11:00pm. Our graduate program was just beginning, and we had graduate students who worked during the day.

I believe that I was the only African American faculty member in the College of Engineering. I served on several University-wide committees, including a committee to search for an equal employment officer and a committee detailing what to do with an outdated nuclear reactor.

While I was on the faculty at Lowell Tech, I traveled on some weekends through small towns in Massachusetts to York Harbor, Maine, to have a lobster feast. I drove through small towns because there were many antique shops to visit along the way. I did not eat in the restaurants of those towns. Instead, I found outdoor locations where the lobsters were steamed. Then I picked a couple of lobsters to eat while sitting on the rocks along the coastline. I could get two lobsters for the cost of a dinner inside a restaurant. I felt that I could have salad, potatoes, and vegetables anytime at home.

I spent the summer of 1974 at my parents' house in Sawdust. I was financially able to fix up the house for my then 67-year-old parents. I put a bathroom and running water in the house—a no small feat.

I hired handy men to do the work. One of them was a cousin who had taught me so much about life on the farm when I was a young boy. I told him that I wanted him to be sober when he came to do the job. He got sober and did an excellent job.

Other handy men did the plumbing, installing hot water heaters. They put in an additional electrical line for the hot water heater and water pump.

When my cousin finished his job, I paid him and decided to buy him a nice bottle of liquor from a liquor store. However, he preferred moonshine. We went to someone's house who sold moonshine in half-pint jars. My cousin took the jar and began to "chug" it. I asked, "What are you doing?" He responded, "Do you want some?" "No," I replied, and he finished chugging it. This revealed the way that many of the moonshine drinkers in Sawdust got intoxicated (DRUNK).

After I returned to Lowell for the fall semester, I received an offer from a former colleague who had worked at Sandia when I was there. He was the author of the first book on computational fluid mechanics. A year after I had left Sandia, he left Sandia to head a unit of Science Applications International Corporation (SAIC). He was offering me a job at SAIC. He also sent me a Request for Proposal (RFP) that looked as if it was written from my résumé. However, I was unable to submit a proposal because we did not have the computational facilities at Lowell. Further, when I was working on a research project, I had to visit the library at Worcester Polytechnic Institute on the weekends to do my research.

Frustrated with the limited facilities at Lowell, I decided to interview for a position elsewhere. In the fall of 1974, I applied to Lawrence Livermore National Laboratory in Livermore, California, and interviewed for the position. At the end of the interview, I informed the Personnel Department that I would not be available until the end of the current academic year ending in 1975.

Although the faculty at Lowell had a nine-month contract, our salary was paid over twelve months. The State of Massachusetts had to call a special session of the Legislature to provide funds to pay our salaries through the summer.

Lawrence Livermore National Laboratories offered me the job but I was not ready to accept. I needed some time to clear my mind and consider my next career steps. I thought about going to Alaska during the summer to prospect for gold. I discussed it with a professor in our department at Lowell. His mother lived or had lived in Alaska, and he told me that mosquitoes were very bad during the summer, so that option was out. I also thought about taking a trip around the world by freighter ship and got information on it. I would write a book while on that trip. However, I figured it would be difficult to get a job in my profession after sailing around the world for a year or more. I did not take that option either.

Instead, I decided to visit my folks in Sawdust and then take a Greyhound bus trip across the U.S. to decide where to work in the fall of 1975. It cost only seventy five dollars for a thirty-day trip to travel anywhere Greyhound traveled and the ticket came with discounts on hotels.

At the time, I had a 1970 Triumph TR6, a British convertible sports car. I drove to Florida and visited relatives on the way.

Daniel Milton, a relative, lived in New Britain, Connecticut. I called him and asked for the name of a motel near his residence. He gave me the location of a place to meet, possibly a convenience store in his neighborhood. I had given him the approximate time in the evening that I would get there. When I arrived, Daniel was coaching little league baseball, so his wife met me. We had never met before, but she recognized me from a photo that Daniel had. They insisted that I stay at their apartment and not at a motel.

My cousin Charles Rolax also lived in New Britain. We spent the night at Charles's apartment playing cards. The next day, Charles gave us a tour of the area. His wife Mary had a garden spot that the company where she worked provided for employees. Charles was the only one who transplanted the vegetable plants. The others just set the pots with plants they purchased on top of the ground. I am sure that they learned how to grow vegetables from Charles's plot.

I spent Tuesday night at Daniel's place because I had not gotten any sleep on Monday night. I left New Britain on Wednesday morning.

My next stop was William Nealy's house in Delaware. I arrived late in the afternoon. William and Shirley were planning to leave for Florida the next day. Their son Bill was a baby. I spent the night at their house and we left Delaware about 4:00pm on Thursday. We drove both of our cars and spent the night at a motel just north of Richmond, Virginia.

On Friday, we drove to Columbia, South Carolina. During the trip, the baby lost his favorite pacifier and would not accept a new one. After we checked into the motel in Columbia, we visited William Rolax at his house until the early hours of Saturday morning. Later that morning, we drove to Quincy, Florida. I drove on to Sawdust, which is ten miles from Quincy, and stayed with my parents.

About a week after I arrived in Quincy, William Nealy came by and said that he was headed to Oviedo, Florida, where his wife and son were, and asked me to travel with him. I took my two pieces of luggage, drove to my sister Mildred's house, and left my car in her carport. I went to Oviedo with William and we had dinner at Shirley's parents' house.

William had an appointment to meet with some university officials at a hotel in Tampa that evening. We drove to Tampa after dinner and met with the university officials. After the meeting, we drove back to Oviedo and I asked him to drop me off at the Greyhound terminal. I bought my thirty-day ticket and checked into a nearby Howard Johnson motel. The next morning, I called my brother James Woodrow and asked him to pick me up at the bus station in Ft. Lauderdale. I visited with him for a couple of days.

I purposely left one of my suitcases at my brother's house. Using my ticket on Greyhound, I then traveled to Chicago and spent a couple of days visiting my lady friend, Margaret Jean Neff. Next, I traveled west to Las Vegas, spent some time gambling, and finally got to Los Angeles on the Fourth of July. I visited my brother Amos for a few days in Los Angeles. My next two major stops were Seattle, Washington, and Chicago, Illinois. After thirty-one days, I arrived back in Lowell, Massachusetts. My car was still in Florida. I rented a car from a Ford dealer for fifty dollars per week while in Lowell.

By then, I had made up my mind to accept the position at Lawrence Livermore National Laboratory. I informed my new Department Chair and the Dean that I was leaving Lowell for a position at Livermore. The Dean asked me to write a strong letter stating why I was leaving. Six months earlier, my former Department Chair had left the University to take a position in industry, and now I was leaving for a national research laboratory. Thus two of the Department's top researchers were leaving within six months. I told the Dean that I was leaving because I felt that my career would stagnate for lack of facilities and infrastructure to do my research. I detailed my needs to do my research, and Lowell's facilities were lacking.

The Dean asked me to outline my concerns and needs in a letter that he could take to the upper administration to help him argue to upgrade the facilities. A year later, after leaving Lowell, I was informed that the Department was going to fill my old position. I was asked if I wanted to return. I responded that I appreciated the offer, but would not return.

I made arrangements to move, and traveled to Quincy to get my Triumph. My car had been sitting in the hot sun for about one and one half months. Seals in many areas had dried out. It needed much work and there was no Triumph dealer in the area. I had some things repaired in Tallahassee, but I left Florida with a leak in the rear end differential.

Every time I stopped for gasoline, I would have the service station attendant pump grease into the rear end differential. In Dallas, I had some more work done. I drove on to Albuquerque and had the rest of the work completed at a service station where my friend Frank Kite worked. Frank loaned me one of his vehicles— the one he called his "Hippy Wagon."

While waiting in Albuquerque, I stayed at the home of my friends Alan and Lois Peterson. I had been best man at their wedding. My lady friend, Jean, met me in Albuquerque and we drove to Las Vegas and spent a few days there. We then drove to the San Francisco area where we toured for a few days. After she left for Chicago, I drove on to Livermore— in the San Francisco Bay Area—to work at Lawrence Livermore National Laboratory.

Lawrence Livermore National Laboratory

I arrived in the town of Livermore and checked into a small motel that had a small cooking area in each room in September, 1975. But there was no phone in the room. You had to go to a pay phone booth outside the building to make a call. The motel was located a few yards from a railroad track. The train awakened me during the night.

The next day, I went to Lawrence Livermore National Laboratory to begin work in the Chemistry Department. I also began to search for an apartment in town. I checked the paper and other sources and saw apartments for rent, but when I showed up nothing was available. I had seen the same "phenomenon" in Poughkeepsie, New York, in 1963. Landlords did not want to rent to African Americans.

People in my Group asked me where I was living. I replied that I was staying at the motel next to the railroad tracks. I said that I was searching for an apartment in Livermore but each time, when I arrived at the apartment office, I was informed that they did not have anything available. Members in my Group asked if I wanted them to check if those places had apartments available. I said, "No." I would look elsewhere.

I met a black man who worked in the Office of Personnel, and he took me to look at apartments in San Leandro and Oakland. The agent at the complex in San Leandro, Lakeside Village Apartments, said that an apartment would be available in one month. We also went to places in Oakland but the surroundings were undesirable; there were prostitutes walking the street.

I applied for an apartment at Lakeside Village in San Leandro. When it was available a month later, I moved in. This was a great place for a single person. It had a recreation building and the recreation staff planned events on a regular basis including Sunday brunches and trips to Reno, Nevada, where there was casino gambling. I made many friends and still communicate with them as I am writing today. We all enjoyed playing bridge, a card game similar to bid whist. If we got four people together, we played contract bridge and sometimes also played sponsored duplicate bridge contests. I lived there for nearly thirteen years. The downside was that I had to commute thirty miles to work, a sixty-mile round trip each day. However, I drove against the major traffic each way.

I was hired at Livermore because of my prior research in developing computational models to understand the behavior of geotechnical (earth) materials from an experimental, analytical, and numerical point of view.

The organizational structure at Lawrence Livermore National Laboratory was quite complex in the 1970s and 1980s during my employment there.

> ➢ There were the traditional vertical business units headed by the Laboratory Director.

- Under the Director there were, in order, Associate Directors, Department Heads, Division Leaders, Section Leaders, and Group Leaders.
- Within each Directorate, Department, or Division there were Programs headed by a Program Manager.

To simplify, the Groups contained the staff with specific expertise and the Programs had a mission and drew support staff from the Groups. More simply, the Groups had the expertise (people) and the Programs had the money.

This type of organizational structure was called a Matrix Organization. Under this structure, a member in one Group may work with members from any Group in any Directorate across the Laboratory on the same Program and have more than one reporting line—their Group Leader and the Program Manager(s).

My Group was in the Experimental Rock Mechanics Section in the Chemistry Department. They were experimentalists trying to develop models of the behavior of geotechnical materials to be used in computer codes. The computer codes would support work in the Earth Sciences K-Division to simulate the behavior of earth materials subjected to strong ground motion resulting from earthquakes and underground explosions.

I was hired to bridge the gap between the experimentalists who developed the models and those who used the models in computer codes. I had two offices: one in the area controlled by my Group and one in the K-Division complex.

During my first year, my section, which contained several groups, was transferred from the Chemistry Department to the K-Division. I was transferred to an existing group in K-Division. I was the only African American in the K-Division.

The same year, I met my former department head from Sandia, Walter Hermann, at a conference in Salt Lake City, Utah. He offered me a staff position to return to Sandia to work in computational earth penetration mechanics. I did not take the offer.

In my first three years at Livermore, I worked on several projects. Those projects included development of models for the study of the mechanical behavior of geologic materials under extreme stress conditions, extracting oil from oil shale *in situ*, and developing codes to monitor underground nuclear explosions.

In my new group in K-Division, I was assigned to work with a group member on a material model that he had sold to the "powers-that-be." The model was to be used in numerical computations to solve problems related to large deformations in earth materials. The concept was good but the formulation and implementation in computer code was inconsistent with the physics. I continuously questioned the group member on the physics of the model. I pointed out the inconsistencies to him.

I did not get a pay raise that year because my Group Leader had that same member of the group provide input on my performance evaluation. I wrote several rebuttals and provided information to rebut each statement in my evaluation. Each time he re-wrote the evaluation, I provided additional information to reject his report. Still, I did not get a pay raise that year. I talked to Paul Brown, my Section Leader, who had been appointed to the position only a couple of months earlier, and explained the situation. He said that he would guarantee that I got a raise the next year.

Several days later, Howard Rodean, the Program Manager of the Seismic Monitoring Program, stopped by my office. We talked about several things. The mission of his program was to develop techniques to discriminate, using seismic data, between underground nuclear explosions, high explosive explosions, and earthquakes. I assumed it to be a general conversation since my friend Ray Chin and I had collaborated on projects that he had supported in that Program. I did not realize that Howard was actually interviewing me for a position on his Program.

After our discussions, I thought no more about it. A few days later, my Section Leader came by my office and told me that it was a job that I could not refuse. He said that I should talk to Howard. Howard explained what he wanted me to do. He gave me one year of support to analyze the current work on the Seismic Monitoring Program and outline future priorities. I accepted the position and continued to work on materials models for geologic materials under intense compressive loading. I completed the work on seismic monitoring and wrote a draft report sometime during December 1978 to January 1979.

As with all papers or reports that I wrote, I asked for comments from people who I thought were knowledgeable on the topic. I got responses from everyone except one person with whom I thought that I had a good relationship. I asked if he had any comments regarding my report. He replied that I had not done my job, and that he was going to report that to the Division Leader. Reminder: I was the only African American in the K-Division. If I had done what he said I should have done, it would have amounted to my solving the whole seismic monitoring problem and put everyone working on the program out of a job—all in one year! I asked him for my report if he was not going to give me comments, and I said that I did not care what he told the Division Leader, but I wanted my report. He refused to return it that day. It took me several days of "begging" to get my draft back. I believe he wanted to talk to his Group Leader in the meanwhile.

I incorporated comments from other reviewers of my manuscript and prepared the report to be published as a Laboratory Report. Prior to publication, a meeting was called which included my Section Leader, the Section Leader of Seismic Activities, a Group Leader in Seismic Activities, and me to discuss my report. They did not invite the Program Manager who asked me to prepare the document. The Group Leader in Seismic Activities told me that he was going to fight me all the way on anything that did not meet his agreement. Then I spoke my piece.

I never got negative responses from the Section Leader in Seismic Activities; he outranked the Group Leader. I believe that the Section Leader appreciated what I had accomplished for his Program and how I was presenting the report at the meeting. Whenever I have confrontations during the day, I go to bed thinking about what happened and wondering if the confrontation was my fault, but I went home that night and slept well. The next day, I went to see Howard to tell him what happened. I considered him to be a mentor. He had reviewed my report and given comments. I asked, "Why did you ask me to do this job?" He got up from his desk and closed his office door. We had a long discussion regarding Seismic Monitoring. He said that the seismologists were fighting him all the way. When he asked them for things or ways to improve their research methods, they would give him only "grocery lists." Howard wanted someone to look at the whole program and make recommendations to improve the methods. And that was me.

I published the manuscript *"Seismic Monitoring: A Unified System for Research and Verification"* on February 6, 1979. The Lawrence Livermore Report UCRL-80670 was written in the first person because I wanted to make a bold statement to those who had challenged me and my work. This book is contained in more than forty libraries around the world. I continued to be supported by the Seismic Monitoring Program.

Sometime in 1979, there was a re-organization of the K-Division, and new people came into leadership from outside the Division. A new person was selected to head the Seismic Monitoring Program; my Section Leader went to head the Containment Test Program for underground nuclear explosions and I obtained a new Section Leader. This was a blessing in disguise.

In my Section, two Group Leadership positions opened, and I applied for one of them. The Section that contained the seismologists had appointed a young geophysicist to a Group Leader position who had been at Livermore for a few years. I was informed that I was going to be assigned to his Group and that I should discuss this assignment with him. I believed that this was their way to fight me relative to my research. I was prepared to leave Livermore without a future job.

I also thought that I had a good court case, based on an earlier threat, if I were forced to join one of the seismology groups. I met with the young geophysicist to try to learn why I was being assigned to his group. Neither of us thought that it was a good idea.

A bit later, I reported to the new Program Manager for the Seismic Monitoring Program. I told him that I would like to continue to work on the Seismic Monitoring Program, but I would leave Livermore if I were forced to join one of the Seismology Groups supported by that Program. I made the statement several times, and then asked if he understood what I was saying. He finally acknowledged that he understood.

That evening, in the parking lot, I met my Section Leader. He asked if I still wanted the Group Leader position, and I replied, "Yes." He said, "You have it but do not tell anyone because I want to announce it at a Section meeting."

I became Group Leader of the Dynamic Modeling Group in the Geo-Mechanics Section of K-Division in mid to late 1979. I received a raise at the beginning of the new fiscal year that began in October.

My first major task was to prepare a five-year Strategic Plan. The plan was due in early January 1980. I completed my plan and gave it to my secretary prior to leaving to visit relatives in Florida during Christmas and New Year holidays. I asked her to type the plan and submit it to my Section Leader by the due date. I trusted her and knew that she would get the job done. I certainly did not want to be the only one who was late.

When I returned from Florida, my plan was the <u>only</u> one that had been completed out of the four or five groups in my Section! I was then assigned to help and assure that the other Group Leaders in our Section prepared their Strategic Plans.

During the first months after I became a Group Leader, I had problems with two members.

One member simply had a problem with having an African American as his Group Leader. I was unable to communicate with him regarding his responsibilities and how he expected to contribute to our mission. He gave me nonsense answers. I told my Section Leader that the group member did not fit the mission of my Group—so we moved him to another group.

The second problem dealt with hygiene. That person was effective in his work but did not bathe often and had a bad odor—a problem for others working with him. I decided to raise the topic of hygiene in a group meeting without singling out any one person. My strategy worked.

As a Group Leader, I had to manage my group's activities but also do major research of my own. A colleague in K-Division worked on a D-Division project regarding how missile silos would respond to nearby nuclear explosions. He was very knowledgeable in the study of fracture mechanics. However, in the Hydro-Fracturing Program, there was a shortage of staff. The leader of that program wanted my colleague to be assigned there—to work on hydro-fracturing to stimulate natural gas production.

My Section Leader told me about their staffing issue, and asked me to take over the job on silo response to strong ground motion. Accordingly, my colleague told me everything he had done on the project. The idea was to develop a link between two computer analysis codes.

Success of the project required two different organizations to work together.

The ground motion computer code resided in the Earth Sciences K-Division and was used to simulate ground motion from underground nuclear explosions. The structure analysis computer code resided in the Mechanical Engineering Department and would be used for structural analysis of the silo resulting from the ground motion and blast.

My colleague in K-Division had interacted with both the D-Division and the Mechanical Engineering Department regarding the responsibilities of each organization. These responsibilities were agreed upon by each unit.

K-Division was responsible for developing a computer code to link the ground motion in the format to be used as input to the structural analysis code for the silo.

The Mechanical Engineering Department would make the necessary changes to the structural analysis computer code. We were assigned a part-time graduate student to work with K-Division to link the results of the ground motion computer code to the structural analysis computer code.

I was not a computer scientist and knew it would take me too long to learn the ground motion computer code. So I put my leadership skills to work.

First I talked to the developer of the structural analysis code regarding the capabilities of his computer code. He gave me an overview and said that I could get a copy of his source code at any time. We developed a good relationship that lasted.

Next I went to a computer scientist in K-Division and explained my problem. I asked if he were interested and how long it would take him to do the work. He was interested and the job would take a couple of months, but he had other current projects. Once I promised I would try to clear him from the other projects, he agreed to work with me. So I talked to his Group Leader with whom I had a good relationship as a fellow Group Leader. I explained my needs and he assigned the computer scientist to my project. The computer scientist did an excellent job in developing the computer code that I needed.

However, the Mechanical Engineering Department was not doing any development with the structural analysis computer code. Whenever D-Division wanted a report on the status of the work, Mechanical Engineering blamed the lack of progress on me. After being blamed for the part-time graduate student's lack of implementation of changes in the structural analysis computer code, and false reports regarding data that I sent him, I realized that my reputation was at stake. The unfair blame was confirmed by a researcher with whom I had collaborated since 1980.

This colleague had a conversation with a "visiting" faculty member from a university that D-Division hired for the summer. When the conversation turned to work in progress, my colleague told the faculty member that he was working with me on inverse problems. The visitor responded, "You don't want to work with him because people in D-Division say that he does nothing and presents false information." I never met that faculty member and don't remember his name or the university where he was employed.

I was grateful to learn what my colleague had heard about me. I related the information to my Deputy Department Head to assure that he was fully aware of my research activities and erroneous statements by an outsider.

Because I was working on other projects during the week, I decided to work at nights and on weekends—the only free time I had—to make the needed changes in the structural analysis computer code. In December 1981, after making the changes, I presented a preliminary report at the DNA Cratering Working Group Meeting in Marina del Rey, California. Someone asked if I had any experimental results to support my computations. I said that I was not aware of experimental results regarding Silo Response to intensive ground motion. No one in the audience stated that they had any such evidence either. Later, a person who had done model experiments made a presentation at the same meeting that showed results similar to my computer calculations, but he never spoke up during my presentation. However, his experiential model results gave me confidence that my computations were on the right path.

I continued my work on the silo problem, wrote a report, and sent the report out for comments. Once I received comments and revised the draft, I sent a copy to D-Division and the Mechanical Engineering Department. I was informed by my Group Leader that there would be a meeting with personnel from D-Division and Mechanical Engineering to discuss my work.

We had had another re-organization in K-Division, and it had become a Department with Groups. I had a new Group Leader, and I was his

Deputy. My Section Leader had left to become Containment Program Manager.

The meeting took place in my Group Leader's office. I was prepared. The night before, I had decided that I would attend but keep my mouth shut and listen.

It appeared to me that the D-Division representative was not happy that the work was done and was looking for ways to discredit me. The first question he asked was, "Why did you write the report?" I responded that I was tired of false accusations from D-Division and Mechanical Engineering regarding my work on the project. I said that I decided to complete the project so that I would not have to work with this group again and could devote my time to other projects. Then the part-time graduate student's supervisor asked why had I written the report and not acknowledged the student's work on it. I looked at the student and said, "Tell me what work you did to complete the project and prepare the document in question." He could answer only that he had contributed nothing. Immediately, his supervisor told him to go back to his office. He left the meeting.

After that, the meeting became a positive discussion on what I had completed. The Mechanical Engineering representative asked if I would send him an electronic copy of my modifications of the structural analysis computer code and files that they could test. I agreed and sent the results after the meeting.

During the meeting, my Group Leader never said one word in my favor to protect me. I found out later that he had applied for a position in D-Division.

My work was later presented at a conference by a Section Leader in Mechanical Engineering and he did not acknowledge me as the one who pioneered this work. He also bragged on the work prior to the presentation. My friend and collaborator on many research papers asked him, "Do you mean Lewis Thigpen's work?" He told me this shortly after I had published my report.

This shows how some people will take your work and claim it as their own. Indeed, this had happened before when I worked at Sandia National Laboratories in Albuquerque.

My Employers

I became supported totally by the Containment Program after my former Section Leader became the Program Leader. He told me that I was his mathematical physicist and that I could work on any problem that I chose. And, if he needed me to address any problem related to containment of underground explosions, I should drop everything I was doing and address that problem. That was the best assignment that any research scientist in the Department could wish for, and many people in the Department were jealous of me. I still held a leadership position as Deputy Group Leader in the Earth Sciences Department.

One day the Containment Program Manager, Frank Morrison, stopped by another person's office—that person had written a computer code and bragged to Department management about all of the things that his code could do. There had been an underground cavity collapse at the test site in Nevada. Frank wanted to understand the cause of the collapse.

In those days, no one usually closed the door to their office. The office was across the hall from mine, so I could hear everything. Frank explained the problem and asked the colleague if he could use his discrete modeling computer code to explain the collapse. He received a negative answer. Frank then came across the hall to my office. He went to my blackboard and explained the problem. I told him that I would begin to address the problem immediately but it would take me some time to research cavity collapse.

I did general research on cavity collapse from several routes including stress distributions in the surrounding area and even sink holes and their causes. I completed a draft report and gave it to Frank. One evening we talked about the report after he had read it. This was after work hours, i.e., after 5:00pm.

When I came to work the next morning, a notice posted on the bulletin board said that Frank had had an auto accident and was killed. The car that he was driving was a small Pontiac sports car. I never liked or trusted the safety of that car after that incident. When I read the announcement, I said "DAMN" to myself because I knew that I was going to have difficulties with others in leadership positions on the Containment Program. Frank had been a strong supporter of my work and respected my judgment in engineering analysis. Now I had lost him. Nevertheless, I continued to be supported by the Containment Program.

Later in 1984, there was another re-organization in the Earth Sciences Department and I was assigned to a new Group Leader. I was appointed to a Team Leadership position in that group. Back in 1982 at a Leadership Laboratory (workshop) in Ojai, California, I knew that this new Group Leader was unable to communicate with people. There were different groups testing leadership skills and the word got around that he fought everyone in his group. Now he was my Group Leader. I tried to work with him and keep him informed of all work-related activities.

Sometime in 1985 or later, the latest appointed Containment Program Manager—who was also the Department Head—came to my office. He offered me a position of managing the entire effort of re-writing the main computer code for containment analysis which was being undertaken by the computer scientists in the Department. I believe that the Group Leader of the computer scientists had suggested that he talk to me, and that my good relationship with the computer scientists was a factor. I informed the Program Manager that I needed to think about the offer at least overnight. I did not want to get put in the situation that I had endured with the Seismic Monitoring Program. I knew politics would be involved. I had established a reputation for getting jobs done. In fact, I had requests from people in other divisions, particularly the Physics Department, to join their organizations.

I accepted the position as Task Leader for the Stress Wave Modeling, Containment Program, but I remained in my current group in the Earth Sciences Department. During this time, the Containment Program Manager brought an outside advisory group of "experts" to evaluate our efforts in stress wave modeling regarding underground explosions. As Task Leader, I made a presentation related to our work. During my presentation to the advisory group, my Group Leader continued to interrupt and criticize my work. This was a shock because I had discussed my presentation with him prior to the meeting. I kept my "cool" and answered his questions and challenges. It also appeared that he was challenging not only me but also the people in the advisory group.

A few days later, we had an internal meeting to discuss the outcomes of that meeting. My Group Leader renewed his fight with me. This time I did not hold back my personal feeling toward him.

My Employers

Following this meeting, the Program Manager said, "We better move Lewis Thigpen to a different Group." I had already discussed with him many months earlier that I was in the wrong Group. As a result, I was assigned to the Containment Program Group led by the Department Head and reporting directly to him. I remained in that Group until I left Livermore Laboratory.

As Project Leader for Stress Wave Modeling in the Containment Program, I was responsible for all work related to computer modeling and small high explosive experiments to develop material models for the computer codes. My leadership rattled one person, one of my former Group Leaders involved in the computational effort, and he soon left the Earth Sciences Department.

For small scale high explosive experiments, a core feature of the stress wave modeling project, I had difficulty getting funding from the Containment Program Manager. It seemed he had difficulty making a decision regarding my projects. Yet, he would listen to those who wanted to carry out expensive full-scale experiments which cost seventy five thousand dollars per day. I learned that his administrative assistant had authority to sign off on ten thousand dollar requests. Therefore, I would talk to her when the Program Manager was away, and she would allocate the funding.

As we continued to work on the project, a member of the team made computer simulations of an underground explosion that showed low energy at the source, and large deformations far away from the source. The Project Leader in charge of full scale experiments wanted an experiment to explain the results, so he called a meeting. I believed that there had to be instability in the computation. I asked a member of my team to attend the meeting with me for support. After the person who had made the computations discussed them, I explained that his calculation violated the First and Second Laws of Thermodynamics. To prove it, all he had to do was an energy audit. The audit showed that the calculation was unstable and did not represent physical phenomena.

During my professional career, I experienced prejudices on trips sponsored by my organization. For example, the Containment Program scheduled the 3rd Symposium on Containment of Underground Explosions to be held in Idaho Falls, Idaho, in September 1985. I was a co-author of three papers and had to make at least two presentations. After checking into the designated motel, I went to the bar, ordered a draft beer, and watched Monday Night Football on the TV. There was a guy sitting on my left at the bar talking to his friends at a table next to the bar. When he turned around and saw me—a black man—he pushed me. I said, "Do not touch me again or I will break this mug across your face." The bartender said to me, "Sir, I can get you a seat at the other end of the bar." I said, "No, I am going to keep my seat here, and you should move him." The bartender called security and they escorted the guy out of the bar. There were people whom I worked with at Livermore who saw what happened and never said a word. The next day, I told my friend Ray Stout what happened.

I collaborated with numerous people on research projects in Livermore, and we published papers on our research. I also socialized with Livermore acquaintances as well as other acquaintances—having lunch together, doing exercises around the parcourse (fitness trail), drinking beer at a local bar, and going on gambling trips to Lake Tahoe and Reno casinos once a year. There was an acquaintance with which I would have lunch at the cafeteria, and we would also walk around the exercise parcourse every day. Another group of us would plan a lunch at a place that required that we take a flight. There was a pilot in our department and we would plan the lunch trip once a month. The restaurant would have a vehicle pick us up at their local airport. There were five or six places that we flew to for lunch.

On Fridays after work, my buddy Ray Chin and I would stop at the local bar and have a beer "or two" and discuss technical problems. For trips to Lake Tahoe or Reno, I did the planning because I knew where there were inexpensive hotels or motels. We would rent a car and I would drive there. I usually gambled most of the night, so someone else would drive home on the return trip while I was sleeping.

I also went fishing with colleagues from work and with friends at Lakeside Village Apartments in San Leandro. My fishing trips included salmon fishing and bottom fishing for cod and other fish. We had a pool (money) for the largest fish caught, and I won the pool twice. I caught my salmon limit every time except once when I stayed in the cabin of the boat because it was raining and too cold. Whenever I caught fish, I gave the largest one to my fishing partner. I gave most of the other fish to friends in Lakeside Village Apartments.

I left Livermore in February 1988 to accept the position as Chairman of the Department of Mechanical Engineering at Howard University. After I left California, I remained friends with many of my colleagues at the Laboratory and with friends at Lakeside Village Apartments.

Howard University

I flew from San Francisco to Washington, DC, on Sunday night, February 21, 1988. My friend Ray Chin was scheduled for the same flight. He had taken a one-year position as a Program Manager at the National Science Foundation (NSF) in Washington and was returning from a visit with his family in Livermore. During the boarding in San Francisco, Ray was not allowed on the flight because of overbooking—he had a low fare round-trip ticket. I was allowed to board because I had a one-way expensive ticket.

Since it did not appear that we would be on the same flight, Ray gave me the keys to his apartment in Arlington, Virginia (Pentagon City). Fortunately, he was able to take the flight after all—and I was relieved. I slept on his couch that night. A week later, I got an efficiency (one-room) apartment in the same building.

Ray explained the Washington area's Metrorail system to me. It had been more than twenty years since I had lived there while a student at Howard, and there was no Metrorail at that time. The next day after my arrival—Monday, February 22, 1988—I went to Howard to take on my position as Professor and Chairman of the Mechanical Engineering Department.

I rode the Metro to work every day during my first nine months. There are two Metro stations near my residence in Arlington—one in Pentagon City and the other in Crystal City. I usually used the Pentagon City Station.

Some evenings, I would meet Ray at the bar at the Days Inn in Crystal City for a beer and then we would go for dinner. One evening during my first months at Howard, I met Ray at the Days Inn where he was having a beer with several white people whom he knew, though he did not work with them at NSF. There was a woman in the group. I had a beer and then Ray and I were going to dinner. The men stated that they had already had dinner. The woman said that she knew of a bar in Arlington where we could get great burgers, so the three of us went there.

We sat at the bar and ordered our burgers and beer. Ray and I were wearing coats and ties. We were having a good time talking to the bartender. There was a white man wearing a coat and tie who was sitting at the other side of the U shaped bar. When he saw Ray and me having dinner with the woman, he said, "A Nigger and a Chink having dinner with a white woman, etc...."

I looked directly at him and said, "If you open your mouth again, I am going to kick your ass out of this bar. Do you hear me? I am going to kick your ass all the way out of this bar." He finished his drink and left the bar without saying another word. I do not know what Ray thought about what I said and I never asked him. This was another example of the prejudice and racism that I had to experience in 1988 and throughout my life, and I was tired of it.

My first year as Chairman of the Department of Mechanical Engineering at Howard was a new awakening and a new experience for me. I shall relate some of those experiences and how I addressed them.

I arrived at the University around 8:30am on February 22, 1988, but the Mechanical Engineering Department office was closed. It was supposed to open no later than 8:30am and close no earlier than 5:00pm. I walked around the building, went to the Dean's office, and sat there until after 9:00am. I finally found someone in the Department office about 9:30am, an hour later than it was supposed to open.

I had informed the Interim Department Chair and the Dean that I would be arriving that day. But there was no office space available for me. It took a couple of days for office space to be cleared for me.

I felt disrespected and asked myself, "Why in the hell did I leave Lawrence Livermore National Laboratory for this position when I had an opportunity to become a vice president at a company in Salt Lake City, Utah?" I was being recruited for that position at the same time I was being recruited by the Dean of the School of Engineering, Dr. M. Lucius Walker, Jr.

I chose Howard because I was an alumnus of the Mechanical Engineering Program and the Dean wanted a mentor for students at this Historically Black College and University (HBCU). My choice was also influenced by what I thought my social life would be as a single man in Salt Lake City.

I scheduled a department faculty meeting for the following Thursday, February 25, and worked with the staff to plan the agenda. At the meeting, I learned that there were many hidden agendas among faculty.

The staff in the Department office typed everything for the faculty on typewriters. I was surprised that the Department did not have computers. There was a word processor but the staff had not learned how to properly use it. One of the hidden agendas was prioritizing typing.

Another hidden agenda was change in leadership. Most people do not want change in operations. This type of behavior is clearly elucidated in Spencer Johnson's book <u>Who Moved My Cheese</u>, a parable that reveals truth about change. This is similar to what the older people said when I was growing up in Sawdust: "You can't teach an old dog new tricks."

There was still another hidden agenda from a faculty member who wanted to know what the Department was going to do for him personally, regarding an appointment that he intensely desired. Having attended workshops on how to conduct effective meetings, I knew how to control the hidden agendas and have a successful meeting.

In my first days at Howard, the office staff acted as if I should know everything about the operations, including preparing personnel recommendations, purchase requests, etc. Some of them had not learned how to prepare those documents themselves. I asked if there were policy and procedures manuals, safety manuals, etc., and was informed that there were none. However, there was a Faculty Handbook and a Non-Faculty Staff Handbook that spelled out the responsibilities of faculty and staff.

Whenever someone called the office, the staff would immediately transfer the call to me without finding out what the caller wanted. Further, they would send anyone who came to the Department—without an appointment—to my office without first contacting me. This included students and people from the external community. To be an effective leader, I had to address these issues first. A leader must have a supportive staff; and the current staff did not want a new leader. This was spelled out in <u>Who Moved My Cheese</u> all over again.

I made a list of things that I needed to learn in short order regarding preparation of documents, policies and procedures, and the operations of the University. Then I made an appointment with Dr. James H. Johnson, Jr., who was then Chairman of the Civil Engineering Department, to discuss my list. He was very organized and helped me immensely in my first two weeks.

Trying to get the office staff to change their old habits was very difficult. In the first place, there was no performance evaluation of staff at the University. Secondly, the staff in other offices, including the Dean's office, arrived to work after specified office hours. It took me more than a year to get major changes done in the Department office.

I had several major, important tasks to address during the first months. They included the preparation of a Self Study Report for an accreditation visit in October, submitting information for faculty raises, submitting teaching schedules, and recommendations of leaves of absence for full-time faculty. I shall discuss each.

My first important task as Department Chairman was to prepare for the October visit by the Accreditation Board for Engineering and Technology (ABET). For each university with an engineering program, the Board required the program to satisfy specific curriculum requirements. Each engineering program had to prepare a Self Study document showing that they met those requirements. During the 1980s and 1990s, ABET emphasized student design, hands-on laboratory experience, and oral and written communications across the curriculum in addition to other requirements. The Self Study had to show how the engineering program satisfied the requirements. Samples of student work were required to be displayed at the ABET visit to show that students were meeting those requirements.

The Department had a Laboratory and Space Committee to take care of undergraduate student laboratory needs. This committee was ineffective. At the beginning of the fiscal year on July 1, 1987, the University had allocated one hundred thousand dollars for equipment upgrades. All purchases had to be completed by mid-April 1988. Yet, as we neared that deadline, no equipment had been purchased. To complicate matters, each piece of equipment had to have the approval of the President of the University before the purchase order could be submitted to vendors.

I asked the committee chair how long it would take for the committee to put together the list of equipment and prepare purchase orders. He said two weeks. But after two weeks, I did not have a report from him. I went to his office and found that nothing had been done. The following week, I did get a list, but no purchase requests. I forwarded the list of equipment to the office of the President for approval.

Guess what? Some equipment on the list had vendors that did not sell that equipment. I had to send another list to the President's office. I asked myself, "What will the President's office think about my handling the job as Department Chairman?"

In the end, we lost about twenty five thousand dollars because of an ineffective Laboratory and Space Committee, and some of the equipment that we purchased was outdated. The Department effectively lost about half of the money allocated by the University to upgrade the laboratories.

I later found out the committee, as a matter of practice, would ask our technician to put the list together with little guidance or oversight on equipment selection. The technician had a habit of stopping whatever he was doing, no matter how important, and work on the task of the last person who asked him do something—whether running errands for students or for someone in another Department. Clearly, the committee had not properly prioritized the purchase of laboratory equipment.

Preparation of the Self Study Report was a great opportunity for me to understand the needs of the Department. I saw where I should focus my efforts to move the Department forward. The design component of the curriculum was unsatisfactory. There was a need to upgrade the equipment in the undergraduate laboratories and place computers in the staff office. I also saw the need to assure that the committees in the Department worked effectively.

It has been said that getting faculty to work together is like trying to herd cats. I found that to be true. I addressed all of those issues as Department Chairman and was successful in all endeavors. I appointed junior faculty whom I could mentor into key positions in Capstone Design and design of engineering systems. Capstone Design is a culminating course offered to undergraduate students in engineering. Students work in teams to design, build, and test prototypes with real world applications. Further, I did not schedule Capstone Design courses during the summer because I knew that the students would not get a satisfactory design experience in six weeks. I sought and obtained support from industry for instructions in our Senior Capstone Design Course. And, I restructured the Laboratory Committee.

During my first year, I tried to ensure that each faculty member got a raise to boost morale. The system was set up with metrics in teaching, research, and service that each member had to meet to be eligible for a raise. I spent many hours on those metrics to avoid punishing anyone, and submitted my evaluation to the Dean of the School of Engineering. I got away with my play on numbers. Every faculty in the Department except me got a raise that year. I had no record in teaching, research and service as Department Chairman yet I was evaluated as a faculty member. Staff raises were decided by the University Administration.

One faculty member asked me for a two-year leave of absence. I said that we had an accreditation visit in October and I would consult with the Executive Committee in the Department regarding his request. The Executive Committee agreed that we needed all current faculty to continue preparation for the ABET visit. I found out that he had been offered a much higher salary for a two-year temporary appointment at another university that was having an ABET visit during the same year as our visit. He was not granted a leave of absence.

However, he left Howard for the temporary position at the other institution, stranding one Ph.D. student and one master's student who were studying under his advisement. The faculty member had earned his Ph.D. in the Department of Mechanical Engineering at Howard, and his former advisor was still on the faculty. Nevertheless, his former advisor would not take on his protégé's Ph.D. student.

As Department Chairman, I had to take all responsibilities for the guidance of these two students. I talked to numerous people across the campus regarding the advisement of the Ph.D. student and found no avenues other than taking on his advisor ship. I maintained contact with the professor at his new institution and invited him to participate in his former advisee's Ph.D. dissertation defense. He returned and participated in the student's defense.

The master's student left the University due to poor grades. In fact, my experience with him taught me another lesson. While advising him during the fall semester 1988, I found that he had registered for a freshman course to increase his GPA. When I addressed him about this, he said that I had access to his records and it was my problem. From then on, I decided not to talk to students without knowledge of their academic performance. I required my office staff to make appointments for any student wanting to see me and to note the purpose of the meeting. I insisted on seeing their records prior to meeting.

The teaching schedules for faculty had to be prepared before the next term of classes, whether summer, fall, or spring. This was a major responsibility of the Department Chairman.

Five adjunct faculty members taught courses in our Department. During my first months, four of them came to me and asked for a raise. It was important for our programs to keep them. In my meeting with the Chairman of the Civil Engineering Department, I had learned about preparing personnel recommendations. I was able to give the adjuncts a raise using funds that I managed by re-allocating the time spent teaching each course. For example, if the time was listed as one quarter time, I increased it commensurate with the raise. This did not require University administrative action, only the approval of the personnel recommendation.

The fifth adjunct faculty member never talked to me. Instead, he communicated with a senior faculty member in our Department who had selfish interests. That senior faculty member told me that the adjunct member would not be available to teach the course, probably for health reasons, but I cannot recall.

I assigned the course to the senior faculty member. However, he wanted to teach only one course per year, as before my arrival. He told me that the course was the adjunct member's course. I informed him that no faculty member owned courses; they belonged to the Department. That course was never offered again.

The adjunct member wanted to be advisor of record for a master's student in our Department. He called me at the office after 5:00pm one day in late 1988 and asked if I would appoint him as the advisor. He probably had been informed that I stayed in the office late in the evening. I said that a graduate student's advisor had to be a member of the graduate school, and first had to be a member of the Department that appointed him. I saw no need to appoint him to our faculty. Therefore he could not serve as advisor to graduate students in Mechanical Engineering. He had been misled by the senior faculty member and others. He began to argue.

After the discussion, I received a letter from him stating that he was going to sever his relationship with Howard. I did not want to burn any bridges that would affect our Department, so I answered his letter, explaining the details of appointments to the graduate faculty. I knew that both of us would be at a meeting in Rio de Janeiro, Brazil, so I wanted to make sure that he received the letter before I saw him there.

I left New York for Brazil in the early hours of New Year's Day, 1989. In Rio, several of us who had relations at Howard were having beer, and the adjunct professor joined us. On the day before he was leaving for home, he told me that I would receive another letter from him. I replied that I would not respond regarding appointment to the graduate faculty.

After returning to Howard, I received his letter containing threats regarding what I had said in Brazil about not responding to a new letter. I placed it in his file. He was trying to test or bully me and I knew it. Later, he wrote a letter to the Dean of Engineering questioning my leadership and copied it to all full professors in Mechanical Engineering and one full professor in Civil Engineering. The Civil Engineering professor was chair of the Howard University Faculty Senate. The most senior faculty member in Mechanical Engineering showed me the letter and said, "I am on your side." The Civil Engineering professor told me that he had received the letter too, and we discussed its contents. He supported my actions.

The Dean of Engineering called me after he read the letter to discuss actions. I preferred to talk in person and went immediately to his office. While there, I learned that the Dean was preparing a response to the letter. His statements would deflect the situation back to me. I said that I would resign and leave the University before I would endorse a recommendation to hire that adjunct faculty member. I do not know what the Dean's response was. However, the former adjunct faculty wrote a letter threatening the Dean. He also got a person who had received a master's degree in Mechanical Engineering to write a letter stating that I was trying to destroy our graduate program. Nothing happened with either of those threats and I remained Chairman of the Department.

Many years later, the former adjunct faculty member called me to apologize. Yet, he still could not let the subject rest without trying to deflect the blame to me. I knew that he had a serious health problem and I just listened, spoke without argument or defense, and wished him well.

Managing the budget and other resources was one of the most important things that I had to take control of in my first months at Howard. My predecessor told me that the Department would nearly run out of funds by the end of the first semester. I spent evenings after the office closed, studying records to find out how the resources were used. I learned that much of our Department's University budget, designated for supplies and expenses, and our discretionary funds from external organizations were being used by two people in the Department—the acting chairman and one senior faculty member—for domestic and foreign travel. The senior faculty member had already been approved and allocated expenses for a foreign trip when I arrived. I allowed the expenses for the trip but informed him that I now controlled the budget and discretionary funds, and that I would control expenses for travel, including travel requests.

The Department also had a scholarship fund of ten thousand dollars provided by an industry sponsor of our program. I saw the need to use this fund for needy students.

I had needy students to come to my office, and promised to help them get registered. I prepared the appropriate documents awarding a scholarship to each of them, and forwarded those documents to the Office of Financial Aid.

I later found out that there were no funds in that account. The Office of the Assistant Dean had used the funds for not only mechanical engineering students, but also for students in other Departments in the School of Engineering. I informed the Office of the Assistant Dean that they should never use funds allocated to the Mechanical Engineering Department without my approval.

Now I had to find funds for the needy students. I wanted them to know that I always lived up to my commitments. I discussed my situation with a faculty member and he provided me with funds from an account under his control. These funds were sufficient to fulfill my promise.

In later years, the Office of the Associate Provost for Research Administration took funds from my discretionary account. My administrative assistant and I searched and found out. I contacted him and the funds were replaced.

In short, the Department Chairman did not have control of money in his budget. Our budget had no meaning. Other offices could access the

Department's accounts and take the funds for their own uses at any time. There were times when my Department ordered supplies using a particular account only to discover that there was no money. The University had taken those funds without notification, and our purchase orders were rejected. I had to use funds that I raised from industry to pay for needed supplies that had been in the budget.

These are only examples, not a comprehensive recounting of all that I had to confront during those years. Over time, I had numerous issues to address as Department Chairman. I shall discuss several of those issues to illustrate what my life was like in that position. I addressed issues from people within and outside the University.

After my first year, we hired a new technician to replace one who left on full disability. However, the new technician disrespected faculty and often would not show up for work. More than a year after he had been on board—after his probation period—faculty in charge of laboratories finally informed me of his poor performance. I personally began to look for him at different times throughout the day and could not find him. I wrote aids to my memory at those times.

I discussed his poor performance and other work habits with him, and he deflected the subject to me regarding my work. I said that I did not need to explain my work to him, but it was important for me as his supervisor to know if he was performing his assigned duties. The university had recently established annual staff evaluations.

At the annual evaluation of staff, I wrote a negative performance evaluation for him based on my observations and reports from faculty members in charge of Department laboratories. As with all written evaluations, I called him to my office and discussed the evaluation personally. He threatened me physically. Sitting in front of my desk with what appeared to be fire in his eyes, he said, "I am right with Jesus Christ, and you better not take money from my kids." I asked him to leave my office.

That discussion took place at the end of the work day. After I closed the office, I went to the Dean's office to inform him of my talk with the technician and the threat. I said, "If anything happens to me, I want you to know this."

Later, this technician had an auto accident and was away on sick leave. After appropriate leave time had elapsed, we contacted him by mail asking him to report or contact the Office of Mechanical Engineering. We received no response. I made an appointment with the Office of Human Resources to discuss how to handle the situation. It was agreed that I should send another letter informing him that his appointment at Howard would be terminated.

I sent the letter but it was returned to my office unopened, marked "wrong address." I placed it in his files. I found out that he had used his sister's address in his employment files. After about a week after the letter was returned, the technician came to my office. I offered him the opportunity to resign. He said that he was not going to resign and threatened to contact the President of the University about things that he thought were going on in the School of Engineering. I told him that it was his privilege but I was preparing paperwork to terminate his employment. My paperwork dismissing him was approved by the University.

There were no templates to complete Department or School of Engineering business. Sometimes Department chairmen waited for someone else to develop templates. I looked at the issue as if I had requested templates, asking myself, "What would I like to see?" Then I answered my own question and was very successful. It seemed that others would say, "There is no need to reinvent the wheel. Let's see what you have;" and they would use my work as a guide.

I had expected a cycle for annual events, but there was none. And there were always new activities that I had to prepare for and develop solutions accordingly.

I had to address complaints from parents regarding their son's or daughter's progress through the curriculum. Parents also had hidden agendas related to other Departments at the University, such as the Financial Aid Office, Athletics Department, or campus housing, and would try to involve our Department in issues of those units.

Some parents called me and tried to get me to change the requirements. For example, two different parents who worked at majority universities said that their son or daughter was being treated unfairly at Howard. I informed them that our curriculum was a contract to obtain a degree from our program, and asked if the institutions where they worked changed the requirements to satisfy a parent's complaints. They replied, "No." Then I asked why they were asking me to change requirements, and the conversation ended. Numerous parents called me regarding exceptions for their sons or daughters, asking me to make changes. My answers were always the same.

One family tried to take advantage regarding their complaint with the University. Their daughter was a student in our Department. She and her parents had an issue with the Athletic Department, but I was unaware of this. She was always given the benefit of doubt. She made an appointment to see me but brought her parents with her without my advance knowledge. The parents made numerous complaints regarding my treatment of their daughter. I was shocked because the complaints were totally false, and this student did not correct her parents. The mother made several negative comments regarding the University, and I had to correct her.

Following the meeting in my office, the mother sent an e-mail to the Dean containing false, negative comments on my leadership. The Dean recognized the false content and forwarded the email to me. This family later invaded a Town Hall Meeting that I had, and tried to record it on video camera. While I was responding to students' questions, the Dean recognized that the son of the same family had a video camera in the background recording the event. The Dean stopped the discussions and asked the son if he had received permission from all to record the meeting. The son said that he had not gotten permission. The Dean said, "You must stop recording and leave NOW." I learned to always pay attention to everything around you at a meeting.

Following the Town Hall Meeting, several students came to me stating that they agreed with my leadership but were afraid to express their opinions in the meeting.

Another challenge was that faculty advisors would send their students to me without helping them or researching information first. I had to figure out a way to prevent this, and I knew it would take time to develop a solution to this problem.

I advised all senior students, but had to take myself out of the loop of advising non-seniors.

My solution was to develop a Mechanical Engineering Department Handbook for faculty and students. It laid out everything that a student or advisor should know from freshman year to graduation.

As the first step, during the summer of 1989, I paid a faculty member to prepare a poster showing all courses in the curriculum. I posted it on my wall to see the prerequisites for each course when a student was sent to my office.

My handbook was developed in 1992, the very first handbook in the School of Engineering at Howard University. Beginning in 2004, all departments in the College were required to have handbooks. My Handbook served as a model for other programs in engineering.

From time to time in the courses I taught, some students wanted to discuss other business in the classroom. During class, students would complain about other faculty or request things such as building a new ladies' restroom on the ground floor. I needed to let them know that I had to separate teaching from Department business. I said that, while in the classroom, I would not discuss business that was not related to my course. Students should make an appointment with my office staff to discuss non-course-related business. I added this statement to my course syllabus.

In the mid to late 1990s, I initiated a special recognition, the **"Department Chairman's Award"** for the most outstanding graduating senior. The purpose was to encourage high academics and service of students in the Department. The award would be given to the senior who had demonstrated high academic achievement and voluntary service to the community and had been a champion of the program at Howard. This award included a plaque and a one thousand dollar check. If no one met the criteria, no award would be given that year. I know of no awards being given after my service as Department Chairman ended in 2004.

I observed that those who asked you to help them the most were the ones who fought you the most. This included both faculty and students. Over my sixteen and one-half years as Department Chairman, there were four faculty members and several students in that category.

Two faculty members filed complaints against me. One was a discrimination complaint with the EEOC and the other was with the University's Grievance Committee. The complaint filed with the EEOC resulted from that person misreading information from the Office of the Dean following an accreditation visit. The complaint filed with the University's Grievance Committee came about because I did not recommend a promotion.

Two other faculty members complained to people across the University because of my course assignments. All complaints were dismissed, but answering those complaints required a lot of extra work on my part.

Some students thought they knew how change-of-grade reports worked and tried to take advantage using their limited knowledge. They knew the process for change-of-grade reports to be sent to the Office of the Registrar. One evening around 5:00pm, when my office staff was preparing to leave, I got a call from a staff person in the Office of the Registrar regarding a change-of-grade report. I walked from the Engineering building up the hill to the Administration building to discuss her concerns. During our meeting, I saw that the registrar's staff person thought she had caught me doing something illegal—as evidenced by her gleeful expressions.

However, Howard's change-of-grade report form was not for grades from courses that students took at other universities in the Consortium of Universities in Washington, of which Howard was a member. The registrar's office knew that this was not standard procedure, so that office contacted the professor at the university where the course was taught. The specific problem was that the change-of-grade form had my alleged signature. The professor stated that he had no contact with me regarding that course.

The staff person showed me the change-of-grade report with my suspected signature. I told her that it looked exactly like my signature, but I had not submitted that report. I sensed something unusual about the form. When I asked if I could see a fresh copy of the form, she did not want to comply because she thought she had caught me in an illegal activity. Once I saw the original form, I compared it to the copy with my alleged signature and realized that the student had scanned my signature.

I suggested that we meet with the Assistant Dean of Engineering the next morning to discuss this matter. During the meeting, I asked for an audit of records of students in my Department. I never received the audit.

A few years later, there was a similar incident regarding change of grades. Again, I asked for an audit. The students involved were not successful in having their grades changed and left the university.

I also had to address problems that had nothing to do with Department business. Here is an example:

A student in our Department of Mechanical Engineering had agreed to give pilot lessons to a student in another Department in the School of Engineering. The student in the other Department had paid for her flight lessons but was not getting them. She talked to a non-University person who sent her to me to address the problem. I told her that this was not a situation that I could address because it was not University business. I said that she should consider getting an attorney.

Any time anyone associated with the Mechanical Engineering Department had a problem, they were told, "See the Department Chairman."

I gained a reputation from the Deans that I served under that, if you want to get the job done, get Dr. Lewis Thigpen to do it. I was assigned or asked to volunteer for numerous important tasks and committees by the Dean. Several examples follow.

- In the early 1990s, I served as chair of the Educational Policies Committee in the School of Engineering and was appointed by Dean M. Lucius Walker, Jr. to a University-wide committee to evaluate educational policies.
- In the mid 1990s, the University obtained an endowed Chair in Materials Science from the Packard Foundation. Dean James H. Johnson, Jr. asked me to volunteer at the next School of Engineering faculty meeting to serve on the Search Committee for a candidate to fill that position. He appointed me to chair the committee. I filled it with members from Chemistry, Physics, Chemical and Electrical Engineering, and Mathematics which involved two Department Chairs.
- In 1997 or earlier, the University decided to merge the School of Engineering and the School of Architecture and Dean Johnson appointed me to the University-wide Steering Committee. The two schools were merged in 1997 and became the College of Engineering, Architecture and Computer Sciences (CEACS) comprised of the School of Engineering and Computer Science and the School of Architecture and Design.

> In the early 2000s, the University prepared a proposal to the Kauffman Foundation to develop entrepreneurial efforts. Dean Johnson appointed me to chair a committee in the College to prepare our contribution to the proposal.
> Further, I served two Deans, Dean James H. Johnson, Jr. (1995 – 2009) and Dean James W. Mitchell (2010 – 2013) and prepared the Institutional Profile for the 2006, 2008, and 2012 ABET Accreditation Visits.

I cherish the confidence that the Deans and faculty in the College had in my ability to get things done and I consider that to be a great honor. I enjoyed seeing students develop from freshman through their senior year and the collegiality of faculty across the University. In the spirit of the legendary Dean Lewis K. Downing and Dean M. Lucius Walker, Jr., my work at alma mater was to advance the University and help those it serves. I am proud to be part of the legacy of those two remarkable leaders at Howard.

From July 1, 1998, to late June 1999, I spent a sabbatical from Howard University as a Long Term Visiting Staff Member at Los Alamos National Laboratory in Los Alamos, New Mexico. There, I pioneered work in computational web transport processes. This work is important to industry in reducing machine downtime during manufacturing. The work was supported by a collaborative agreement between industry and the Laboratory.

In June 1999, before I returned to Howard, I was called by the Chair of the ASME National Mechanical Engineering Department Heads Committee to serve as Vice Chair. I was elected as Vice Chair of the ASME National Departments Heads Committee at the ASEE Annual Conference and Exposition in Charlotte, NC.

Prior to leaving Los Alamos, I made a presentation of my work to my Group members and I was also invited and made a presentation of my work to two other groups that supported and encouraged my efforts.

As I was about to leave Los Alamos, there were several going-away receptions for me. One was hosted by Pete Miller, an Associate Director at Los Alamos Laboratory. He encouraged me to stay at the Laboratory. Of course I could not stay because I was obligated to return to Howard for at least one year following my sabbatical.

After I returned from sabbatical to Howard in 1999, I was contacted by a search committee for a high profile management position at Lawrence Livermore National Laboratory (LLNL). I was familiar with the responsibilities of that position. It meant that I would have to be available "24/7." At my age and health condition, I did not think my body could take it, so I did not follow up for an interview. I learned that several people at LLNL had recommended me for the position.

Back at Howard, my first major task was to lead the effort in preparing for an accreditation visit from the Accreditation Board for Engineering and Technology (ABET). This was to be a landmark visit because it would reflect major changes, established by ABET, in the way engineering programs were evaluated. I had begun this effort prior to my sabbatical but found that nothing had been done during my absence.

Using my leadership skills and knowledge of faculty, I formed three sub-committees to work on specific requirements of the accreditation process. There were three faculty members whom I had to place with great care. No two of them were on the same committee because they would only argue and nothing would get done. I assigned myself and one of them to a two-person committee that had the most work to do. We were successful in our efforts. As I have stated earlier, other Departments requested electronic copies of my Self Study Report as a guide in the preparation of their reports.

In 2000, following our success in accreditation, I informed the Dean of Engineering that I was going to give up the position of Department Chairman when my current appointment ended, and return to the ranks of the faculty. Department Chairs had three-year renewable appointments. The Dean formed a search committee for a new Chair. However, it was two years before a new Chair was appointed.

My major accomplishments at Howard University as Chairman of the Mechanical Engineering Department included curriculum innovations, introduction of new graduate programs, obtaining resources to advance student learning, promoting outreach and diversity, and enhancing the reputation of the Department to the external community.

In the area of curriculum innovations, my efforts began in 1988 and ended in 2008 when I retired. In 1989, I restructured the Senior Capstone Design courses to include industry-sponsored senior design projects with an industry liaison who was appointed to the faculty without compensation (WOC) from the University. The liaison could participate in all aspects of the conduct of the course.

This is how I acquired our first sponsor, Sundstrand Corporation, an aerospace company in Rockford, Illinois.

One evening after 5:00pm, I answered a call from a recruiter from Sundstrand Aerospace. He wanted to talk to one of our graduate students. I replied that I would contact the student and have her call him. He then asked if there was something that his company could do for our Department. I explained my interest in getting industry to support our Capstone Design course.

I must say that I had discussed this with many recruiters on campus prior to this telephone discussion. The Sundstrand recruiter said that he would get back to me. I thought to myself, "I have heard this from other recruiters and probably nothing will happen."

Well, my thoughts were wrong. The recruiter called me a few days later, inviting me to come to Rockford to discuss my needs with the Vice President of Engineering, Richard "Dick" Spencer. I went to Rockford and met with leaders at Sundstrand. They gave me an overview of the corporation and we went to a restaurant for lunch.

The waitress asked me first what I would like for a drink. I said a Michelob beer. Then Spencer said, "I like a person who knows what he wants. He did not ask what kinds of beer you have. He just stated what he wanted. I will have a Michelob also." He then turned to the person in the leadership position below him and said, "I like the project that the professor has discussed with us. What are you going do about it?" The manager responded, "I am going back to the office and see that the project goes forward."

We implemented the Sundstrand projects in the fall semester 1989. During the preceding summer, I assigned the most junior faculty member in the Department as faculty of record. Sundstrand assigned one of their young engineers to work with us on the Capstone projects. I charged the Senior Projects Committee to overview our selection of projects.

Throughout the 1989-1990 academic year, I worked with and mentored my junior faculty member to ensure that my initiative was a success.

The engineer from Sundstrand was appointed as a faculty member Without Compensation (WOC) and came to the University every two weeks for design reviews with our students.

I planned a banquet to honor our sponsor and student teams. The banquet took place after the teams made their final presentations at the end of the academic year. Officials from Sundstrand, including Dick Spencer, attended the presentations and banquet. Photos were taken by Sundstrand. I presented a plaque to Sundstrand to acknowledge our appreciation for their support of our program.

About a month after the banquet, I received a call from Sundstrand requesting me to visit them in June to talk about our relationships. I agreed to attend. However I broke a bone in my left foot about a week before I was supposed to visit.

I informed Vice President Spencer of my situation. He said that he would like me to make the visit if possible and would have someone pick me up at O'Hare Airport in Chicago. From the conversation, I knew that it was important for our program and Sundstrand that I make the trip. Sundstrand had gotten a new President and CEO, Harry Stonecipher, who wanted to show their relationships with Historically Black Colleges and Universities (HBCUs). I agreed to go.

At O'Hare, Spencer's valet brought a wheelchair to the gate and took me to his limousine for the trip to Rockford. I had lunch the next day with Spencer in the executive dining room and later met with President and CEO Harry Stonecipher in his office.

At that meeting, there were reporters from the local newspaper and members of the Department of Defense from the Chicago area. The newspaper published the contents of our meeting and I received a copy. I received a certificate signed by Stonecipher and Spencer for my efforts in educational outreach. I also presented a plaque to Sundstrand recognizing their support for Mechanical Engineering at Howard University.

Sundstrand Aerospace supported our program for seven years. Subsequently, Stonecipher left Sundstrand Aerospace and became Chief Executive Officer of McDonnell Douglas and later the Boeing Company. He orchestrated the merger between McDonnell Douglas and Boeing.

I acquired other sponsors for our Capstone Design Course including Boeing Helicopter, General Motors, and Sandia National Laboratories. At the time of the writing of this memoir, Sandia Laboratories has sponsored Capstone Design projects for more than ten years.

In 2002, we offered a new undergraduate program curriculum that reduced the number of credit hours from a maximum of 141 to 128 credit hours. Because the pendulum swings very slowly in an academic institution, it took several years for the curriculum committee to present a DRAFT to the Department. The new curriculum had a product realization stem in which students began their first semester in college taking design courses in a sequence that ended in the Senior Capstone Design Course.

Having experience working in industry and national laboratories, I knew that design teams were made up of people from different disciplines, so I solicited different Departments at the University to join our Capstone Design Course. By 2002, I formed a multidisciplinary Capstone Design Course that included students and faculty from Mechanical Engineering, Electrical Engineering, Chemical Engineering, Business, and Art.

In February 2004, I was informed that Howard University had been selected as a Partner for the Advancement of Collaborative Engineering Education (PACE) Institution. This selection was the result of a proposal that I and colleague Professor Emmanuel K. Glakpe wrote. The PACE grants provided $70.6 million in "in-kind funds," the largest in the history of Howard University.

The PACE Program linked General Motors (GM), UGS (Unigraphics Solutions Inc.—now part of Siemens), Hewlett-Packard (HP), and Sun Microsystems to support selected academic institutions worldwide to develop product life-cycle management (PLM) teams of the future. It provided Howard with new computer hardware and software that gives students experience with tools to enhance their success in the workplace. The PACE office was located at General Motors in Warren, Michigan.

The celebration of Howard's selection for membership in this prestigious program took place on campus in October 2004. It was hosted by President H. Patrick Swygert and Dean James H. Johnson, Jr., College of Engineering, Architecture and Computer Sciences. Representatives from other PACE institutions attended. I met the PACE Integrator from Virginia Tech and we discussed collaborations.

In 2005, I joined Virginia Tech, Technische Universitat (Darmstadt, Germany), and ITESM (Monterrey, Mexico) in the development of a Global Engineering Design Course as part of the PACE Program. Shanghai Jiao Tong University (Shanghai, China) joined our team in 2006. The course was set up in teams with students from each country on each team. Video conferencing was our major means of communications, although students also used e-mail, Skype and Gismo. Each institution gave one lecture. There were also guest lecturers.

The course is offered to undergraduate seniors and graduate students as an elective. Projects are obtained from the automotive industry and awards are given to the top three teams. Judging is done by people from GM and other industries after the final student team presentations. This course is the first and only global collaborative engineering course offered in engineering at Howard University and probably at many universities in the United States. Thus far, the course has continued to be offered since fall 2005.

New programs were developed in mechanical engineering under my leadership as Chairman. In 1997, interdisciplinary graduate programs at the master's and Ph. D. levels in Atmospheric Science and in Material Science were approved. The interdisciplinary programs involved the Mechanical Engineering Department, the Electrical Engineering Department, the Physics Department, and the Chemistry Department.

In 1996, I developed a Computer Aided Design and Instructions Laboratory to enhance student learning. This laboratory has computer workstations, video conferencing capabilities and numerous computer software packages used in design and instruction. It is open twenty-four hours a day, seven days a week, and is referred to by students as "The ME Lab." This laboratory was developed with funds that I raised from industry.

I served as Principal Investigator and Co-Principal Investigator of projects resulting in more than $6,000,000 from government agencies and private industry to support graduate student research.

In 1992, for faculty advising, I prepared the first Department Handbook for faculty and students in Engineering at Howard. Other engineering programs at Howard began to develop handbooks in 2005 and some used the Mechanical Engineering Department's handbook as a guide. My handbook is still used today, with little modification.

In 1995, we hired Sonya T. Smith, Ph.D., the first female faculty member in the history of the Department of Mechanical Engineering at Howard. She advanced rapidly and served as Chair of the Department (July 1, 2011 – July 7, 2015). A Fellow of the ASME, she currently serves as President-elect of the FY 2019 Sigma Xi Board of Directors, the Scientific Research Honor Society.

My diversity and outreach activities to enhance education and research, and the reputation of the Department also include my personal activities in the external community. Between 1988 and 2013, I served on more than one hundred external committees, panels, and advisory boards and chaired many of those entities. The majority of committees and boards evaluated candidates for graduate student fellowship grants. Other committees and boards outlined processes to enhance research and education and develop new programs.

I was appointed a member of the Advisory Committee of the National Science Foundation (NSF) Mechanical and Structural System Division in 1990. I served for two years. One of the committee's charter goals was to provide advice on allocating limited resources to many outstanding research proposals from University faculty members. The chair of the committee was a professor in my Department when I was in graduate school at IIT more than twenty years earlier—what a small world!

In 1991, I was invited and served on the Visiting Committee of the Massachusetts Higher Education Coordinating Council. Our mission was to evaluate a proposal from Johnson and Wales University in Providence, Rhode Island, to establish technology programs in Massachusetts and make recommendations.

Other advisory committees on which I served related to education, outreach, and research for several organizations including the Indiana University-Purdue University External Advisory Board for Mathematics and Undergraduate Education (1996-1998); the External Advisory Committee, NSF Research Experience Undergraduate (REU) Virginia Tech (2006-2008); and the Mechanical Engineering Visiting Advisory Committee, United States Naval Academy (2008). The latter committee consisted of two admirals and me.

I served as Chair of the National Mechanical Engineering Department Heads Committee (MEDHC) in 2000-2001. I also served as Chair of the

American Society of Mechanical Engineering (ASME) Committee on Engineering Accreditation (EAC) for two years (2005-2007). I am the first and only African American to serve in those two positions so far.

I served as a member of the ASME Board of Directors Center for Education in 1999-2003 and 2007-2010.

Through my service on panels, boards, and committees, I was able to make significant impacts on engineering education, outreach, diversity, and research at Howard, around the United States, and internationally. Details regarding committees, panels, and boards that I served on are in my professional résumé.

I retired from Howard University on August 31, 2008. The following year (2009), Howard University offered a buyout for administrators. The Dean of the College of Engineering, Architecture and Computer Sciences, James H. Johnson, Jr., decided to retire and accept the buyout.

At that time, there were two Schools in the College, the School of Engineering and Computer Science, and the School of Architecture and Design. The Dean was also the Director of Engineering and Computer Science.

Architecture was managed by a Director of Architecture and Design who would become Acting Dean of the College. For the other entity— the School of Engineering and Computer Science— the College had to appoint an Acting Director during the search for a new Dean.

Dean Johnson asked if I was interested in becoming the Acting Director. I responded that I had just retired and was not interested. However, I suggested that Ramesh Chawla, Chair of the Chemical Engineering Department, would be a good candidate. Dean Johnson agreed and recommended him for the position. Professor Chawla served in that position for a year.

Chapter 12

Major Achievements

I was a high achiever in my youth and graduated salutatorian of my high school class at age 15 in May 1954. Following more than a year of farm and construction work as a common laborer, I joined the United States Army on September 2, 1955 at age seventeen and advanced to the grade of E-5. In August 1958, at age nineteen, I separated from active duty and joined the Army Reserves. As a non-commissioned officer (NCO), I taught courses at our Reserve meetings prior to and during my first year as a college student in 1959 and continued until I completed my obligation in 1961.

I earned a Bachelor of Science degree in Mechanical Engineering, *magna cum laude,* from Howard University in June 1964 and the Master of Science and Ph.D. degrees in Engineering Mechanics from Illinois Institute of Technology June 1967 and January 1970, respectively. I am the recipient of the Illinois Institute of Technology 2006 Alumni Professional Achievement Award for outstanding achievements in my profession.

I retired Professor Emeritus of Mechanical Engineering at Howard University on August 31, 2008, after a more than a forty-year distinguished career of leadership and contributions to research, service, and education. I served as Chairman of the Department of Mechanical Engineering at Howard University from January 1, 1988, until June 30, 2004. Prior to my appointment at Howard, I held positions of leadership at Sandia National Laboratories (1969-1973) and at Lawrence Livermore National Laboratory (1975-1988). At Sandia National Laboratories, I was a member of the Technical Staff and Project Leader for Earth Penetration Mechanics and

Water Entry Phenomenon. At Lawrence Livermore National Laboratory, I held the following positions: Task Leader of Stress Wave Modeling Containment Program, Earth Sciences Department, 1985-1988; Team Leader Solid and Wave Mechanics, Earth Sciences Department, 1984-1985; Deputy Group Leader Earth Sciences Department, 1982-1984; Group Leader Dynamic Modeling Group K-Division, 1980-1982; Assistant Program Manager Seismic Monitoring Program, K-Division, 1978-1979; and Member of the Technical Staff, 1975-1978. I was also an Assistant Professor in the Civil Engineering Department at Lowell Technological Institute, now University of Massachusetts at Lowell (1973-1975). I am a registered Professional Engineer (PE) in the District of Columbia.

As an accomplished researcher, I made significant contributions to research on non-linear wave (energy) propagation in geologic materials. This research included constitutive modeling; coding constitutive models for computer analysis; and developing computer application codes to discriminate energy emanating from earthquakes and underground high explosive and nuclear energy sources. I performed the first three-dimensional (3-D) computations dealing with soil-structure interactions under intense loading from ground motion emanating from nuclear energy sources. I am also a pioneer in computational earth penetration by a projectile into rock. I pioneered and published work on the analysis of stress distributions in *in-situ* oil shale rubble columns during retorting (a process to extract oil from shale deposits *in-place*), earth penetration mechanics, water-entry phenomena, and web transport. I was elected Fellow of the American Society of Mechanical Engineers in 1998 for my pioneering work in earth penetration mechanics, and I co-authored a patent on water-entry phenomena. I have more than sixty publications that I authored and co-authored as a result of research in engineering, science, and education.

Extremely active in the American Society of Mechanical Engineers (ASME), I served on the Center for Education Board of Directors for more than ten years (1999-2010). I am the only African American so far to have served as Chair of the ASME National Mechanical Engineers Department Heads Committee (2000-2001) and Chair of the ASME Committee on Engineering Accreditation, where I was elected to two consecutive terms (2005-2006 and 2006-2007). I also served as the Chair of the Mid-Atlantic Regional Mechanical Engineering Department Heads Committee (MEDHC) from 1996-1998. I served on the planning committee for the MEDHC Education Conferences and as a Mechanical Engineering Program Evaluator for the Accreditation Board for Engineering and Technology (ABET). I received an ASME Certificate from the ASME Center for Education for serving as Chair of the Committee on Engineering Accreditation 2005-2007 which reads *in grateful appreciation for his dedication and substantial contributions to the area of engineering accreditation through serving as Program Evaluator and leader of the Committee on Engineering Accreditation.* I received the ASME Council on Education 2000-2001 Award for advancing engineering education as chair of the national Mechanical Engineering Department Heads Committee. I also received the ASME International 2003 Dedicated Service Award for dedicated voluntary service to the society marked by outstanding performance, demonstrated effective leadership, prolonged and committed service, devotion, enthusiasm, and faithfulness. Further, in July 2010, I received the ASME Board of Governors Certificate as a member of the Board of Directors Center of Engineering Education 2007 – 2010.

During my professional career I was invited to and served on numerous advisory boards and/or committees which include the United States Naval Academy's Mechanical Engineering Program Advisory Committee (2007-2008); the Virginia Tech Research in Undergraduate Education National Science Foundation External Board (2006-2008); the Indiana University—Purdue University External Board for Mathematics and Undergraduate Education (1996-2000); the U.S. Department of Energy's Panel on Seismic Monitoring of Underground Explosions (1992); the Massachusetts Higher Education Coordinating Council (1991); and the National Science Foundation Mechanical and Structural Systems Division Advisory Committee (1990-1992). I was also invited and served as a chair and reviewer of manuscripts for numerous journals and on review panels of graduate fellowship and undergraduate programs.

As a leader, teacher, and innovator in engineering education, I was recognized in Engineering at Howard University for teaching innovations. This achievement included the development of a multidisciplinary senior capstone design course in mechanical engineering involving industry-sponsored projects that brought together students and faculty from mechanical engineering, electrical engineering, chemical engineering, fine arts, and business to work on the same year-long project. It also included the implementation of a team-taught course on global engineering design involving student teams and faculty from Virginia Tech; Howard University; Technische Universitat Darmstadt, Germany; Tecnologico de Monterrey (ITESM) Monterrey, Mexico; and Shanghai Jiao Tong University, Shanghai, China.

I also provided resources and served as advisor for both graduate and undergraduate student research. My contributions to proposal grant writing helped provide more than six million dollars to support graduate student research and develop laboratories for undergraduate instructions. In addition, I was the key faculty member involved in bringing the Partners for the Advancement of Collaborative Engineering Education (PACE) Program grant of $70.6 Million to Howard University in 2004, the largest "IN-KIND" contribution in Howard's history.

For my contributions to engineering education, I received the Outreach Award from Sundstrand Aerospace Corporation in 1990 that reads *in recognition of his extraordinary effort and assistance to the development of outreach to Historically Black Colleges and Universities;* the Howard University 2008 Faculty Senate Inspirational Interdisciplinary Project Award; and the Virginia Tech 2007 XCaliber Award for Excellence in Technology-Assisted Teaching and Learning for a Global Team. I also received the 1991-1992 Teacher of the Year Award and the 1997-1998 Supporting Faculty Member of the Year Award from the Howard University Student Chapter of the American Society of Mechanical Engineers. The Student Chapter of the American Society of Mechanical Engineering gave me a T-shirt with the names of all members of the graduating class in 1992 printed on the back. This was my first class of freshmen during my service as Department Chairman to graduate and I have never worn the T-shirt. I have kept it as an award to remember. The graduating class of 1998 gave me a pyramid and pen set that I keep on the coffee table in my family room. **Overall, I have received more than fifty honors and awards.** I am also the co-author of one U. S. Patent, number 5,014,248.

My latest honor is becoming a recipient of the Albert Nelson Marquis Lifetime Achievement Award, May 13, 2019. The plaque reads: *The*

Marquis Who's Who Publication Board is pleased to recognize Lewis Thigpen, PHD, PE as a recipient of the Albert Nelson Marquis Lifetime Achievement Award an honor reserved for Marquis Biographees who have achieved career longevity and demonstrated unwavering excellence in their chosen fields. The inscription is signed by the Marquis Who's Who Biographee Editor-in Chief, Fred M. Marks.

Chapter 13

Activities and Retirement

On Being Single

Living a single life has been both by choice and circumstance. During my early adult years, although I met many wonderful women, I felt that I was unable to support a family. Prior to earning my bachelor's degree, there were many times when I wondered where my next meal would come from. It was my decision to remain single until I could take care of a family. This meant that I would complete graduate school and obtain successful employment. By circumstance, I have never married, and have remained single. I have no regrets that I do not have a family of my own because I have three sets of marvelous surrogate children.

My first surrogate child is Janice L. Maxwell, the daughter of my late sister Mildred. I first saw Janice in August 1958 when I returned from active duty in the U.S. Army in Germany. At that time, as I recall, Mildred was separated from her husband Wylie Maxwell. I would babysit Janice later that year when Mildred was working as a school teacher. Wylie passed away early in Janice's life. Many years later, Mildred married Leroy Ross and had another daughter, Monica Ross. After Mildred passed away, Janice has looked to my sister Isabel and me for support as surrogate parents. I always hoped that she would obtain a college degree but that has not happened so far.

My brother Amos's children, Traci N. Thigpen Weatherspoon and Steven C. A. Thigpen, are my next set of surrogate children. They lived in Los Angeles, and I lived in San Leandro, California from 1975 to 1988.

During those years, I visited them often. Basically, they grew up around me. I could get an inexpensive round-trip flight from San Jose to Los Angeles and would spend many weekends there. I remember going on outings with Amos, his wife Dorothy, and their children to a farm to pick vegetables, as well as to San Pedro for seafood.

When Traci and Steven were young, I hid Easter eggs for them. Each time, I made a map of where I hid the eggs. I hid the eggs several times because they enjoyed hunting so much that they would say, "Uncle Lewis, hide them again." I also cooked burgers and hot dogs on the grill at their neighborhood block parties. The whole street block was blocked from traffic during the parties.

We occasionally took trips together. We traveled to Las Vegas in my brother's camper, and even to Reno, Nevada, in a rental car from San Leandro. In Las Vegas, Amos parked his camper in the lot for campers at Circus Circus Casino. I would take Traci and Steve to breakfast at the restaurant and then upstairs at the casino to play kids' games, which I called kids gambling because they won prizes. They had to pay to play those games.

On another occasion, I believe that they took a flight to Oakland and rented a car at the airport. They picked me up in San Leandro and we went to Reno together. On the way to Reno, we stopped at the State Capitol in Sacramento, California, to tour the Capitol grounds.

Traci called me _her_ uncle as if I had no other nieces or nephews. I attended all of Traci's and Steven's high school and college graduation events.

One time in 1976, when Traci and Steven were very young, Amos, Dorothy, Traci, and I went to Las Vegas. Steven was less than one year old, and he had gone to Quincy, Florida, with his parents' good friend Bertha Williams to visit family. Bertha became a good friend of mine in later years.

We did not have hotel reservations in Las Vegas and had to wait for rooms. We went to a fast food restaurant for breakfast. The restaurant had a slot machine. Traci put her quarter in the machine and hit two cherries, which gave her three coins back. She came back to our table so happy. I told my brother that he could get into trouble for letting a kid gamble. I then told Traci that I would take her to a casino when she became twenty-one years old.

When Traci turned twenty-one, I was Chairman of the Mechanical Engineering Department at Howard University in Washington, DC. I flew to Los Angeles and we went to Las Vegas. I gave her one hundred dollars to gamble. At the time, her mother Dorothy and Aunt Annell were on travel in South Korea.

Traci knew that I loved Tina Turner. During Tina's comeback, she was having a concert at the Hollywood Bowl in Los Angeles. Traci and her mother bought me a ticket for the concert for my birthday. My cousin Ruby Gunn told them that I was not going to come all the way from Washington, DC for a concert and she (Ruby) would use my ticket. But Traci knew that I would come to the concert—and I did.

I participated in Traci's wedding by walking down the aisle with her and Amos. Most of the family from Florida attended the wedding.

When Steven was a young boy and knew I was visiting on a holiday, he waited outside the house for my arrival. I traveled to Los Angeles from Alexandria, Virginia, to attend Steven's high school graduation. After the graduation, while we were celebrating in the back yard of Amos's house, a neighbor informed us that Amos's Jeep Cherokee had been taken. She also told us who she had thought had taken it. Traci and Steven decided to go look for the vehicle. But I said, "No, do not do that. Report it to the police." This was a time that they would not listen to me and they left the house. Amos was not home at that time.

Traci and Steven did not find the vehicle. It was later recovered at a place where cars were being shipped out of the United States.

Many years later, I traveled to Los Angeles from Alexandria to attend Steven's wedding. He was disappointed that other members from the family in Florida did not attend.

Traci and Steven always call to wish me Happy Fathers Day.

Kashira M. Turner and Krystle L. Jones is my third set of surrogate children. They are the daughters of Michelle Turner, a friend. They grew up around me in the Washington, DC area. We shared many activities before they moved from the local area in Germantown, Maryland, to Richmond, Virginia, in August 2015. When Kashira was three years old, I took her and her mother to Disney World in Florida. While there, and after I purchased a cone of ice cream for Kashira, some birds (sea gulls, I believe) dived down and took her ice cream. I didn't know that birds were around waiting to take kids' ice cream. She cried. I purchased another cone and protected it from the winged thieves.

I took Kashira and Krystle to local amusement parks, circuses, and movies, and to Hershey Park in Pennsylvania. They loved to visit me at my house for cookouts and to spend the night. I always celebrated their birthdays with them and took them out to dinner.

When Kashira and Krystle were young, I shot movies of them making presentations on stage. I have given them many of my photos and movies of their activities. In the future, I will give them copies of what they do not already have.

I am the only father that they know. Their biological fathers have ignored them and not supported them in any way throughout their lives. I have helped support Kashira and Krystle and attended major events including high school and college graduations.

In June 2013, I rented a seven-passenger van and took Kashira, her sister Krystle, her mother Michelle, and a friend of Kashia to Kashia's graduation from the University of Chicago. Kashira had just returned from Jerusalem where she spent her last quarter while enrolled at the University of Chicago. For health reasons, I did not attend Kashia's master's degree ceremony in Pasadena, California, but I supported travel for her mother and sister.

In 2016, I attended Krystal's high school graduation ceremony in the Richmond, Virginia, area. I took her mother Michelle, sister Kashira, and three of her friends to dinner afterwards to celebrate.

Kashira and Krystle always wish me Happy Father's Day. Here is a typical message from Kashira: "Thanks for always being there for me and my family since we were born. You have been a dad to me and my sister all these years. We are so grateful for you."

Hobbies

My hobbies have included playing cards, fishing, gardening, and collecting things. I developed many friendships through my hobbies in cards and fishing.

I learned to play whist at a very young age. We had shoe boxes full of cards that Uncle Buddy Ray gave us. He ran a pool room and there was probably gambling on the side. My sister Gladys, brother Amos, cousin Ruby, and I learned to play whist with those cards. We later played bid whist at the Cypress Inn every week until I joined the Army. I learned to play blackjack in the Army. However, my favorite card game is contract bridge.

From almost as far back as I can remember I loved to go fishing. Growing up in Sawdust, Florida, we fished on Juniper Creek and Lake Talquin in Gadsden County. There were several places to fish on Juniper Creek depending on the species of fish we wanted.

After I returned from active duty in the Army in 1958, I fished in the Apalachicola National Forest with my brothers for sunfish and small catfish. I had not been fishing during my three years in the Army. We fished off the sides of the unpaved roads that were built throughout the forest during the Great Depression in the 1930s to provide jobs for unskilled workers under the Work Projects Administration (WPA) of FDR's New Deal. My father worked as a common laborer in building those roads. You had to be careful to look out for venomous snakes such as cottonmouths/water moccasins that may be hiding in the brush on the edge of the road where you were fishing. Sometimes we took my first cousin Adel's six-year-old son, Ervin Omega Gilliam, Jr., with us. This was the best place to take a young boy fishing because he could always catch fish and he loved it. I can still picture the smile on his face when he caught his first fish. It was not "fishing" but "catching"— fish always took your bait whenever it hit the water.

I have also fished in New Mexico for rainbow trout and northern pike; the Gulf of Mexico out of Panama City, Florida, for red snapper, trigger fish and grouper; the Gulf of Mexico out of Carrabelle, Florida and Tate's Hell State Forest off Florida State Highway 65 in Franklin County for sea trout; the Florida Keys for yellow tail snapper; the Chesapeake Bay in Maryland and Virginia for blue fish, sea trout, croaker and assorted bottom fish; the Atlantic Ocean out of Delaware for assorted bottom fish; and the San Francisco Bay Area and several places in Alaska for halibut, salmon, ling cod, and other bottom fish.

Tate's Hell State Forest is named after Cebe Tate, a local farmer who lived near Carrabelle, Florida He went into the swamp either looking to find a scrub cow to feed his wife or to chase a panther that kept attacking his livestock. As folklore has it, there are different versions of a story. Cebe Tate went into the swamp with his shotgun and hunting dogs. After a few hours he was separated from his dogs. He got lost in the swamp and lost his shogun in the mud. He sat down by a tree to rest and was bitten by a snake. Lost and disoriented for a week from the snake bite and drinking muddy swamp water, he ran blindly through the swamp. Finally breaking through a clearing of the underbrush near the town of Carrabelle and barely able to speak, he lived long enough to murmur the word, "My name is Cebe Tate, and I just came through hell." His adventure took place in 1875; since that time the area has been known as Tate's Hell. There is a plaque at the entrance that describes his adventure.

From 1991 to 2014, I made an annual trip to Alaska to fish for salmon and halibut. My brother James Woodrow joined me in 1992 and we fished together most of the years after 1998. There were years in between that he did not join me. I have fished on the Kasilof and Kenai rivers for Coho (silver) and Chinook (king) salmon in Soldotna. I have fished for halibut in Homer and Ninilchik. And I have fished for salmon and black bass in Resurrection Bay in Seward.

Growing up on a farm in Sawdust, I learned to love gardening and growing a variety of things. Over the years, in spring and summer, I grew vegetables in pots on the deck of my house in Alexandria, Virginia, and found it to be therapeutic to look at them after a pressing day at work.

I liked to collect things I saw that were interesting. My collections include an old nickel coin slot machine, a 1898 Japanese military sword, Lladró figurines, a juke box, 55-gallon drums, an old tractor, a Budweiser train set, souvenirs from my travels, vinyl records, and paintings. But the collection creates a problem when you want to downsize and move to a smaller place. "What should I do with this collection?" I am having this problem because I did not plan ahead.

Community Service

I grew up in a community where helping others was a way of life. As a child, I learned that service to others was very important. Throughout my life, I have been involved in community service. I should emphasize that my service activities were voluntary, without compensation. However, some of them during my professional career provided funds for travel expenses. In the following, I shall relate some of my community service activities.

When I was very young, I participated in Sunday school activities at Union Chapel AME Church in Sawdust. Mr. A. D. Paul was the Sunday school superintendent. The Thigpen family and Mrs. Ola Clark's family were very involved in Sunday school activities. I participated in plays at Christmas and Easter, acting out scenes related to the birth and Resurrection of Christ. Children from those two families including my cousin Ruby Gunn participated in those plays but I remember that my sister Mildred and Mrs. Ola Clark's daughter Fannie were very involved in the production of the plays. Everyone had their part to remember, and I was given the male part that had the most lines because I could memorize long speeches in a short time. We used bedspreads as robes because no one had resources to purchase robes. For historical purposes, I need to state that Mrs. Ola Clark replaced Mr. A. D. Paul as superintendent. Later, after Mrs. Clark moved to Detroit, Michigan, my sister Mildred became superintendent.

In the early 1940s, access to Union Chapel was a one-lane dirt trail from the unpaved road past Sawdust School. To help clear the land during the construction of a two-lane unpaved dirt road to the church, I cut brush, and picked up roots. I also helped plant raspberry plants along the side of the road, but the raspberry plants never produced raspberries. We now had a two-lane dirt road instead of a one-lane dirt trail.

As a high school student in Quincy, I did some tutoring on a small scale. Community service activities were not required as they are now in the Virginia area where I live and in schools in Washington, DC and Maryland.

After I graduated from high school, Mrs. Ruby Gilliam Francis would ask me to recite a poem at funerals at Union Chapel to comfort the family.

She knew that I could recite poetry and suggested a poem each time. Two of the poems were "If" by Rudyard Kipling and "On His Blindness" by John Milton.

During my service in the U.S. Army, many soldiers had not completed high school. When I was stationed in Germany, 1956 to 1958, the University of Maryland sponsored a program on our base where one could get his high school diploma. Two or three soldiers in my company were studying for the GED (General Education Diploma). I tutored them in mathematics and science. I also tutored mathematics to a soldier who planned to become a plumber and was studying to get his license when he returned home.

My voluntary service includes my contribution to the world's community health. During my early years in the Army in the mid-1950s, I volunteered to take the vaccine developed by Jonas Salk for polio. There was no follow up with me regarding my vaccination or statements regarding my contribution to the World Health Organization. However, I knew that President Franklin D. Roosevelt had had polio and I wanted to do my part in eradicating this health problem around the world. My brother James Woodrow wrote an award-winning short poem about the Salk vaccine when he was in the ninth grade, "To Kill the Germs Unseen Be Sure to Take the Salk vaccine."

I entered college at Florida A&M University in 1959 as a pre-engineering student. During my first semester, after fellow students saw my prowess in the chemistry class, a group of five or six students asked me to tutor them. We would meet once a week at a student's house for the session. Tutoring was very helpful for me because I had to prepare in advance and learned from their questions. Other voluntary work at FAMU included grading papers for my advisor, Mr. Blake, in his Graphic Statics course. My brother-Amos was in that course—I graded his papers rigorously and gave him no breaks.

After I entered Howard University in 1961, I tutored non-engineering students in the physical sciences on a small scale basis. The School of Engineering and Architecture had a tutoring program. As a senior, I joined that program and volunteered to tutor engineering students in engineering subjects.

As a graduate student at Illinois Institute of Technology (IIT) in Chicago, I volunteered my services as well. In 1966, Robert Naftzger, a classmate, was the leader of a bicycle club for youth at a local church. One weekend we took the group to a dairy farm in Wisconsin. The farmer, Mr. Brown, had a youth hostel on his property. We arrived with the boys and their fathers on a Friday night. The boys had an enjoyable weekend. They had a show on Saturday night and mimicked Farmer Brown milking a cow by twisting the fingers of a glove—not the way one milks a cow by hand, but it was fun. Farmer Brown had milking machines to milk his cows. They also mimicked "Mr. Bob," as they called Robert Naftzger. Farmer Brown lived alone and he enjoyed the show.

A couple of things I remember are that it rained that Saturday night and the roof on the building that we stayed in leaked. On Sunday morning, the fathers took their children to church. Bob and I decided to go to a local restaurant for breakfast. After we got into my car, I found out that the rain had caused the wheels to sink in the soil and we were unable to move. We had to wait until Farmer Brown distributed the manure that was loaded on a wagon attached to his tractor to pull my car out of the bog. We did not go to the restaurant.

Bob later became leader for the Boy Scout Troop at his church. I had a car and always went to weekend campouts to help take some of the boys and to serve as assistant leader.

There were two Boy Scout camps where we went for weekend campouts. We went on Friday evening and returned to Chicago on Sunday evening. Some of the boys' parents would drive out to the camp on Friday evening to take their kids and return on Sunday evening to pick them up. At the camps we would check out tools such as axes and shovels, and we would get permission to cut down a tree for firewood. We would let each boy participate in cutting the firewood.

On the evening of my first trip to the camp about sixty or more miles from Chicago, something very interesting happened. All of the boys wanted to use the shovel to dig a hole and we let them do it. I was curious but said nothing to Bob. The next morning one of our IIT classmates, Jim Skirdulis, brought his son who was between two and four years old. This little boy was also most interested in digging a hole.

I wondered, "Why is it important to these kids to dig a hole in the ground?" I then realized that all of them had grown up in the city where they saw only asphalt and concrete.

On a weekend trip to the second camp, it got very cold. The boys were not prepared to camp out in twenty degrees. Fortunately, the latrines at the camp had electric heaters. The boys spent their nights sleeping in the heated latrines.

We took our own food and cooked it over campfires. On Sunday nights, after we got the Scouts home safely, Bob and I would clean up and go downtown Chicago to George Diamonds Steak House for a great meal. I volunteered with Bob and his troop for one or two years.

My professional life includes Sandia Laboratories, Lowell Technological Institute, Lawrence Livermore Laboratory, and Howard University.

My volunteer service involved more than one hundred panels and committees including leadership positions in professional organizations. This alone represents more than 365 days of volunteer work. I have also served as a technical reviewer for more than eight professional journals.

My professional positions began in December 1969 when I joined Sandia Corporation as a full time employee. A coworker restored a Model A Ford car each year and raffled it to support students on service trips to another country. One year, I helped in the restoration.

During my retirement, I have continued to support and mentor students on their Capstone Design Projects and to participate in Design Reviews in the Mechanical Engineering Department at Howard University.

I served as unpaid secretary/treasurer and a director of my Homeowners Association, Indian Run Commons Homeowners Association, Inc., for more than twelve years. I volunteered because it was important—and no one else wanted to serve. I served from 2005 until early 2017 when my health would not allow me to continue.

Professional Organizations

My current memberships in professional organizations include the Society of Sigma XI, the Scientific Research Society; the American Society of Engineering Education; and Fellow of the American Society of Mechanical

Engineers (ASME). Only two percent of the organization's more than 140,000 members have attained the grade of Fellow.

I am also a member of Tau Beta Pi, the Engineering Honor Society and a Registered Professional Engineer (PE) in the District of Columbia.

Prior to retirement, I also held memberships in the American Geophysical Union; the New York Academy of Sciences, the oldest scientific organization in the nation; the American Institute of Aeronautics and Astronautics; and the Society of Rheology.

Retirement

I began planning to retire from Howard University when I was sixty-eight years old because I was tired of fighting the traffic each morning on I-395 and the bridge across the Potomac River from Alexandria, VA to Washington, DC. I was already receiving Social Security payments and a pension from the University of California. Lawrence Livermore National Laboratory was managed by the University of California, so I was a University employee. I retired from the University of California in 2000.

Prior to retiring from Howard, I wanted to know what my pension would be. I was assigned an advisor regarding benefits based on my last name, but she was new at her job and would not return phone calls or e-mails.

One day, I was in the benefits office on another matter, so I made an appointment to meet with my advisor. It turned out that she was not knowledgeable enough about retirements to help me. I then requested another benefits advisor.

It took me two years to complete planning for my retirement. On August 31, 2008, I retired as Professor Emeritus. After retirement, I chose to remain in my house in Alexandria where I had lived for twenty years. This allows me to continue to participate in activities at Howard and use its facilities for research as needed.

My professional activities have not changed significantly since I retired. I continue to visit and participate in some activities in the Mechanical Engineering Department at Howard University, and I have traveled to forums on behalf of the Department. I give invited lectures on Project Management to support the Capstone Design course and the Global

Design course. I participate in major design reviews of the Capstone Design course. At the college level at Howard, I consult on accreditation issues.

External to the University, I continue to serve as a chair or member of the American Society of Engineering Education Graduate Fellowship Review Panels. I also continue to serve as a Technical Reviewer of journal articles.

In my leisure time I write, read, watch television, listen to music, and travel. During my writing, I use the TV or music as a background. I have prepared a manuscript on the history of Mechanical Engineering at Howard University that I hope to publish.

My favorite TV programs are news, weather, sports, old Western movies, the history channel, the travel channel, and Music TV, particularly blues.

My favorite music includes classics, rhythm and blues, jazz, rock & roll, and country & western. My car radio is set on those stations. I also play blues CDs when driving.

My travel includes trips that support two of my hobbies: fishing in Alaska and playing blackjack at casinos. I travel to Las Vegas, Nevada, and Biloxi, Mississippi, at least once a year. At the casinos, I budget the money that I will play.

My health is not as good as it was when I retired in 2008. I now suffer with peripheral neurology in my fingers and have difficulty walking. My difficulty walking may be arthritis but my doctors have not diagnosed it. This caused me to give up my annual fishing trip in Alaska.

After I retired from Howard in 2008, my former Dean, M. Lucius Walker Jr., Archer S. Mitchell, Jr., and I looked out for each other. All three of us were single at that time—and I never married. We maintained close contact until Walker passed away in 2013 and Archer passed away in 2017.

I still maintain contact with my good friends Robert Naftzger and his wife Mary and former coworkers at Lawrence Livermore National Laboratory (LLNL) and Howard University. I talk with coworkers and friends from LLNL often, particularly Ray Stout and Ray Chin. I talk to Steve Nielson and Patrick Reardon who were coworkers during my sabbatical at Los Alamos National Laboratory in New Mexico. I meet regularly with coworkers from Howard University. Robert Reiss, Emmanuel

Glakpe and I plan luncheons to socialize. Robert and I schedule lunches to meet with retired staff from Mechanical Engineering. I maintain personal contact with Mrs. Carolyn Drakeford, my administrative assistant when I was the Mechanical Engineering Department Chair. I also communicate regularly by phone with staff members Dr. Mary Frances Stubbs and Ms. Romaine Peace who worked in the Office of the Dean of Engineering prior to their retirement. I still maintain contact with my former Dean, Dr. James H. Johnson, Jr., who retired in 2009 and took a position at the U.S. Environmental Protection Agency.

I have had a rewarding and successful life, and have enjoyed my career in engineering and science. If one asked me if I have been all I can be, I would say, "No," because I believe that there is always more one can do.

Today when people ask, "What are you doing in your retirement?" I respond, "Hell, I go to the doctor all the time." I do not have any major worries regarding aging. However, I think about my health and not being able to take care of my personal needs alone. After visiting my friend Archer S. Mitchell, Jr. in a nursing home and observing the people living there, I do not want to have to live in one.

Chapter 14

My Travels

I have a passion for new places, new people, new sights, new foods, unique discoveries, unusual experiences, and broad education. I love to travel. It helps to fulfill this passion, wanderlust, and curiosity. It is this passion that has driven my journey from Sawdust and around the world in eighty years.

I am privileged to have traveled in six of the Earth's seven continents: North America, South America, Europe, Asia, Africa, and Australia. The only continent that I have not been to is Antarctica. I have also traveled to islands in the Caribbean Sea and Pacific Ocean.

As you read these pages, I hope that my very detailed experiences will become vivid. Even if you do not visit any or all of these places in your lifetime, perhaps these memories will bring the places alive for you.

North America

In addition to the United States, I have traveled extensively in Canada and Mexico. Major cities that I have visited in Canada include Windsor, Toronto, Vancouver and Montreal.

My first trip to Canada was in 1965. At the time, I was on spring break from graduate school at Illinois Institute of Technology in Chicago. Two friends from Sawdust, Fannie and Vesta, were living in Detroit. They were the daughters of Mrs. Ola Clark. I had not seen them in more than ten years, but we kept contact and still do today. I took the Greyhound bus to Detroit and stayed at the home of Fannie and her husband. One evening, Fannie and her husband took me across the border to Windsor, Canada, to see the sights. Windsor is on the Detroit River between Lake St. Clair and Lake Erie.

In May 1980, while working at Livermore Laboratories, I traveled to Toronto to attend the American Geophysical Union meeting. I made a presentation on methods of modeling synthetic seismograms relating to earthquake behavior. While there, I took a sponsored tour to Niagara Falls on the weekend. The tour bus had to go through a series of locks to change elevations. I saw Niagara Falls from the Canadian side; I had been told that this was the best place to observe it.

On this tour, I talked with Brian Kenneth, a well-respected scientist from England in computational seismology. He said that Ray Chin, my colleague from Livermore, had told him that I had found an error in his (Brian's) computer program. Brian also told me that someone else had found the same errors. The computer code had originally been developed by Fuchs and Mueller in Germany; Brian had modified it for his needs. In my modifications of the code at Livermore, I had to understand all of the physics. This is one example of why we attend conferences in the engineering and science profession. We talk to each other about what we have done and solicit comments.

My second trip to Toronto, in June 2007, while I was at Howard University, was to attend an American Society of Mechanical Engineering Center on Education Board meeting.

In June 2002, I went to Montreal for the annual summer meeting of the American Society of Engineering Education.

In the 1980s, while at Livermore, I traveled to Vancouver to a meeting related to Applied Mathematics. I was traveling with Ray Chin and a couple of mathematics professors from different universities. After about a week in Vancouver, we headed to a meeting also related to Applied Mathematics at the University of Washington in Seattle.

Before leaving Vancouver, we turned in the first rental car and picked up another one that we could take to the U.S. as a one-way rental. We left Vancouver on a Saturday and drove to a ferry for transport to Washington State. I do not remember the name of the place where we stayed on Saturday night. On Sunday morning, Ray and I found a Laundromat because we had another week left on our trip. We took the ferry to Seattle on Sunday evening, checked into a hotel, and spent the next week there before returning to the San Francisco Bay Area.

I have been to every state in the United States except South Dakota. I have driven my automobiles in a majority of those states including every state east of the Mississippi River except Michigan and Minnesota, and many west of the Mississippi River.

In a location in New Mexico called Four Corners, there are four states that meet—Utah and Colorado on the north, Arizona and New Mexico on the south. In 1973, I drove there and placed my feet on all four states at the same time.

One winter in the late 1970s, I traveled from California to Minneapolis, Minnesota, with Ray Chin in his automobile. Ray and I stopped in every little town across Nevada that had a blackjack table.

I have traveled to every state in the mainland U.S. by ground transportation except South Dakota. To get to the two other states—Alaska and Hawaii—I went by air and rented cars to see the countryside.

I traveled to Alaska to fish for salmon, halibut and black bass every year for more than twenty years beginning in 1991. I visited numerous parks including Denali and observed wildlife such as bear, moose, and caribou. In Alaska, I have seen the effects of global warming. Glaciers that I visited can no longer be seen from where I saw them in 1991. Bear Glacier off of Resurrection Bay in Seward now has a beach where there had been ice.

In April 1990, I visited two of the Hawaiian Islands, Oahu and Kauai. I spent most of my time in Honolulu on Oahu but took a side trip with my friend Robert Reiss to Lihue on Kauai, where we had a rental car. We went to a luau in Honolulu and dined on pig cooked in an imu (earth oven), haupia (coconut pudding), poi (Hawaiian taro starch), many other dishes, and plenty of booze. We listened to live music and watched skilled performances of the hula. I also took a photo with one of the Polynesian women performers. Until they performed at the luau, I did not know that black people from Samoa were part of Polynesia.

In summer 1975, on a thirty-day trip across the U.S., I traveled to Montana, Nebraska, and North Dakota. They are the three states that I have traveled to only by Greyhound bus. I have flown to major cities in all but thirteen states.

My Travels

I have traveled extensively in Mexico driving my own car and with others. My first trip to Mexico was to Juarez, across the border from El Paso, Texas. I went in the summer of 1964 when I worked at Sandia Laboratories. I traveled with a coworker from Sandia in his car and a friend of his who was a Catholic priest at the College of St. Joseph on the Rio Grande. We spent Saturday night at a hotel in Juarez. That evening, we visited clubs in town. The priest, who was wearing regular clothing, was the only one getting propositioned by prostitutes.

The next morning, we attended service at a Catholic church. The church looked like an ordinary building in a poor neighborhood from the outside, but had the ambience of a rich neighborhood inside, with gold trimmings and plaques. Having never been in a Catholic church before, I tried to follow what others were doing, standing up and sitting back down several times. I did not know what was being said in Spanish or Latin.

I traveled with friends to Juarez several other times prior to my major trips into mainland Mexico. One time in Juarez, someone said that I looked like Poncho Villa or words to that effect. Another time, my friend Archer S. Mitchell, Jr. and I went to a bull fight. We had to wear coats and ties because Archer wanted to sit in the Sportsmen's Club where you had to dress properly. We left my car on the U.S. side in El Paso and had to ride to the stadium on a bus filled with local people. Everyone was begging us because we looked very prosperous.

The interesting and worst thing that happened at the bull fight is that the bull ran into a picador's horse and gored the horse. People tried catching the bull by the tail to pull him away, but the bull killed the horse. They didn't kill the bull. My thoughts were that they had the "cow" by the tail but it did not save the horse. *"Catching the cow by the tail" was an expression on our farm when I was a child. It meant that you are relating a story incorrectly. Expressions come to reality and I saw a worst case of it here.*

During the summer of 1970, my lady friend Jean and I drove my Triumph TR6 Roadster from Albuquerque to Juarez. Our ultimate destination was Acapulco.

I bought auto insurance from Sanborn Insurance for international protection and got a detailed map of our route. The map was actually a book that pointed out interesting places along the route, and we took several side trips. Whenever we stopped for lunch, I parked my car near the restaurant where I could get a seat by a window so I could see it. It had a luggage rack on the trunk with a large suitcase containing most of our clothes. We had a smaller suitcase inside the trunk.

The first day, we drove to Chihuahua and spent the night. I asked for an air conditioned room. That night, the fans were blowing hot air. I learned that I should have asked for <u>refrigerated</u> air. We did not drive at night because there were too many animals, especially donkeys, on the road. Other major cities that we drove to en route to Acapulco were Zacatecas, Mexico City, and Taxco. We were unable to find a room in Mexico City because of the International Soccer Tournament, so we spent the night in Taxco. The next morning, we drove to Acapulco and spent several days there. We met people from around the world who had come to see their team compete in the World Cup. When their team lost, they came to Acapulco to vacation.

We drove back to Mexico City, took pictures of a famous mural on the Central Library of the National Autonomous University of Mexico, and visited some ruins nearby. I cannot recall the names now, but there were two pyramids, the sun and the moon, and I climbed both. The moon pyramid was the scariest to climb because the steps were almost vertical. After leaving the Mexico City area, we traveled northwest and spent a night in Guadalajara. Next, we went to Mazatlan and spent a few days there. We bypassed the city of Tequila because Sanborn Insurance stated that people might step in front of your car on purpose. We then headed back to the U.S. via Guaymas and Hermosilla. We entered the U.S. in Nogales, Arizona. The whole trip took two weeks.

The next year (1971), Jean and I drove to Mazatlan via Nogales, for vacation. On both trips in Mexico, I drove my 1970 TR6 English sports car.

Also in 1972, I flew to Merida, Mexico, spent a night there, and then flew to Aruba in the Caribbean. On the way back from Aruba, I spent another two nights in Merida. On my return trip, I was able to see the Mayan influence on Merida. I will discuss details in a later section where I relate my travel to Aruba.

In summer 1973, my brother James, his wife Betty, daughter Stephanie, and our sister Isabel visited me in Albuquerque. I rented the empty apartment next to mine for them during their visit. We toured the

Albuquerque area including a trip to the summit of the Sandia Mountain. Sandia in Spanish means watermelon; when the sun is at a specific angle, the mountain looks like a slice of watermelon. Later, we drove to El Paso, Texas, and walked across the border to Juarez, Mexico. When we were crossing the border, Isabel did not want the custom agents to look into her purse until I explained that we were entering another country.

After we got back to Albuquerque, James and his crew left his car with me while they traveled to Los Angeles by bus to visit our brother Amos. Stephanie was three years old at that time. When they were leaving, Stephanie said, *"Uncle Lewis you want me to stay here with you, I'll have a fit."* Stephanie was joking with me and had no intention to stay with me and I understood her joke. Yes, young children do have a sense of humor. They returned from Los Angeles by bus with Amos's wife Dorothy and daughter Traci, and checked into a motel. I met them at the motel and we visited for one or two days. Then they drove back to Quincy, Florida.

My last trip to Mexico was in May 2005, while I was at Howard University, when I flew to Mexico City for the Partners for the Advancement of Collaborative Engineering Education (PACE) Annual Forum. The meeting was in Mexico City, but we stayed in a hotel in Toluca and traveled by bus to Mexico City each day.

Islands in the Caribbean Sea

I have visited three islands in the Caribbean: Aruba, Jamaica, and Trinidad and Tobago.

My trip was to Aruba on a research expedition with oceanographers from Texas A&M University probably in summer of 1971 or 1972. I was working at Sandia Corporation in Albuquerque. My mission was to test a Marine Sediment Penotrometer that we had developed. We flew from Albuquerque to Aruba to meet Texas A&M's ship, The Alaminos.

Our plane was a DC-3 owned by the Atomic Energy Commission (AEC). Sandia Corporation was part of the AEC at that time. This was basically a cargo plane used for Laboratory travel on special projects with a few seats for passengers. We loaded our equipment and boarded the plane. After boarding, the pilot informed us that there was a problem with the carburetor and we had to wait a couple of hours until it was repaired. We flew from Albuquerque to Kelly Air Force Base in San Antonio, Texas, where we left the U.S.

The plane did not have the capability to fly the complete trip to Aruba without stopping, so we flew to Merida, Mexico, where we had hotel rooms reserved. While going through customs late at night in the Merida airport, officials requested money to expedite our entry. We had to "grease their palms." They also requested money for their boss. We arrived too late to get dinner. We spent the night in the hotel and had the hotel prepare lunches for our trip on to Aruba the next day. Another thing about the plane—it did not have climate control. It was either too hot when the heat was turned on or too cold when the heat was turned off. We completed the two-day flight and checked into a hotel and had just enough time to get dinner before restaurants closed in Aruba.

Aruba is a very small island, nineteen miles long and three miles wide. Basically everything is imported. Two things that I remember about Aruba were (1) they had one of the world's largest oil refineries and (2) there appeared to be no poverty. There were people who had cars and nowhere to drive them. The day after we arrived, we unloaded our equipment from our private plane and boarded the ship that night for our research in the Caribbean. After a few days, we returned to Aruba from our research at sea on Friday. That night I went to a casino to play blackjack. The next morning we left Aruba.

We spent Saturday and Sunday night in Merida and toured the city on Sunday. On Monday, we saw some areas on the Yucatan peninsula by air on our way home. We went through customs at Kelly Air Force Base in San Antonio and then flew home to Albuquerque.

During summer 1972, I traveled from Albuquerque to Quincy in route to Montego Bay, Jamaica. I visited my relatives in Sawdust and Quincy. I decided to travel to Ft. Lauderdale to visit my brother James and fly from there to Jamaica. My sisters Mildred and Gladys drove me to Ft. Lauderdale and took their kids with them and visited Disney World in Orlando on the way. They had tickets already through the school system. Gladys's son Carl Dewayne Rhowe was about five years old and the only one who used all of his tickets. Each of us would stand in line and take him on a ride. Mildred's daughter Janice was fourteen years old. We left Disney World and drove to James Woodrow's house in Ft. Lauderdale.

My Travels

I flew from Miami to Montego Bay on a Saturday. Dewayne was disappointed because he thought that he was going to Jamaica too.

I had not made hotel reservations in Montego Bay. The customs agent asked where I was staying because I needed an address to enter the island. I gave them the name of a guest house where my lady friend Jean had stayed a few years before. I got through customs and checked into the guest house. The accommodations included breakfast. On Sunday morning at breakfast, I met a businessman from Kingston. He took me to his office and other places. He spoke the Queen's English perfectly, but when he talked to a local Jamaican, I could not understand a word he said. I met another Jamaican at the guest house the next morning at breakfast and he invited me to visit him at his house when I came to Kingston.

During my first days in Montego Bay, I rented a motorcycle to travel around the local area. However, it rained every day, so I turned in the motorcycle and rented a car. From the guest house in Montego Bay, I visited Ocho Rios, Fern Valley, and Negril. The car was built like British car—steering wheel on the right with driving on the left side of the road. I had no problem shifting gears with my left hand and adjusting to drive on the left.

The Negril beach was completely isolated; I could have just put on a bathing suit on the beach. I then drove to the main area of Negril. All I can remember was a large building, and meeting some Americans. They told me about the food and said that I should order the fish fry. The fish was cooked in coconut oil and I did not like it.

On my way to Ocho Rios, I saw signs that said, "Come see the man who puts his head into a crocodile's mouth." This show took place in the evening. I stopped there one afternoon and talked to the owner. He told me that he raised crocodiles and there were many baby crocodiles at his facility. However, he said that in the show he used an alligator that he had trained from a baby. In my travels I saw women washing clothes in streams along the road. The houses were very small.

I decided to travel around the island without having hotel reservations along the way. I knew of guest houses or motels en route. On the first day of this trip, I stopped at a place in the mountains and got a room without a problem. I met several people and we played darts in the recreation room.

The next morning, I traveled to Kingston and got a room at a guest house. I called the person who had invited me to visit him. Since I did know the area, he picked me up and took me to his house. I figured that he had a salary similar to mine. He had children but he must have been separated or divorced from his wife. Yet he had a full-time housekeeper taking care of his house and children. We drank rum punch, ate, and had very good discussions about our lives and how he was able to have a full-time housekeeper. He then took me back to my guest house.

I went out that evening to try to get a feel of what Kingston was like—from the waterfront to shopping areas. The next morning at breakfast, I met a woman from Africa who was working at a center outside of the city. I believe that was a Saturday and we went downtown to a movie; I do not remember what the movie was about. On Sunday morning, she asked if I would take her back to her place of residence. We both checked out of the guest house and I drove her home.

I continued my trip around the island back to Montego Bay. I had a map and took side trips away from the main road. It had been raining and there were low areas where water was across the road. I followed cars in front of me and did not worry about the puddles.

However, when not following anyone, I reached a large puddle and drove slowly into it. It drowned out the engine and my car was stuck in the water. I took off my shoes and socks, rolled up my pant legs, got out of the car, and pushed it out of the water. My adrenaline was pumping and I was scared. I got the car restarted and continued on my trip. I hoped not to get into a situation like that again.

I stopped at Discovery Bay and observed the sea for a while. When I arrived back in Montego Bay, I checked into a motel for the rest of my stay. In Jamaica, I did not read any newspapers or listen to news on radio or TV. I hoped to get a surprise that the war in Vietnam was over when I returned home, but it was still raging. I flew back to Miami and my brother James picked me up at the airport. The next day, I flew home to Albuquerque.

During the Christmas 1991/New Year 1992 holidays, I traveled to Port of Spain, Trinidad and Tobago to the wedding of my graduate student, Richard Gordon. He had completed the requirements for the Master of Engineering at Howard in December 1991. I arrived on Saturday, December 28, 1991, and returned home on Thursday January 2, 1992.

I learned how to get around in the city on local transportation. My students were amazed with my abilities—they saw me waiting for a jitney on the street when they came to see me at my hotel prior to the wedding. That day, Richard and another mechanical engineering student from Howard University took me to visit people on the island. At each home, the residents rolled out a cart with beverages including rum and food and cakes. Everyone I met was so gracious. It was similar to how we visited people when I was growing up in Sawdust and we had no phones. You just dropped in to visit and that was no problem.

That evening, my students took me to the campus of the University of the West Indies. There was reserved parking for Department Chairmen. I thought to myself, "Education is very important. Leaders in education are well respected here." As a Department Chairman at Howard, I paid for parking but had no reserved space. This showed me the respect for education in the West Indies compared to the United States. Later that evening, Richard took me to his parents' house. The next day, before the wedding, another student of mine at Howard took me to visit his family members and to shopping centers.

On the day of the wedding, I gave a toast to the bride and groom at the reception and danced with Richard's mother on the first round. I was treated as a family member and Richard was my intellectual son. The next day, I flew home. In the Port of Spain airport, I bought my first Lladró figurine, and it is one from the Black Legacy Series. En route home to Alexandria, Virginia, we went through customs in Puerto Rico.

South America

Brazil is the only country that I have traveled to in South America. I went to a conference in Rio de Janeiro with Robert "Bob" Reiss, a colleague in my Department at Howard University. Bob planned our itinerary.

The conference was the first Pan American Conference on Applied Mechanics. I was scheduled to make a presentation on my research work.

The sponsors had booked a hotel and flights for attendees. But Bob and I wanted to make our own reservations. Bob contacted a travel agent, Manuel, to make arrangements for our flight and first night. Manuel booked us on the same flight that the conference had booked for other attendees.

On New Year's Eve 1988, we left Washington for John F. Kennedy (JFK) Airport in New York, bound for Rio de Janeiro. As the calendar turned to 1989, we were on the plane waiting to depart JFK.

The travel agent had also contacted someone in Rio—Pablo—to meet us at the airport. When we arrived, there were people with signs for conference attendees to follow them to the buses. And, there was Pablo holding a sign with "REISS" on it. It became a joke that Reiss had his own travel agency and Pablo worked for him.

Pablo had made arrangements with a hotel for our first night. We had a room at the Sheraton for the remainder of our stay. At the opening ceremony of the conference, we were told about crime in the area and how careful we should be in the city. This made us afraid to leave our hotel. Tours were scheduled for sights in and around the city.

On the second night of the conference, returning from a tour, Bob and I agreed not to let fear ruin our trip. We got off the bus at Copacabana Beach. We went out every night for dinner and shows, making our trip enjoyable. One night we went to dinner at a great place and enjoyed the ambience and everything about it. After dinner, we got a taxi to go to our hotel. After we got into the car, we observed that the driver had not turned on the meter. Several times, we asked him to turn it on. He finally pulled a cable from the meter showing that it was not connected. We got out and walked back to the hotel. At other times, taxis would drive with the lights off and through <u>red</u> lights. I don't know why.

One day, Bob and I were sitting at a table around the pool at the Sheraton. The hotel was at a private beach on the South Atlantic Ocean. A colleague came by in his bathing suit and asked how we liked swimming in the ocean. Joking, we said "great" although the water was very cold and we did not swim in it. Our colleague walked down to the ocean and put his foot into the cold water and jerked it out. He tested the water at several different places to see if the water was warm enough a few yards away to swim. We watched him and laughed. He came back to our table and said, "You two love the cold, but it is too cold for me." He was always very serious and never joked. Because of his seriousness about everything, we never told him that we were joking.

Currency inflation was so bad in Brazil that restaurants published daily prices at the day's currency rate. They had a general menu with no prices and a supplement that showed the price for that day. On Saturday, our last day in Rio, the Sheraton had a brunch that consisted of meat from all parts of the pig cooked in numerous ways. I do not remember what they called this special, but Bob and I had it. However, I was careful of what I ate because I did not want stomach trouble on my trip back home the next day. At the airport Sunday morning, I tried to spend all of my Brazilian money because it would be worthless in the U.S.

Bob and I arrived at Kennedy Airport on Sunday night and spent the night in a motel near the airport. The motel had a shuttle service to the airport but they were slow in coming. It was suggested that we hire a private van in order to make our flight to Washington.

Prior to the arrival of the van, a flight attendant needed to get to the airport. We told her that we had a van en route. The van driver forced her to pay full fare because he had not been informed that there would be three people. This was my first experience with hiring cars in New York City. I have seen similar situations around the world where taxis and what the drivers charge are not regulated. When we got to the airport, the flight attendant took us to the front of the check-in line to assure that we did not miss our flight.

Europe

I have been blessed to travel in ten countries in Europe: Germany, Spain, France, England, Holland, Belgium, Italy, Austria, Czech Republic, and Poland. In some cases, I connected with strangers who became co-travelers and friends. This seemed to be quite common and safe in Europe.

From May 1956 to August 1958, I was a soldier in the United States Army in Germany. During that time, I used my leave to travel to Spain, France, England, Holland and Belgium.

My first trip for more than one day off base was to visit my older brother Amos, an Infantry soldier stationed in Heilbronn, Germany. Amos would not travel, so I visited him on a three-day pass before he returned home in 1956. I arrived on a Saturday and spent two nights in his barracks. Amos, one of his soldier friends, and I went to a bar on Sunday. When the waitress came, I was waiting for Amos to order but he did not open his mouth. I finally ordered a beer and he ordered one next. I was only seventeen years old. We did not drink before we left home, and I thought that Amos would make the first order.

The first place outside of Germany that I traveled to was Barcelona, Spain. As a soldier, I did not have a passport. Travel to Spain required special papers to enter. I always wore civilian clothes, not a military uniform, outside of Germany. I took a train and traveled through France. I was supposed to change trains in Nice, France, but I was asleep and ended up in Marseille. I had to purchase a ticket in Marseille to Nice to get back on my trip to Barcelona. I did not speak French so I had a problem trying to buy the ticket. I took some money out of my pocket, flashed it in front of the agent, and said "Nice." Then he gave me a ticket. I learned the value of the "green back"(dollar). The green back was an international language when I was stationed in Germany.

I arrived at the train station in Barcelona that night. When the customs agents saw my papers, they said "American" and moved me to the front of the line. At the station, I met three Englishmen. We took a taxi and got rooms at the same hotel. I shared a room with one of them. The next morning, after breakfast, the four of us went to the market together. I had never been to such a market before. The market had meats, vegetables, clothing, and numerous other things for purchase. There were also restaurants. We went upstairs to a restaurant for lunch and I ordered steak. The Englishmen ordered a tray with several appetizers such as octopus and squid that I had never eaten before. They also ordered their main dish. At first, I was hesitant to try the appetizers but then decided to try them. From that experience—throughout my life—I decided to try foods that were a regular part of the cuisine of other cultures.

The next night, the Englishmen moved to another hotel but I remained in the original one. If you came back late at night, the door was locked and you had to clap your hands to get someone to open the door. Every morning, I went down to the Mediterranean seaside to relax, look at the coast, and decide my activities for that day. Of course, I went to a bull fight. At night, I went to entertainment clubs and bars. Most interesting were the bars. You stood at the bar and ordered drinks, but they also had snacks that you could order such as small birds like sparrows. I liked eating the birds because I had eaten them back home.

I met many people in Barcelona. Oddly, some asked if I was from Norway. How strange it was for a black man to be asked if he were from a Scandinavian country.

I traveled to Paris from Germany with a soldier friend from Virginia, and we shared a room. Many of the French could speak English, but would not do so unless they were challenged. For example, I took a taxi to an American Express office. The driver appeared to be traveling in circles, building up costs on the meter. I asked, "Do you know where in the hell you are going?" He replied, "I have been all over the world and never got lost." Aha! He had pretended that he could not speak English!

I developed a love for French food, and it is one of my favorites today. The hamburger included a sunny-side-up egg on top. Now, I prepare my own hamburgers that way. I made sure that I visited the Eiffel Tower on the Champ de Mars and the Arc de Triomphe (Arc of Triumph) at the western end of the Champs-Élysées. I was unable to reach the top of the Eiffel Tower because of construction on the upper level.

I flew from Frankfurt (Germany) to London on Lufthansa Airlines with a soldier friend from North Tonawanda, New York. This was my first flight on an airplane and it was first class all the way, including white tablecloths. We stayed at the Airmen's Club in London, where U.S. military paid only one dollar and fifty cents per day. The Airmen's Club had a cafeteria and a bar with slot machines for gambling. I traveled around London by subway, bus, and taxi. I made sure to see the Tower of London, Number 10 Downing Street (Office of the Prime Minister), and Buckingham Palace where I saw the Changing of the Guards. I also saw Big Ben from the bridge across the River Thames. I had heard of Big Ben before I went to London but did not know that it was a clock.

My next travel was to Amsterdam and a side trip to Brussels in spring 1958. I traveled to Amsterdam with a black soldier from Evergreen, Alabama. As we left the train station in Amsterdam, a woman solicited us to stay at her house. Naturally, we ignored her request and asked a taxi to take us to a place for housing. Well, he took us to the house of the same woman who had met us at the train station. We took a room in her house. She had a daughter and several other people staying there. It was a great place to stay. She served breakfast as part of our room charges and all tenants sat at the table for breakfast.

One thing about Amsterdam comes to mind—the number of bicycles. You had to be careful to keep from getting run over by a bicycle when crossing the street.

My friend and I took a bus tour from Amsterdam to the 1958 World's Fair in Brussels. This was the first place that I had been where people that you did not know wanted to take pictures with you—and these were not black people.

When I returned to Base at Ayers Kaserne, I found out that I had been promoted to SP-5 (grade of E-5, a sergeant). This was in the late spring or early summer 1958, shortly before I was scheduled to return home from active duty.

In September 1991, while I was Chair of Mechanical Engineering at Howard, I flew to Italy via Paris. I was traveling with Robert Reiss, a fellow Howard professor, to the Florence Modal Analysis Conference, 16th International Seminar on Modal Analysis. The plane left Paris early, before our luggage was loaded. We had to wait at the airport in Milan until the next plane arrived with our luggage.

In the Milan airport, we met Reiss's Ph. D. graduate student, Oscar Barton, who had arrived on an earlier flight from the U.S. to attend the conference. In the terminal, we had one of the most expensive lunches that I have ever had.

After our luggage arrived, we took a train to Florence for the conference. We stayed in Florence several days and found time to tour the city.

After the meeting ended, we took a train trip to Rome for a few days. We visited the Coliseum but were unable to visit the Vatican. It basically rained most of our time in Rome.

We took the train from Rome back to Milan and arrived at night. We did not have a room reserved, so the graduate student, Oscar Barton, got on the pay phone at the station to find us one. While he was on the phone, four or more policemen were kicking and screaming at a man who was on the floor. The man was unarmed. This was a true case of police brutality; I had never seen such before. Oscar found us a room and we took a taxi to the hotel. The elevator was so small that the three of us could not take our luggage and ourselves to our room at same time. After putting our luggage in the room, we found a place nearby for dinner. The next day, the three of us flew home.

In August 1999, I traveled via Frankfurt, Germany, and Vienna, Austria, to make a presentation at the International Conference on Engineering Education in Ostrava, Czech Republic. I flew from Washington Dulles to Frankfurt, Germany and changed planes. I flew from Frankfurt to Vienna, Austria and arrived on Saturday, August 7.

The following Monday, August 9, I left Vienna and took a train to Ostrava. Prior to my trip, I wanted to guarantee an assigned seat with a view. So I purchased a first-class round trip ticket from Vienna to Ostrava and returning from Prague to Vienna. I arrived at the train station in Ostrava that evening and went to a currency exchange in the station to cash an American Express travelers check for transportation to my hotel. The currency exchange sent me to a nearby bank, but the bank would not accept my travelers check. This was the first time in more than forty years of travel that I could not cash a Travelers check. I continued to question the teller and explained my situation. She asked if I had some Austrian money. Fortunately, I had some. I exchanged the Austrian money for Czech money. The cost of the trolley to my hotel was less than one U.S. dollar. The woman trolley operator pointed out my hotel when we reached the nearby stop.

The next morning, I took the trolley to the University of Ostrava and picked up my registration materials. In my conference tote bag, along with the schedule, was a can of beer. We were greeted by government officials at the opening ceremony.

On August 11, 1999, at the University of Ostrava, I saw my first and only total solar eclipse. We were given eclipse glasses to watch it. I tried unsuccessfully to photograph the eclipse looking through those glasses.

This was one of the most enjoyable conferences that I ever attended. There were social events for each evening including concerts and outdoor activities with food and entertainment. There were buses to take us to the events. At one of those evening outdoor activities, I took a photo with Alexandra, the coordinator for all activities. I sent her a copy of the photo.

The final day of the conference was in Prague the following Saturday. On Friday evening, a special, exclusive train took the attendees to Prague. Several railroad officials greeted us. Food and drinks were served on the train. I believe that many of the activities were politically motivated to showcase the Czech Republic to the world. We checked into a hotel in Prague.

At the conference, I had become friends with an educator and researcher from Norway. Friday night, he and I went out to see the sights in Prague.

I did not see any black people other than myself attending this conference. After the Saturday morning session, I went back downtown to take photos during daylight.

I was on a tight schedule. I left Prague that afternoon to take the train back to Vienna to fly back home on Sunday morning, August 15. On the train, I went to the car that sold beverages to get an original Budweiser beer. The sales people did not understand English but they said "Sprechen sie Deutsch." So I made my order in Deutsch (German). I arrived in Vienna on Saturday evening. When I was checking into the hotel, the person at the desk gave me an upgraded room. My hotel was directly across the street from the entrance to the airport building to check in for flights. I left Vienna Sunday morning to return home. I changed planes in Frankfurt.

On July 12, 2010, I left for Gliwice, Poland, via Frankfurt, Germany, to attend the International Conference on Engineering Education and Research. This was the beginning of my flight "around the world" in one continuous trip. I traveled with Professor Horace Whitworth from Howard. We arrived in Poland three or four days before the conference began. After checking into my room, I found that there was no air conditioning. The bed and shower were the smallest that I had ever seen. I went downstairs and asked if I could get an air-conditioned room. It turned out that the hotel had only a few and none were available. The bed was so short that I banged my head on the pillow-height headboard several times. The shower in the room was so small that I could hardly turn around without bumping into its walls.

The room rate included breakfast, so I ate breakfast at the hotel. Horace was very picky about food and did not want to go to any restaurant that did not have several people eating there. Therefore, we usually ate our evening meals at a pizza shop where there was a crowd. The menu was posted with a picture of each pizza. From the time I was in the Army as a teenager, I had heard Polish jokes. On the menu was a picture of a pepperoni pizza. To me, pepperoni is a hard, dry Italian sausage spiced with pepper. This pizza showed a crust with green peppers on top. I thought, "This is the greatest Polish joke I've ever seen or heard of."

While in Gliwice, we hired a car to take us to the Auschwitz concentration camp. This was a network of German Nazi concentration and extermination camps built by the Third Reich during World War II. More than one million people, mainly Jews, were starved, tortured, and murdered. Above the gate to the main entrance was a sign "ARBEIT MACHT FREI" which means "work will make you free." You could see signs of all of the horrific things done to people because of their race. I took photos wherever we were allowed to do so.

We returned to Gliwice that evening. There was very little to do for entertainment in Gliwice. Horace and I found a place to hang out in the afternoons and drink beer when we were not exploring the city.

I left Gliwice on Sunday August 18, on my way to Seoul, Korea, via Frankfurt as part of my flight around the world. The event in Seoul was the 2010 Partners for the Advancement of Collaborative Engineering Education (PACE) Global Annual Forum. Horace remained in Gliwice until the end of the conference there.

Asia

I have traveled to three countries in Asia: Japan, China, and South Korea.

In November 1992, I flew from Dulles Airport to Osaka, Japan, via San Francisco, California. I was traveling with a faculty member, Naren Vira, in the Mechanical Engineering Department at Howard to a conference on manufacturing. When we arrived at the Osaka airport, we took a bus to a rapid transit station and rode to the end of the line. From there we took a taxi to our hotel.

After breakfast at the hotel the next morning, we took a taxi to the meeting venue. Interestingly, the men's room had both eastern and western style toilets. I was familiar with western style toilets—the women's room had commodes and the men's room had commodes and urinals. But here in Osaka was an eastern style toilet built with an opening in the floor instead of a commode. One would squat to do his business. I had never seen eastern style toilets in a men's room before. I have no idea what the women's toilets looked like.

The conference took place during the week of the presidential election in the United States on November 3, 1992. There was a large TV monitor in an open area in the building. We saw the announcement in the middle of the day that Bill Clinton had won and everyone cheered.

In the afternoons, Naren and I took breaks to tour or shop for souvenirs. We took the rapid transit and one afternoon visited a Buddhist temple. At the end of the conference, we took a tour to Kyoto. The tour included travel, lunch, Geishas modeling and performing in a theater, and time for shopping. The next day—Sunday, November 8 in Japan—we left for home. It might seem strange that we arrived in San Francisco on the same Sunday morning, thanks to the International Date Line and time zones. We had breakfast in the San Francisco airport while waiting on our flight to Dulles. This was the first time I had breakfast at a restaurant in two different continents on the same day.

In 2006, I traveled to Beijing with Horace Whitworth, a colleague from Howard University, to a meeting sponsored by the American Society of Mechanical Engineering and its counterpart in China. The event ran from March 30 to April 4. In Beijing, I took a tour to the Great Wall of China. But, at sixty-eight years old, I walked only a short distance up the wall because I did not have the energy. Returning from the Great Wall, the bus stopped at a shopping center for those who wanted to make purchases.

One evening, I attended a banquet for all conference attendees at the Great Hall of the People, west of Tiananmen Square. I also visited Tiananmen Square with three colleagues and we paid for a tour of the Forbidden City on the north end of the Square. The Forbidden City served as the Imperial Palace for twenty-four emperors during the Ming and Qing Dynasty (1368–1911). Before traveling to Beijing, I had paid for a tour at the end to the conference. Horace also took that tour.

I checked out of the hotel on the evening of the last day of the conference, and the tour bus took us to another hotel in Beijing. Our main tour guide traveled with us throughout our tour. During the tour, we met local guides who were familiar with the areas that we visited. After we checked into the hotel, our bus took us to a restaurant for dinner. This restaurant was famous for Peking duck, and on the wall were photos of famous visitors. One of them was President Bill Clinton. No, I did not get my picture on the wall!

We left Beijing the next morning on a flight to Xian and checked into a hotel. The local tour guide knew the area and worked with our main guide. They took us out to dinner that evening. The next morning after breakfast, our guides took our luggage and had it checked in to save time when we got to the airport that evening for our trip to Shanghai.

In Xian, we visited the site of the terracotta warriors that was discovered in 1974 by workers digging a well. They found life-sized clay soldiers poised for battle and notified Chinese authorities who dispatched archaeologists to the site. The archaeologists found thousands of warriors. At the time of my visit, they had not completed excavating the site. The terracotta warriors were created to protect the first emperor of China in his after-life. After visiting the site, our tour stopped at a place that sold artifacts. On my travels in China, our tour always stopped somewhere—a restaurant or a shopping area where someone wanted to sell you something, including fake Rolex watches.

We left Xian and flew to Shanghai. At the airport in Shanghai, another local guide met us and took us to our hotel. We toured Shanghai for two or three days. The numerous sites we visited included the Confucian Temple of Shanghai honoring Confucius, Yu Garden built in 1577, the Jade Buddha Temple, the Shanghai Museum, the 468-meter tall Oriental Pearl Radio and TV tower, the shopping street, and the Historic Buddhist Temple Complex. Horace and I took pictures with a few monks at the Temple Complex at their request. On the grounds of the Shanghai Museum, one woman asked if I would take a photo with her. Her husband took the photo. One evening we went to a Chinese acrobats show at the Shanghai Circus World. The tour ended on Saturday evening. Horace left on Sunday morning, and I left on Monday morning for home via Tokyo, Japan and Houston, Texas.

On Monday, July 19, 2010, I arrived in Seoul, South Korea from Frankfurt, Germany, on my flight around the world. I attended the Partners for the Advancement of Collaborative Engineering Education (PACE) Annual Forum in Seoul. At the opening reception on Monday evening, I took a photo with one of the female performers who were part of the entertainment for the evening. The Forum ended on Thursday.

The next day, Friday, I took a tour to the demilitarized zone (DMZ) between North and South Korea. At one place when I got off the tour bus, a couple of women asked to take a photo with me.

We went to one of the underground tunnels that the North Koreans had dug to enter South Korea. Prior to entering the tunnel, we were given hardhats. However, our tour guide did not wear one. The tunnel from the South Korean side was high enough for me to stand up and walk but we were continuously going deeper and deeper downhill. I began to wonder why we had to wear hardhats. I found out why when we entered the portion that the North Koreans had dug. In that section, you had to bend over and at times banged your head on the rock above. Our guide was short and she could stand up throughout the tour of the tunnel. The first section was dug by the South Koreans, probably as part of a tourist attraction.

The difficult part for me was returning to the entrance of the tunnel where we began the tour. I had to walk uphill all the way. There were benches along the way and I took advantage of them. A young man walking behind me in another tour group asked me if I was okay. I responded that I was, but he walked with me all the way out of the tunnel. I thanked him for his consideration. I was about one month less than seventy-two years old. By the time I reached the exit, my tour group was already out of the tunnel.

You will find people all over the world who will try to help you if they think you need help. And I have tried to help people in need all of my adult life.

When I got out of the tunnel, I turned in my hardhat. Then I retrieved my personal things from a locker, items that I was not allowed to take into the tunnel such as my camera. I bought a hydration drink at the store above. We went to another shopping place in the DMZ, and I bought a Korean beer. I went outside to drink it and have a smoke while others in my tour group shopped. I believe the beer was made in North Korea, and I liked it. The tour bus returned to Seoul and stopped at a gift shop for the group to purchase gifts. We then returned to our hotel. Secretary of State Hillary Clinton and Secretary of Defense Robert Gates had toured the DMZ two days earlier, on Wednesday July 21. I left Seoul the next Saturday morning. We flew east, stopped in Tokyo, and continued across the Pacific Ocean, completing my flight around the world on Sunday,

July 25. The journey had begun with my flight to Gliwice, Poland on July 12—a total of thirteen days.

Africa

I have traveled to only one country in Africa—the Ivory Coast (Côte d'Ivoire). The purpose was to attend an International Conference on Power Systems Operations and Planning in Abidjan on January 14-17, 1997.

This conference was planned by the Chair of the Electrical Engineering Department at Howard University. I traveled with two students from the Department of Electrical Engineering, a female senior undergraduate student and a male graduate student. We traveled on Air France from Dulles Airport near Washington. We left Dulles one evening and arrived at Charles De Galle Airport in Paris before lunch the next morning.

There was only one Air France flight each day to Abidjan. So after a layover of many hours at Charles de Gaulle, we arrived in Abidjan that night.

The Electrical Engineering Department Chair was on the tarmac welcoming our flight. We took a charter bus to the hotel. All meals were covered by the sponsors of the conference. The first three days were filled with presentations and workshops. Presentations were translated into English or French simultaneously. Each attendee wore an earphone for their language. I served in three different roles during the first three days: Session Chair, Session Co-Chair, and Panel Member of a Workshop.

On the third day, there was an awards banquet. To my surprise, I received an Award of Excellence. When my name was called, two ladies escorted me from my table to receive the award.

On the last day, we took a tour to another city where the Prime Minister lived. The chartered buses did not have toilets. At one place along the road, the buses took a "pit stop"—both men and women had to go in the bushes to do their thing.

As we traveled, I saw women carrying heavy packages on their heads and houses made of thatched roofs. Along the way, we toured a power plant.

Then we went to observe the Prime Minister's compound from our buses. The compound was surrounded by water containing either alligators or crocodiles. We visited a large basilica built by the Prime Minister and given to the Vatican in Rome. The Prime Minister was a Catholic.

Around 4:00pm we went to lunch (a late one) at the residence of the president of the power company. His house was in a village. There were large tents in his yard with tables. To my surprise, he invited me into his house for a tour. During lunch, I sat at the table with him. I have never been honored or respected as a Department Chairman more than at this conference. The president's neighbors were there to welcome us, and there was dancing. During the dancing, when an item was given to someone, that person had to dance. I was one of those chosen. I handed my movie camera to someone to record me dancing. Passing the "dance item" around was a way of making sure that special guests were asked to dance, getting everyone involved, and increasing the fun. That evening, we went back to Abidjan for dinner—a little after midnight!

The next day, several of us took a taxi to shop for souvenirs. I left Abidjan around 11:00pm and arrived in Paris around 6:00am the next morning. My flight was scheduled to leave Paris for Dulles at 2:00pm, but a problem with the plane delayed our departure until after 4:00pm. I did a lot of window shopping at Charles de Gaulle while waiting for my flight home. We arrived at Dulles late that night.

I really enjoyed my trip to Abidjan—including its warm weather. When I arrived at Dulles, it was very cold. I pulled my coat out of my luggage as soon as I could. When I got to the parking lot, I had to scrape snow and ice off my car.

About a week later, the faculty from the Electrical Engineering Department returned from Nigeria. Unbeknownst to me, they had been sponsored by a power company in Nigeria following the meeting in Abidjan. I was then informed that I had also been invited by the same company but no one on Howard's planning committee had told me. The company had reserved a room for me at a five-star hotel and it had to be canceled.

REVELATION: Positions of leadership in education might be taken for granted in the United States but are highly respected in some countries in the Caribbean and Africa.

Australia

In 2007, I attended the International Conference on Engineering Education and Research in Melbourne, Australia. At the conference, which ran from December 3 to 7, I presented two papers and chaired a session.

I traveled with a colleague, Horace Whitworth. Another colleague, Emanuel Glakpe, arrived later. The trip to Melbourne required several changes of planes. From Washington Dulles, we flew to Los Angeles on United Airlines. From Los Angeles we flew to Sidney and changed planes for Melbourne.

While in Melbourne, we visited local attractions and I tried foods that I had never eaten before, such as kangaroo and emu. There was free transportation to many sights including the market for food, clothing, and dining. Some activities were sponsored by the conference, including a banquet and dancing in the evenings. All three of us— Horace, Emanuel, and I—took a day-long tour outside of Melbourne. On the last day, I did my laundry at the hotel laundry room (I never packed clothes for more than a week). We left Melbourne the next day and took a side trip to Auckland, New Zealand.

New Zealand

Other than Australia and Japan, the only other island in the Pacific that I have traveled to is New Zealand. Horace, Emmanuel, and I went to Auckland, New Zealand, in December 2007 after leaving Australia. We visited many sites including museums related to history, original natives, and art galleries. We also took a ferry to another island and a bus trip to a winery. The food was great, and I enjoyed Auckland.

There are always unusual things to see when you travel. I walked past stores that sold marijuana in different forms. In all of my travels, I had not seen a store that openly sold marijuana before. We stayed in Auckland for nearly a week. As in all of my travels, I purchased souvenirs for family and friends back home.

After the long flight across the Pacific Ocean, we arrived in Los Angeles. At the international terminal, we went through customs. We then had to take a bus to another terminal and go through security for the flight to Washington. One of the security personnel opened my carry-on bag and took out a wooden boomerang that I had purchased in Australia. She spent at least a minute looking at it from numerous angles. As a young person, she probably had never heard of or seen a boomerang before. She finally placed it back into my bag.

Chapter 15

Natural Environmental Events

I have experienced numerous natural events including hurricanes, earthquakes, volcano eruptions, solar eclipses, and melting of glaciers.

I experienced many severe storms when growing up in Sawdust. However, I never heard the word hurricane during my early years. That is probably because we did not have radio communications with the outside community. I remember coming home from working on Maxwell Strom's tobacco farm during a severe storm. The lightning had hit pine trees on our farm and a strip of bark was removed from top to bottom. I banged my elbow on a chair when I entered our house and hit the ulna nerve— "the funny bone" as we called it—and thought I had been struck by lightning.

As an adult, I have experienced the effects of hurricanes in Florida and Virginia including several days of power outages. A flight from Tallahassee was delayed for three days. Today it appears that hurricanes are getting much stronger. Is this related to global warming? I believe that it is, and it's something for everyone to worry about in the future.

I have experienced earthquakes in four different states. The first was in 1968 when I was a graduate student in Chicago. I was not aware that the shaking was an earthquake because my neighbors living above me always were wrestling in the evenings but not early in the mornings. That morning, I wondered why they were wrestling so early while I was still in bed. Later that day I was driving my car with my lady friend and heard on the radio that there had been an earthquake that shook Chicago and surrounding areas. I believe the epicenter was at a fault in Missouri.

My next earthquake experience was in Albuquerque. I was living in an apartment on Palomas Avenue. One night, I was awakened by rattling that seemed to come from my entrance door. I did a stupid thing by getting out of bed and opening the door without a weapon to check whether someone was trying to break in. Later, I learned that we had an earthquake—that was what caused the rattling noise.

I experienced numerous earthquakes when living at Lakeside Village Apartments in San Leandro, California. However, my friends there seemed to think that I could predict when an earthquake would happen, because I was always away when one occurred. When a major earthquake created much damage at Lawrence Livermore Laboratory, I was in Grass Valley, California. That evening, when I arrived home, my phone was ringing. My sister-in-law Dorothy was calling to see if I was okay. I received similar calls from friends all over the U.S. My Section Leader at Lawrence Livermore National Laboratory called to inform me of the damage there, and said that I should not report to work the next day.

The following Saturday, while I was in a restaurant in Oakland talking to a friend about the recent earthquake, there was a strong aftershock. The following week at work, we evaluated ways to protect employees from future earthquakes. I became the Safety Officer in our trailer (office area). My task was to assure that safety was a number one priority. There were four Groups in our Section, and I was a Group Leader at that time. I held a Leadership position until I left Livermore in February 1988. I maintained the position as Safety Officer simultaneously. Some Group Leaders and technical staff gave me problems but had to listen to me and follow safety rules.

Another earthquake happened on a Saturday morning when I was sitting in my living room. I saw a kid riding his bicycle outside. When I heard a loud bang, I thought he had run into the wall around my patio. I rushed to see if he was hurt but saw no one. Later I heard on TV that we had experienced an earthquake. The bang came from the primary "pressure" wave. I did not experience the shaking from the secondary "shear" wave.

Earthquakes on the East Coast are very rare. But, on August 23, 2011, after I retired, I experienced an earthquake at home in Alexandria, Virginia. I stood in a door opening during the shaking from the secondary "shear" wave, as I had been taught. I had to have my front door reset following the earthquake; my insurance did not pay for it.

In 1991, I began taking an annual fishing trip to Alaska and took side trips to tour the state. On my second trip in 1992, I experienced the eruption of Mount Spurr. The volcano spread so much ash that it closed the airport in Anchorage.

When the eruption took place occurred, my brother James Woodrow was fishing on the Kasilof River with Steve Nielson and Albert "Bert" Abey. They were fishing the <u>float boat</u> of our main fishing guide, Bruce "BUBBER" Schwartz. At the time, after fishing on Ron's boat (another fishing guide) on the Kenai River with Patrick "Pat" Reardon and Glen (Pat's co-worker at Los Alamos Laboratory), I was asleep. Pat, Glen and I had caught our limit of salmon early that day. While fishing, Pat and Glen got their lines tangled and wrapped around the outboard motor. Ron was trying to free the lines and I hooked a thirty-five-pound fish and yelled "Fish On." We were fishing for Silver salmon and I thought that I had hooked a record-breaking one. When I brought this huge salmon to the anchored boat, Ron looked at it and yelled "Oh, that's a King" and cut the line and went back to clearing Pat's line from the motor. I was very disappointed. King salmon were out of season at that date.

How did Bruce Schwartz come to be called BUBBER?

BUBBER told us that John Madden (former coach of the Oakland Raiders and TV football analyst) said that anyone who weighed more than three hundred pounds should be called BUBBER.

A few years after the eruption of Mount Spurr in 1992, Steve's three sons came on one of our annual fishing trips to Alaska. We chartered a plane in Kenai and flew across Cook's Inlet to sightsee and look for brown bear. We flew within about a fifty-yard radius around Mount Spurr and it was smoking. Steve's oldest son was sitting next to me and asked if it was safe flying so close to the volcano. I encouraged him that it was safe; there was nothing else that I could say. We did see bears. We also saw migrant workers from Mexico camped on the beach, harvesting razor-back clams for commercial use.

In the 1990s, I visited Portage Glacier off the Seward Highway, forty-eight miles from Anchorage, Exit Glacier in Seward, and Bear Glacier at Resurrection Bay. They were covered in ice. Since then, I have seen the effect of global warming. By 2014, there was so much melting that some places no longer had ice. Bear Glacier now had a beach. Icebergs were floating in the Bay.

On August 11, 1999, I experienced a total solar eclipse at a conference in Ostrava, Czech Republic. I tried unsuccessfully to take a photo while using eclipse glasses to protect my eyes. As in many of my travels, I was in the right place at the right time to experience an event that very few people have the opportunity to observe.

Chapter 16

Family Get-Together

When I was growing up, we celebrated on the 20th of May each year. As previously explained, May 20, 1865, was the day that Confederate forces in Florida formally surrendered in Tallahassee, and the slaves were freed under President Lincoln's Emancipation Proclamation. The Proclamation had been issued on January 1, 1863—over two years earlier!

Later, during the 1980s, my sister Leatrice and Cousin Adell Gunn Gilliam (Aunt Carrie Thigpen Gunn's daughter) began planning and sponsoring family Fourth of July together. The celebrations took place at my mother's house in Sawdust or at Leatrice's house in the St. Johns community in Gadsden County.

We also began to have family get-togethers during the Christmas holidays. The first Christmas get-together was probably at my sister Gladys's house with just a few of us. I traveled from San Leandro, California, my brother James Woodrow came with his wife Betty and family from Ft. Lauderdale, and William Lloyd Nealy (Aunt Carrie's grandson) came with his wife Shirley and family from Houston. Gladys would fry fish and shrimp or cook southern food.

Later, William and I decided to have a fish fry on the day after Christmas at my mother's house in Sawdust. The first year began small with only members of Aunt Carrie's and my father's family. As time went on, the event expanded significantly. Attendance extended to more of the family with roots in Sawdust. On the Thigpen side were the Gunn and Porter families (Gunn, Gilliam, Nealy, Rolax, Jordan, and Milton). On my mother's side were the Brown families. See my family tree in the Appendix to understand how the families are related.

We began cooking fish, shrimp, burgers, and hot dogs outside because there was not enough room inside the house. We also had raw oysters on the half shell. My niece Sharon L. Green prepared dishes out of conk shellfish. We had two 55-gallon drums in which we built fires for heat for the large group of people in the yard. We had to cut wood for the heat and shop for more than a day for food and drinks. The get-togethers lasted through 2014. They ended at our house in Sawdust when James Woodrow and I felt that it was too much work for us to prepare for the event and clean up after it, due to my health. No young men were available to take over.

Aunt Carrie's grandchildren Pinky Gilliam Hall and Erving Omega Gilliam, Jr. alternated a family celebration on Christmas Day at their houses in Tallahassee the day before our celebration in Sawdust.

Further, Aunt Carrie's granddaughter Celeste Nealy Holman began a family celebration a few days prior to Christmas after she and her family moved from Virginia to Tallahassee.

Other major celebrations that I have participated in were my mother's 90th birthday celebration on December 28, 1996, and my sister Leatrice's 85th birthday celebration in March 2014.

My brother James Woodrow and his wife Betty suggested that we have a celebration for my mother's 90th birthday. We planned it for the Christmas 1996/New Year 1997 week when most of the family and others could attend, and we communicated our plans with the rest of our siblings. Junior Smith was from Sawdust and owned a soul food restaurant in Quincy; we chose his facility for the venue. My sisters Leatrice and Isabel took charge of getting the invitations out since James Woodrow and I did not live in North Florida.

I wanted all of the immediate family present. I promised to pay for the trip of anyone who said they could not afford it … and I did. The planning was excellent and all of my mother's children and grandchildren attended. Most of our cousins and people from the neighborhood in Sawdust attended too. Relatives from Virginia, California, Georgia, Texas, Tallahassee, Mariana (in Florida), and other places also attended. I was the master of ceremony. The pastor of Union Chapel AME Church,

Reverend Ervin O. Gillian, Sr. spoke. Celeste's three-or four-year-old granddaughter Victoria also spoke. My niece Traci from California added a new touch; she purchased roses for the children and grandchildren to present to my mother. This celebration allowed me to meet and communicate with relatives and people whom I had not seen in many years. More than one hundred people, including family, friends, and neighbors, signed the guest list for this special celebration.

We celebrated my sister Leatrice's 85th birthday at James Woodrow's house in March 2014. This was a surprise party. The planners were Leatrice's daughter Sharon L. Green; James Woodrow and his wife Betty; and Isabel. I traveled from Virginia. Close relatives and friends from Florida, Georgia and other places came to the celebration. More than sixty people signed the guest list.

My paternal grandmother Emma Gilliam Thigpen (right)
and her oldest daughter Laura Thigpen Jordan

Aunt Lucy Thigpen Rolax
Courtesy of Herschell Rolax and Sonya Rolax-Jackson

Rubin Jordan Jr., Aunt Carrie Thigpen Gunn and
her daughter Adell Gunn Gilliam
Courtesy of Celeste Nealy Holman

Aunt Addie Thigpen Hall (left) and my mother Emma Adaline Ray Thigpen

My father Alonzo Thigpen Jr. and mother Emma Adaline Ray Thigpen

Replica of the house where I was born
Painted by my brother James Woodrow Thigpen from plans provided by me from memory

Replica of the Sawdust School House that I attended
*Painted by my brother James Woodrow Thigpen from
plans provided by me from memory*

Lewis Thigpen at age ten in seventh grade

Lewis Thigpen at age twelve in ninth grade

My first photo in dress uniform in the U.S. Army at Fort Knox, Kentucky, in 1955

Socializing with fellow soldiers at the Enlisted Men's Club at Ayers Kaserne in Kirch-Göns, Germany, in 1956

Taking a break during a field training exercise in Germany

In my dress uniform outside the barracks at Ayers Kaserne in Kirch-Göns, Germany, in winter 1957-1958

I am standing on the right during field training in Germany in 1958

A fellow soldier and I use our steel helmets to wash up during a field training exercise

Standing on a lower level of the Eiffel Tower in Paris, France

U. S. Army photo of C Company 7th Tank Bn. in 1956.
I am on the back row, sixth from the right.

Big Ben and surroundings. I took the photo while standing on the bridge over the Thames River in London, England.

At the World Fair in Brussels, Belgium, in 1958.
The Atomium is in the background.

My sister Mildred during her early years as a teacher of Mathematics and Science

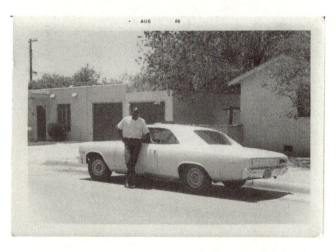

My "muscle car," a 1966 Chevrolet Chevelle 396 Super Sport

My 1970 Triumph TR6 British Roadster

My visit to Rockford, Illinois, in June 1990
Sundstrand Today courtesy of Sundstrand Corporation, 1990

My visit to Florence, Italy, in 1991 to attend the Florence Modal Analysis Conference. I am standing in the foreground.

Fourth of July Celebration 1993. From the left: I am standing in a black shirt and white shorts; my mother Emma is sitting in front of me; Ruby Francis is in a straw hat in front of my mother; and Janice Maxwell is standing on the right of Ruby Francis. Rev. Ervin O. Gilliam Sr. is on the right.

Fourth of July Celebration 1995. Left to right: siblings Leatrice, Lewis, Gladys, James Woodrow; my mother Emma; and my sister Isabel.

At Gladys's house during the Christmas holidays in the late 1980s or later. I am sitting in her kitchen drinking a beer while she prepares southern food for a small group of family members.

My mother's 90th Birthday Celebration. Front row: her children Isabel, James Woodrow, Lewis, Gladys, and Amos (his back to the camera). Back row: grandchildren Traci Thigpen (behind Isabel), Sharon Green, Monica Ross, and Janice Maxwell.

My mother's 90th Birthday Celebration

My mother's 90th Birthday Celebration

My mother's 90th Birthday Celebration

The Thigpen men in the early 1990s at the family house in Sawdust. Left to right: brothers, James Woodrow, Amos, and Lewis. Far right: Amos's son Steven.

At the Great Wall in China in 2006

Site of the Terracotta Warriors that I visited in Xian, China, in 2006

Receiving the Alumni Professional Achievement Award from Illinois Institute of Technology (IIT) in Chicago, May 5, 2006. I am in the middle. IIT President Lewis Collens is on the right.

Receiving the 2007 Virginia Tech XCaliber Award for Excellence in Technology-Assisted Teaching and Learning for a Global Team, August 26, 2007. President Charles W. Steger is on the left. A colleague at Virginia Tech on the right.

My tour of the DMZ in Korea on July 22, 2010

Leatrice's 85th Birthday Celebration in March 2014. First row, left to right: Gladys, Leatrice, Isabel, and Lewis. Back row: James Woodrow and Leatrice's daughter Sharon.

Leatrice's 85th Birthday Celebration. I am in the middle.

Left to right: my grandnephews Christian Renfroe, Seth Long, and Albert Jackson "AJ" Arnold (shooting ball) playing basketball during Leatrice's 85th Birthday Celebration

Janice L. Maxwell (my niece and surrogate daughter) in the mid-1960s

My nephew and niece Steven C. A. Thigpen and Traci N. Thigpen (my surrogate children) in the late 1970s.

Surrogate daughter Kashira M. Turner in the middle to late 1990s

Surrogate daughter Krystle L. Jones at her seventh birthday celebration in February 2007 at a Red Lobster Restaurant in Germantown, Maryland

Surrogate daughter Kashira and I at her graduation at the University of Chicago, June 15, 2013

Surrogate daughters Kashira and Krystle at Kashira's graduation at the University of Chicago, June 15, 2013

Our catch of halibut on a fishing trip in Alaska in August 2011. Right to left: Sterling DuPont, Lewis Thigpen, James W. Thigpen, another crew member, and Captain Joe Simpson (standing) of Simpson Charters in Ninilchik, Alaska.

Holding a silver salmon that I caught in Resurrection Bay out of Seward, Alaska

My brother James Woodrow (left) helping me land a halibut.
Painting courtesy of James Woodrow Thigpen

A 250-pound halibut caught by a fisherman on our boat during my fishing trip with James Woodrow out of Homer, Alaska, in August 2006.
Photo courtesy of James Woodrow Thigpen

Chapter 17

Friends

I have had numerous friends during each stage of my life from childhood through retirement. I shall name and talk about them in each stage.

Charles Damion Rolax was my best friend when I was a young child. He was also my second cousin. We remained friends through our adult lives. I was best man in his wedding. Charles passed away several years ago. His brother James Lloyd Milton and I have been close friends since I was an undergraduate in college. We communicate regularly. Daniel Milton is the first cousin of Charles and James Lloyd. He is also my distant cousin. We have been friends since I graduated from high school.

Friends from my undergraduate years in college include John Owens, whom I met at FAMU in 1959; and Hailey Baker, Aubrey Walker, Archer S. Mitchell Jr., and Charles Watkins at Howard University. I communicated with those friends on a regular basis. Unfortunately, Archer passed away on February 23, 2017, and Aubrey passed away in early 2019. I still communicate regularly with John, Hailey, and Charles.

As a graduate student at Illinois Institute of Technology, one of my first friends was Thomas Hilliard. We first met in the graduate student dormitory. Tom introduced me to the night life in Chicago, and through many of his friends and acquaintances, my studies in Chicago were more meaningful. One year, we shared an apartment. Through Tom, I met my lady friend Jean.

Tom was pursuing a Ph.D. in clinical psychology. I earned my Ph.D. before he completed his. Sometime after I left Chicago to work at Sandia Corporation, we lost contact. However, I subscribed to *Ebony Magazine*, through which I found that Tom had served as a consultant for Angela Davis's attorney's jury selection for her 1972 trial. I contacted him in San Francisco. We remained friends until he passed away in the mid-1980s at an early age.

I remain personal friends with Robert Naftzger, Ray B. Stout, and Robert Reiss, whom I met at IIT in 1964.

I introduced Robert Naftzger to Mary Owens, and served as best man in their wedding in 1969. Over, the years, I have visited them in Chicago. They visited me in Virginia in 2017. About two years later, on January 20, 2019, we had a great time together at their daughter's house in Falls Church, Virginia.

Ray Stout and I also worked together at Lawrence Livermore National Laboratory. That was after he left Bettis Atomic Power Laboratory in West Mifflin near Pittsburgh, Pennsylvania. We talk often about the old days at IIT but mostly about national politics. We had a long visit in late May 2018. That visit included a trip to museums in Philadelphia and back to Washington to several Smithsonian museums on the Mall.

Robert Reiss earned his Ph. D. degree and I earned the Master of Science degree from IIT in June 1967. I knew that he accepted a faculty position at Howard University in 1977, but I had no personal contact with him until I saw him in 1982 at the 19th Annual Meeting of the Society of Engineering Science in Rolla, Missouri. The next time I saw him was in 1985 when he visited Lawrence Livermore National Laboratory as Acting Chair of the Mechanical Engineering Department at Howard to secure support for the mechanical engineering program. Three years later—on January 1, 1988—I became Chairman of the Mechanical Engineering Department at Howard. Bob and I have remained close since. We have traveled to many places around the world together. Once or more a year, since the early 2000s, we go to Las Vegas to gamble. We play black jack and bet at the race and sports books in a casino where one can bet on all sports. Bob retired from Howard in May 2017.

I became friends with Zeora "Zeke" Hercey, George Reis, William "Bill" Patterson, and Frank Kite when I worked at Sandia National Laboratory in Albuquerque, New Mexico.

I believe you develop friends through common interests. Zeke loved the outdoors and had a cabin in the Jemez Mountains. We would go fishing and camp out at his cabin or in his camper trailer. My last communication with Zeke was in the early 2000s.

George Reis loved mathematics. We would meet for coffee and donuts at the Laboratory cafeteria and talk mathematics. We would also go out to the range and fire our pistols. I lost contact with George after I left Sandia in 1973.

Bill Patterson had season tickets to the University of New Mexico basketball games for himself and his two sons. Bill's oldest son did not show strong interest in attending those games, so I purchased one of his season tickets and we attended those games. I became very close to Bill and his family. My last contact with Bill was probably in the early 1980s.

Frank Kite was old enough to be my father. We became friends and had a routine of leaving Sandia Laboratories to have lunch on Fridays. On some Friday evenings, we would stop at a local bar and socialize. There were automobile race tracks in Albuquerque that had three categories of racing on Saturday evenings: Super Stock, Sportsman, and Hobby Stock. Frank had a son who raced cars in the Super Stock racing division.

After Frank's son got married, he quit racing automobiles. By then, Frank had retired from Sandia. Frank said that he had been involved in racing for a good part of his life, and now he was going to race a car in the Hobby Stock Division. The Hobby Stock Division was set up to assure that you did not spend much money because someone could claim the engine for one hundred dollars. Everyone who raced in the Hobby Stock Division knew the rules of the Division. I worked with Frank to build a vehicle. We rebuilt a 1957 Cadillac to race in the Hobby Stock Division in 1973. Most of our work was done in the evenings after I left work, so the process took some time. It was nearly halfway through the season before we were able to race our car, but we came in at third place in the season.

I left Sandia Laboratories in Albuquerque in 1973 to take a position with Lowell Technological Institute in Massachusetts. Two years later, I was moving from Massachusetts to work at Lawrence Livermore in California. On the way, I drove through Albuquerque. When I arrived, my Triumph TR6 sports car needed work, so I made an appointment at the Triumph dealer. I also contacted Frank. He said that he was working at a place where the work could be done. So I cancelled the appointment at the Triumph dealership and took my car to where Frank worked. He loaned me his van, which he called his Hippie Wagon, to use until the work on my car was completed. Once I got my car back, I continued on to Livermore, in a suburb of San Francisco.

Frank's daughter worked at Trans World Airlines (TWA). And Frank and his wife were able to get free passes to fly on TWA. One day, while I was at LLNL, he called me and said that he and his wife were going to Las Vegas but would fly to San Francisco on their way to take me to dinner. I met them at the San Francisco airport, the three of us squeezed in my sports car, and we had dinner at Fisherman's Wharf. Frank and I maintained contact through Christmas cards but later lost contact.

At Lawrence Livermore National Laboratory, I made many new friends. They included Raymond "Ray" C. Y. Chin, Albert "Bert" A. Abey, Ray Lorenson, and Anna Marie Ayres.

I met Ray Chin when I began to work at Livermore in 1975. He shared an office with a coworker of mine. We immediately became good friends because of our similar interests in science and mathematics. I must say that Ray was my closest friend throughout the years after we met. I became close with his family and we traveled together, formed a partnership with Gerald Hedstrom, and of course fished together. I spent nights at his house after major dental surgery. He helped in whatever I needed and vice-versa. We remain friends today.

Bert and I worked in the same Department at Livermore. A pilot in our Department was waiting to get accepted into medical school. We would often fly out for lunch at restaurants with others. I even got a chance to fly the plane myself. Once a year, we scheduled a trip to Reno, Nevada, or Lake Tahoe, California, with other participants.

Beginning in 1990, after I moved to Alexandria, Virginia, Bert scheduled annual trips to Alaska, which I joined, to fish for salmon and halibut. But that year, I broke a bone in my foot and had to cancel my trip. I began fishing in Alaska in 1991. Two years later, in June 1993, Bert planned the trip for the Kenai River in Soldotna, which is on the Kenai Peninsula, south of Anchorage. The fishing was on the Kasilof and Kenai Rivers. However, he and I planned a side trip to Barrow, prior to the arrival of other members of our fishing crew. Barrow is on the northern tip of Alaska, on the Arctic Ocean.

Bert arrived at the Anchorage airport a couple hours before I did. He made sure that my name was on the rental car when I arrived, something he had not done the past two years. We flew to Barrow to spend couple of days there.

One evening, we were to go to dinner with a couple whom we had met on our tours. Bert was very concerned about his diet and exercising. Before dinner, as he headed out to run in the cold weather, he said, "If I am not back in thirty minutes, call 911." He always joked around and our fishing crew kidded him about our love for mayonnaise, which he did not eat because of his diet, so I never thought anything about his statement. When he returned from his run, I was lying on my bed due to a stomach virus. I believe he took a shower and flopped on his bed. Then I heard heavy breathing ... but, a little later, nothing. I called him because we were supposed to meet the couple. He did not respond. I ran to the desk to get emergency help. The hospital was only about a short half block away. I went to the hospital with the emergency team. While waiting at the hospital, I was informed that Bert had passed away. This was one of the saddest days in my life.

In retrospect, I believe that Bert had a premonition regarding his life based on things that he did and said in Anchorage and Barrow.

The doctor asked for the phone number at Bert's home and called his wife. Since this was a case for the police, the constable contacted me. He was unhappy that the hospital had contacted Bert's wife without assuring that someone else was there when she received the bad news.

I was obviously a suspect. The room with all of our belongings was searched for foul play. I moved to another room in the hotel that night. I was probably the only black person in Barrow at that time. I was being watched the whole time after Bert passed away.

A Native Alaskan who worked at the hotel invited me to his house to console me. Under different conditions, I would have enjoyed that visit. I returned to the hotel and went to a restaurant the next morning for breakfast, where I received a phone call from the constable. He had made arrangements with the airline for me to leave Barrow for Anchorage with Bert's body.

Pat Reardon was going to join us on the fishing trip. I called him to let him know the situation. Per the suggestion of the constable, I also met with a minister. I went out that evening to a feast that Native Alaskans were having on the beach of the Arctic Ocean with the couple whom Bert and I had met. I still had problems with my stomach and had no desire to eat whale. I left before the eating began.

After the constable concluded his investigation, I left with Bert's body for Anchorage. The constable took me to the airport that evening. At this time of the year, it really never got totally dark at night. When I got to Anchorage, I picked up the rental car and drove to the Sheraton. The next day, Pat Reardon arrived in Anchorage and stayed in the room with me.

When Bert's wife arrived, I went to the garage under the Sheraton to get his things from the trunk of the car. After she placed Bert's things in her rental car, we drove both cars to an Italian restaurant for dinner.

She parked directly in front of the restaurant in the only space available. I parked near the front and saw a sign in the space saying, "No parking." The space was reserved for the Rug Doctor store, which was closed at the time. Pat said, "This is Sunday evening. No one is going to worry about this." Well, when we came out of the restaurant my rental car had been towed away. I went into the phone booth in the restaurant to call the number of the towing company. Inside the phone booth, a sign said that you would be towed if you parked in the Rug Doctor space. There was no such sign anywhere else, so there had to have been collusion between the restaurant and the Rug Doctor's business. It cost me about one hundred fifty dollars to get my rental car back. We were all mourning the loss of Bert, so having to deal with a towed car bothered me more than it would have under normal conditions.

Bert was cremated. We had a memorial service on the Kenai River where his ashes were sprinkled. During the service, tears came to my eyes as I spoke words of reflection on our friendship.

I met Ray Lorenson and Anna Marie Ayres at Lakeside Village Apartments in San Leandro, California, where I lived during my years at Livermore. We all loved contract bridge, a card game, and whenever we got four people together we played bridge. Ray Lorenson and I also fished for salmon in the San Francisco Bay. Whenever I went fishing, I shared my catch with Anna Marie. I still maintain contact with Ray and Anna Marie. I last saw Anna Marie in the summer of 2016 when she and her friend visited the Washington area.

On my first trip to Alaska in 1991 to fish for salmon, I met Patrick Reardon and Steven Nielson at the airport in Anchorage. They were part of our Alaska fishing group. At that time, I was Chairman of the Mechanical Engineering Department at Howard University. After that, we had many Alaska fishing trips together.

During my one-year sabbatical from Howard that began July 1, 1998, I worked at Los Alamos National Laboratory. There, I worked with Pat and Steve. I still maintain contact with them by phone and Christmas cards. I saw Pat quite recently, when he, his wife Bettina, and son Sean visited me Thanksgiving 2017 for dinner.

I met Emmanuel K. Glakpe who was a faculty member when I interviewed for my position at Howard. We became friends and worked together on numerous research projects. We have continued to remain friends since my retirement in 2008.

Chapter 18

Some of My Favorite Things

Poetry and Quotations

I grew up in a family who were members of the Union Chapel African Methodist Episcopal (AME) Church in Sawdust. As a young child, I was taught a prayer to say before going to bed: "When I lay myself down to sleep, I pray to the Lord my soul to keep, If I should die before I awake, I pray to the Lord my soul to take, Amen." When I got older, we said the Lord's Prayer every night before going to bed. I also had to memorize the 23rd Psalm.

After I became an adult, I began to question teachings of the Christian Church. I had discussions with numerous ministers, and they all believed that Christianity was the only true religion. With all of the different religions on earth, I have been unable to accept that concept. I believe that religion is a way of life and one should live it. My religion can be categorized simply in three words—The Golden Rule: "Do unto others as you would have them do unto you."

I have learned several special poems during my lifetime that I believe relate to living and life. These include "If" by Rudyard Kipling; "Thanatopsis" by William Cullen Bryant; "On His Blindness" by John Milton; "As You Like It" Act II, Scene VII by William Shakespeare; "Macbeth" Act 2, Scene 1, by Shakespeare; "The House by the Side of the Road" by Sam Walter Foss; "Annabel Lee" by Edgar Allen Poe; and "Love and Face Life" by Rico Fonseca. When I was young I recited "If"

261

or the last stanza of "Thanatopsis" at several memorial services at Union Chapel AME Church.

I have a plaque in my home office with the following quotations: "I decline to accept the end of man" by William Faulkner; "Tis not too late to seek a newer world" by Martin Luther King, Jr.; and "True Peace is not merely the absence of tension, but it is the presence of justice and brotherhood" by Martin Luther King, Jr.

Two family sayings that I have tried to live by since I was growing up are "Any job worth doing is a job worth doing well to the best of your ability," and "Don't put off until tomorrow what you can do today." However, in my retirement, I do put off things until tomorrow—or even the next day.

Favorite Foods

This is a very difficult topic to characterize. I shall describe my favorite foods in terms of regional categories and in specific meals.

I grew up eating Southern food which included meat from domesticated animals and vegetables grown on the farm, fish, and wild game. The key things that stand out about Southern food are the recipes for cooking all parts of pork, chicken, fish, wild game, vegetables, and desserts such as cobblers. I try to prepare Southern food but I am no match to my sisters Leatrice, Gladys, and Isabel in preparing it the way it was when I was growing up.

I learned to appreciate French food when I was a soldier stationed in Germany in the middle to late 1950s and visited Paris. I try to cook simple meals such as burgers and duck à l'orange the French way, but when I want a great French dinner, I go to a recognized French restaurant.

I began eating Chinese food when I was a student in college in Washington in the early 1960s because it was inexpensive and I could afford it at local restaurants. It became a favorite when I moved to California in 1975 and went to restaurants in San Francisco and Oakland with my friend and coworker Ray Chin. My favorite Chinese food is Cantonese.

The first Italian food I had was when I was a soldier in Germany. There was a pizza shop in Kirch-Göns within walking distance from our base at Ayers Kaserne. The pizzas were great. Further, some soldiers were of Italian descent. Their parents would send to them packages of non-perishable food and they shared with all of us. When I moved to Virginia in 1988, I lived in Pentagon City, within walking distance to the Portofino Restaurant in Crystal City. This has been one of my favorite restaurants for more than thirty years. If I have visitors and they love Italian food, I take them to Portofino's.

I was introduced to Mexican food in Albuquerque in 1964. The Mexican food that I love is what I enjoyed in Albuquerque and Santa Fe. The food is not Texas-Mexican (Tex-Mex) or food in Old Mexico. The type prepared in New Mexico is uniquely different from Tex-Mex and Old Mexico, and I cannot further explain the differences. It is the preparation that I love.

I found a small Mexican restaurant in Vienna, Virginia, that claimed to prepare New Mexico-style food. The food was prepared in the New Mexico style that I love. However, it has become a chain of restaurants in Northern Virginia and the cooks do not cook "New Mexico" style. The original restaurant does not exist now and the chain has cooks probably from Central America.

When I think of food of any regional category or name, the preparation is more important than its name. These are dishes that I love but do not place in any of regional categories.

My favorite seafood includes lobster, crab, fish, and oysters. My favorite lobster menus are steamed Lobster, Lobster Thermidor, and Lobster Newberg. I like both blue crab and Dungeness crab. My favorite whole crab is Dungeness because it takes less effort to take the meat from the shell after it is cooked. I love soft shell blue crab cooked in butter and crab cakes. I love fried fish; my favorites are sun fish, small whole catfish and crappies. One small sun fish that I like is called red eyes. The red eyes are no more than three and one half inches long. We fried them whole very hard and ate bones and all. And, I like raw oysters on the half shell with Tabasco sauce and horseradish.

My favorite beef cuts are New York steaks, filet mignon, and prime rib, all cooked medium rare. I also like medium rare hamburgers with a sunny-side-up egg on top with tomatoes, onion, lettuce, and mayonnaise on a poppy seed bun. My favorite seafood and beef cuts are prepared at restaurants or at my siblings' houses, but I cook my favorite hamburgers myself. I believe that all great foods are in the preparation and not the ingredients.

I also love fried quail, but in recent years I have been unable to find it at supermarkets where they previously were. Whenever I visit Amos and his family in Los Angeles, I bring back quail. His wife Dorothy takes me where I can get it; she vacuum packs and freezes the quail for me to take home to Alexandria. I prefer quail to chicken or turkey on any day.

I grew up dining on a special meal on New Year's Day. This meal is based on superstitions. The major dishes are black-eyed peas, hog jowl, rice, and collard greens. Each dish represents Peace, Joy, Riches, and Greenback dollars, respectively. The meal includes other meats, vegetables, and desserts as well.

Do not wash clothes on New Year's Day because you may wash away a family member that year. No woman should enter a house on New Year's Day before a man enters. Men get up early on that day to visit their neighbors to assure that no woman visits first. If a woman is the first person to enter, she will bring bad luck. These rituals continue today by some members in my family. I participate when I visit them during the New Year holidays.

Blues Music

I have listened to blues music throughout my life. There are blues songs that have moved me, inspired me, and marked points along my journey. These songs not only bring back memories, but are as relevant to personal relationships, politics, and other issues today in 2019 as they were decades ago. The lyrics of "You Done Tore Your Playhouse Down" by Robert Clifford Brown (Washboard Sam) and "You Don't Miss Your Water (Till Your Well Runs Dry)" by William Bell relate to love and money.

Many blues songs have hidden meanings. I suggest that the above two songs have strong hidden political connotation applicable to President Donald Trump today. If the Republican leadership in Congress does its job in protecting our country, Trump will end up singing William Bell's song and the Republicans will sing Washboard Sam's song.

When I was growing up, I heard a blues song titled "Black, Brown and White" by Big Bill Broonzy (William Lee Conley Broonzy Bradley) that contained so much that I have observed and experienced in racial relationships—not only in the Jim Crow South but throughout my journey around the world.

The lyrics consist of five verses about:
1. A black person having to work for a living;
2. Not getting served in a place (bar or other establishment, e.g. apartment, drugstore, etc.);
3. Being ignored at an employment office;
4. Receiving unequal pay for equal work; and
5. After becoming successful in one's chosen work, asking "What are you going to do about old Jim Crow?"

Each verse ends with: *"If you are white, should be all right, if you are brown stick around, but if you are black, get back, get back, get back."*

Big Bill Broonzy was born on June 26, 1893, in Mississippi and obviously experienced Jim Crow there. He died on August 15, 1958, in Chicago.

My personal experiences relating to the lyrics in "Black, Brown and White" are expressed throughout this memoir.

PART V
Embracing a Changing World

Chapter 19

National Leadership

This chapter summarizes the political and military history of our country during my lifetime.

I have lived under the leadership of fourteen Presidents of the United States. Those Presidents are respectively, Franklin D. Roosevelt; Harry S. Truman; Dwight D. Eisenhower; John F. Kennedy; Lyndon B. Johnson; Richard M. Nixon; Gerald R. Ford; James Earl Carter; Ronald Wilson Reagan; George H. W. Bush; William J. Clinton; George W. Bush; Barack H. Obama; and Donald J. Trump.

I was born in 1938 during Franklin Delano Roosevelt's (FDR) second term as President, which began in 1937. World War II broke out in September 1939, one year after I was born. Germany captured France in June 1940. Roosevelt was re-elected for a third term in November 1940. On December 8, 1941, one day after Japan bombed the U. S. Naval Base at Pearl Harbor, the United States declared war on Japan. Roosevelt was reelected to a fourth term in 1944. However, three months after his next inauguration in 1945—on April 12—he passed away in Warms Springs, Georgia. Vice President Harry S. Truman then became President.

The war ended in Europe in 1945, a few months after Truman became President, and the U.S. could now concentrate on ending the war with Japan. The U.S. was successful in the first atomic bomb test (the Trinity) and now had weapons of mass destruction. The schedule to drop two atomic bombs on Japan was approved by President Truman after Japan refused to surrender. Hiroshima was bombed on August 6, 1945, and Nagasaki was bombed three days later. The two bombs killed more than one hundred thousand people in Japan. Japan surrendered the day after the second bomb exploded. The Second World War ended, and I was seven years old.

Following the end of World War II, I learned that jet propelled air planes had been developed. Further, the scariest development that I heard about in the late 1940s was the development of an H-Bomb. People talked about the H-bomb destroying the world. There were no explanations of what their words meant. This thought came to me during my early period of critical thinking: "Question what you hear and read." My question was why the President, his administration, or anyone would develop something that would destroy the world. The question is still being addressed today.

In 1948, sickened by the violence and abuse suffered by black soldiers returning from overseas from World War II, Truman issued Executive Order 9981, which led to the integration of the military. Truman was reelected President in 1948. The United States entered the Korean War in 1950. Truman did not run for reelection in 1952 and Eisenhower was elected President.

Eisenhower was inaugurated in January 1953, when I was a junior in high school. An Armistice was signed six months later between North Korea, China, and South Korea to end the three years of fighting on the Korean Peninsula. During the fall of 1953, I became friends with veterans of the Korean War who returned to earn their high school diplomas. The Military Forces were completely desegregated during Eisenhower's first term as president. I entered the integrated Army in September 1955. During my three years of active, there were possible military conflicts that I would have had to serve in, the Suez Canal Crisis in 1956 and the Lebanon Crisis in 1958, but I did not participate in either.

We now travel on the interstate highway system that was created by an Act signed by Eisenhower in 1956. Further, I received a NASA Fellowship for support in Graduate School at IIT in 1964. NASA (National Aeronautics and Space Administration) was created in 1958 during my last month on active duty in the Army in Germany.

After I returned home, Fidel Castro overthrew the Batista government and came into power in Cuba in 1959.

John F. Kennedy (JFK) won the presidential election in 1960 against Richard M. Nixon, Eisenhower's Vice President. Shortly after his inauguration in 1961, Kennedy permitted a band of exiled Cubans to carry out the Bay of Pigs invasion. The Cubans were trained and financed by the CIA in an attempt to overthrow Castro, who was aligned with the Soviet Union. The attempt failed.

The United States and its allies were engaged in the Cold War— economic and political crashes— with the Soviet Union since the end of World War II in 1945. Now, Cuba was dependent upon the Soviet Union for military and economic aid. In 1962, the U. S. had high altitude spy planes patrolling the globe. In October 1962, the pilot of a U–2 spy plane photographed a Soviet ballistic missile being assembled in Cuba. This created the Cuban Missile Crisis. President Kennedy addressed the nation on TV about the presence of the missiles and explained his decision to enact a naval blockade around Cuba. He stated that, if necessary, military forces would be used to end this threat to our national security. For about two weeks, I thought that we might have a nuclear war. Through diplomacy, the crisis ended when the U.S. agreed with Soviet leader Nikita Khrushchev's offer to remove the missiles from Cuba.

During his short term as president, JFK decided to launch the mission to the moon. On July 20, 1969, almost six years after Kennedy's assassination, Neil Armstrong and Edwin "Buzz" Aldrin became the first humans to land on the moon. Armstrong was the first person to walk on the moon. He took his first step and made the famous statement, "That's one small step for man, one giant step for mankind." I stayed up late that night to watch on television coverage of the moon landing.

John Fitzgerald Kennedy was assassinated on November 22, 1963, as his motorcade traveled through Dallas, Texas. He was a very popular president, and I believe the country was as sad as I was. Vice President Lyndon Baines Johnson (LBJ) was sworn in as President. I spent the weekend watching the news on TV. Lee Harvey Oswald was charged with the murder. Two days later, Oswald was fatally shot by Jack Ruby, a local nightclub owner, on live television in the basement of Dallas Police Headquarters. I saw the execution on live TV.

LBJ was able to get Civil Rights bills into law proposed by JFK because of his political skills. However, Johnson escalated the U. S. involvement in Vietnam that had begun in 1954. By the end of 1965, there were probably more than 200,000 American ground troops fighting in Vietnam. There was unrest in the U.S., and LBJ did not run for reelection in 1968. Robert Kennedy entered the Democratic presidential primaries. Martin Luther King, Jr. was assassinated on April 4, 1968, in Memphis, Tennessee. Two months later, on June 6, 1968, Robert Kennedy was assassinated in Los Angeles, CA. Hubert Humphrey became the Democratic candidate for president in the 1968 general election.

Richard M. Nixon "Tricky Dick" defeated Humphrey and was inaugurated in January 1969. At this time, there were probably more than one half million U.S. troops fighting in Vietnam. The Vietnam War ended when the U.S. forces withdrew in 1973. Saigon was captured and unified under communist control in North Vietnam in 1975. The Nixon Administration faced two major scandals: the Watergate burglary during the 1972 presidential campaign; and the resignation of Vice President Spiro Agnew in 1973 for bribery, extortion, and tax evasion during his tenure as governor of Maryland. Following Agnew's resignation, Gerald R. Ford was appointed Vice President in 1973. On August 9, 1974, following the passage of three articles of impeachment a month earlier, Nixon resigned. Ford became president, and Nelson Rockefeller was appointed Vice President.

Ford pardoned Nixon for his crimes on September 8, 1974. There were controversies regarding Ford's pardon that he tried to calm. Ford had to deal with inflation and then shift to stimulating the economy when the recession became a serious problem. Tensions were high in the Middle East and the U.S. did not want another war after the 1967 six-day war. The Ford Administration helped persuade Israel and Egypt to an interim truce agreement by providing aid to both countries. President Ford won the Republican nomination for president in 1976 but lost to his Democrat opponent and champion of human rights, Governor Jimmy Carter of Georgia.

Carter had to deal with rising energy costs, mounting inflation, unemployment, and continuing tensions around the world. He had some success in many of these areas through deregulations and the establishment of new energy policies as well as departments within the Administration.

In international affairs, Carter helped bring "good" relations between Egypt and Israel through the 1978 Camp David Agreement. He also obtained ratification of the Panama Canal treaties and established full diplomatic relations with China that had begun under the Nixon administration. Although Carter had a number of achievements in domestic affairs and on the international scene, there were setbacks. The seizure of the U.S. embassy staff in Iran as hostages dominated the news during the presidential election year in 1980. I believe Iran's actions and continuing inflation contributed to Carter's defeat to Ronald Reagan in 1980. An attempt to free the embassy staff by helicopter failed. Carter continued to negotiate over the hostages and Iran released the Americans the same day that he left office. I have always thought that Ronald Reagan somehow made a deal with Iran. This was another chapter in my critical thinking: "Why did Iran release the embassy staff on the day that Jimmy Carter left office?"

Ronald Reagan survived an assassination attempt a couple of months after his inauguration in 1981. Following his recuperation for several weeks, he went back to work. Reagan implemented policies including tax cuts intended to spur economic growth, and advocated for increases in military spending and reductions in social programs.

These were now policies called Reaganomics and not "voodoo economics" as described by George H. W. Bush during the Republican primaries in 1980. Bush became Reagan's Vice President.

Reagan escalated the cold war with the Soviet Union and announced the Strategic Defense Initiative to develop space-based weapons to protect the U.S. from attacks by Soviet nuclear missiles.

Reagan sent a peace-keeping force of Marines to Lebanon after Israel invaded it in 1982. More than a year later, in 1983, two suicide truck bombers attacked the Marine barracks killing more than two hundred Americans. The perpetrators were suspected to be Hezbollah along with Iranian and Syrian involvement. Reagan also sent U.S. forces to lead an invasion of Grenada, a small island in the Caribbean, the same month.

In November 1984, Reagan was elected to his second term by the largest margin of electoral votes ever, against Walter Mondale and Geraldine Ferraro who won only one state—Mondale's home state of Minnesota (by a narrow margin)—plus the District of Columba. I voted for the Democratic ticket. During his second term Reagan forged relations with the Soviet Union leader Mikhail Gorbachev and challenged him to tear down the Berlin Wall that was a symbol of communism. About two and one half years later, the wall was dismantled. However, the administration was involved in the Iran-Contra Affair, a political scandal that involved secret weapons transaction and other activities prohibited by the Congress.

George H. W. Bush won the Republican nomination for president in 1988; he and his running mate Dan Quayle defeated Michael Dukakis in the general election. Bush sent troops to Panama to overthrow the regime of Manuel Noriega who was threatening the security of the Canal. He also sent more than 400,000 troops to free Kuwait after it was invaded by Saddam Hussein of Iraq. The battle was called Desert Storm. Although Bush had success in the military activities, there was discontent on the home front, and he lost the 1992 presidential election to William Jefferson "Bill" Clinton.

Prior to Clinton's election, inflation was very high. In the 1980s, I built a house in California and had to get a variable interest loan at sixteen percent. I purchased my present house in Northern Virginia in 1988 at a high interest rate. When I purchased my current house, the average price of housing was increasing at twenty seven percent per year and interest rates were high. When Clinton left office in 2001, we had the lowest inflation in three decades. But the value of my house decreased significantly. Of course, as inflation decreased, more people were able to own homes; we had the highest home ownership in the country's history. During his administration, we had sustained period of peace and dropping crime rates. Clinton proposed the first balanced budget in many years and was successful in obtaining a budget surplus. I remember that, on one of my annual fishing trips to Alaska, I argued with some of my Republican fishing partners that Clinton was going to be successful in balancing the budget.

In 1998, the House of Representatives impeached Clinton regarding his indiscretions with a young female White House intern. He was tried in the Senate and found not guilty of the charges. He maintained his popularity. Vice President Albert Gore, Jr. lost the presidential election to George W. Bush in 2000, **an election ultimately decided by the Supreme Court of the United States**.

Bush was inaugurated in January 2001. On the morning of September 11, 2001, four commercial airplanes were hijacked by terrorists. Two of the planes were intentionality crashed into the twin towers of the World

Trade Center in New York; a third plane destroyed part of the Pentagon in Arlington, Virginia; and the fourth crashed in Pennsylvania after passengers tried to retake it. I was driving to work on Interstate 395 in slow moving traffic across from the Pentagon when the third plane crashed there. I saw what appeared to be the tail of the plane immediately following the crash. It was reported that three thousand people were killed in the September 11, 2001, terrorist attacks.

The Bush administration accused Osama bin Laden and his terrorist network for the attacks and charged the government of Afghanistan for harboring Osama bin Laden and his followers. The American-led war in Afghanistan commenced in October 2001 as a direct result of the September terrorist attacks. The Afghanistan government was quickly toppled but whereabouts of Osama bin Laden remained elusive. The U.S. still has troops in Afghanistan today as I write this memoir. Bush also ordered the invasion of Iraq, an attack called "Operation Iraqi Freedom," in March 2003. Following photographs of abusive treatment of prisoners at a prison in Iraq by American soldiers, it was discovered in 2004 that captured Afghanistan military and others who were sent to the Guantanamo naval base were tortured. Bush was elected to a second term as president.

On January 20, 2009, Barack H. Obama was inaugurated as the first African American President of the United States. I attended his inauguration on the Mall in Washington. This was an historic event for African Americans and for the nation, and I would not have missed it. Thus I stood on the Mall with a crowd that was estimated to be the largest number (1.8 million was reported by one organization) of people to ever attend an event on the Mall. It was reported in the news and on TV that, on the day of Obama's inauguration, Mitch McConnell, the Senate Minority Leader, was plotting to make Obama a one-term president. When Obama was inaugurated, the country was in an economic downturn. It was referred to as the "Great Recession" in comparison to the "Great Depression" that ended in 1943, during World War II. Efforts to stabilize the economy included appropriating billions of dollars to Chrysler and General Motors with the government assuming percentages of ownership of those two automakers; the Federal Reserve purchasing Treasury bonds to pump money into the economy; and the passage of hundreds of billions in spending measures. Within two years, the efforts to stabilize the economy began to produce positive results. Obama also signed his signature Patient Protection and Affordable Care Act (ACA or "Obamacare") on March 23, 2010, with no support from Republicans in Congress. Since the passage of Obamacare, the Republican members of Congress have tried to repeal the Bill for more than nine years, without success.

The U.S. was also involved in the wars in Afghanistan and Iraq when Obama was inaugurated. The elusive Osama bin Laden, architect of the September 11, 2001 terrorist attacks, was killed by American Special Forces in a fortified compound in Pakistan in May 2011. Obama was elected for a second term in 2012. Throughout the Obama administration, the United States was involved in military activities in the Middle East. These include Afghanistan, Iraq, the revolt in Libya, and the Civil War in Syria.

Donald J. Trump defeated Democrat Hillary Rodham Clinton in the 2016 presidential campaign based on Electoral College votes. The news media has continuously reported in the first three-plus years of Trump's Presidency that there was illegal foreign interference (Russian) during the campaign that favored Trump's election. I believe that Trump began his campaign in 2011 with the "birther conspiracy," claiming that Obama was born in Kenya and therefore was ineligible to serve as president. During the presidential campaign, Trump ran on a slogan "Make America Great Again." I interpreted the slogan to mean that he wants to take America back more than 180 years to when Andrew Jackson was president. Trump's hero, Andrew Jackson (1829-1837), was a rich man who built his wealth on the backs of slaves. Jackson is also remembered for his cruelty to Native Americans and the "Trail of Tears," where he wanted to clear territories east of the Mississippi River for white settlers. Thousands of Cherokees died on the trip to Oklahoma. Trump hung a portrait of Jackson in the Oval Office after he became president. Like Jackson, Trump is a champion of white supremacy.

On January 20, 2017, Trump was inaugurated as the 45th president of the United States. Early in his presidency, Trump issued executive orders to undo the accomplishments of President Obama. He also tried to repeal the Patient Protection and Affordable Care Act (ACA or "Obamacare").

I believe that Trump is a man of no moral values who cheats, lies, disrespects the law, verbally attacks others, and you name it. Trump does these things to push through his program and consolidate power within the presidency. He has taken the attitude that the Executive Branch is exempt from the checks and balances of the Constitution. His first three years have been filled with scandals regarding collusion with Russia during the 2016 presidential campaign, obstruction of justice, and questionable and unqualified appointments to his Cabinet.

Congress is supposed to be the Legislative branch of federal government, co-equal with the Executive and Judicial branches to provide checks and balances on each other. But the Republican members of Congress have their champion of white supremacy—Donald Trump—and support him to preserve it. They understand the changing demographics in the United States and have worked to stack the Supreme Court and other Federal judgeships with Trump appointees. They show that they do not care about the responsibilities of Congress that require checks and balances.

Chapter 20

Military Service in the Family

It is important to acknowledge and honor the military service of family members in my memoir. Members of my family have served during and since World War II through Desert Storm. There may have been other family members who served in World War I and in other periods, but my memoir reflects only those whom I have known. I salute all veterans on the Thigpen, Brown, and Ray sides of our family.

After the United States entered World War II in 1941, my father was called by the draft board, but he was not drafted into service because he had too many children. However, my father had one brother and two sisters who had sons and cousins who were drafted and served during World War II. His brother Johnnie had two sons, Alfred Thigpen and Ellis "Tugar" Thigpen, who were drafted. His oldest sister Laura had one son whom I know of, Lonnie Jordan, who served. My father's sister Lucy had two sons, James Rolax and Robert Rolax, who served. After Robert returned home, he told me that he served in Germany. I do not know where James served.

Another relative who served during World War II was a distant cousin, Gerry Gunn. He told me that he served in the Philippines. There may be other family members in the military during WW II, but I have no knowledge of their service.

On my mother's side, I believe Uncle Eddie Brown may have also served in the Army during the WW II. Veterans of the Korean War include Aunt Lucy's youngest son William Rolax and my brother Amos Thigpen. Amos was considered a Korean War veteran because he entered the Army prior to January 1955. William was also a veteran of the Vietnam War, and he retired from the military. Through William's service, this meant that Aunt Lucy had three sons to serve in the military, the most of any of my father's siblings.

I served in the Army during the Suez Canal Crisis in 1956 and the Lebanon Crisis in 1958.

My distant cousin Jesse "Little Jesse" Campbell served in Vietnam. Little Jesse was a point man for his platoon in Vietnam.

My nephew Carl Dewayne Rhowe served in Kuwait as a marine during Desert Storm.

Other veterans include Larfield Thigpen and his brother McKinley "Kenny" Thigpen. They are grandsons of Uncle Johnnie Thigpen.

On my mother's side, there may be family members in addition to Uncle Eddie Brown who served in the military. I have written about veterans whom I know on the Thigpen and Brown sides. There may be others on the Ray side of the family.

Chapter 21

Continuing Education

After earning the Ph.D. degree, I knew that technology was rapidly changing. I needed to continue my education for future challenges and opportunities.

My education continued in discussions with older men, mostly Mr. Willie Campbell and Mr. Harry Gilliam, when I visited my parents in the Sawdust Community. We talked about life in general and how they had coped with life's ups and downs. I went fishing with Mr. Willie and we did as all fishermen do: talk when the fish are not biting. When I saw Mr. Harry, we talked about my work on the Fletcher farm when I was young, and we discussed life in general. I learned from those men when I was young to always analyze the actions of everyone you meet regarding what their relationship to you means—good or bad. Do not take everything they say at face value. Assess their actions and activities.

Continuing education has been both formal through workshops and courses and informal through discussions with experts, and just by relating to people and observing their behavior. Between 1972 and 2005, I completed more than twenty-five continuing education workshops or courses. All except seven were related to management, leadership, and human relations.

1) I took my first continuing education course, a technical workshop, at Pennsylvania State University in 1972 when I was employed at Sandia National Laboratories in Albuquerque.

2) I had nine continuing education workshops at Lawrence Livermore Laboratory between 1980 and 1983 and nine workshops between 1988 and 2002 at Howard University related to management, leadership and working with people.
3) I attended one-or two-day leadership workshops scheduled by the Dean of Engineering, Provost, or President of Howard.
4) The last workshop, in 2005, was a one-week course that I sponsored at Howard to teach students and faculty in engineering on the use of the NX computer-aided design software code. I invited faculty and students from all departments in the School of Engineering. In addition to mechanical engineering faculty and students, I invited one faculty member from each of the other departments— civil engineering, electrical engineering and chemical engineering. The instructor was a General Motors employee. Because of my relationship with General Motors through the Partners for the Advancement of Collaborative Engineering Education Program (PACE), I had to pay only for the travel expenses of the instructor.
5) In 1998-1999, while on sabbatical at Los Alamos National Laboratory in New Mexico, I took five courses in Spanish in the evenings at Santa Fe Community College.

Early in my career, I learned that the Ph.D. degree was not the end of my education but a means to continued learning. I sought out experts and interacted with those who could help me both within my organization and in the external community in areas for which I had no expertise.

During my first year at Sandia National Laboratories, I worked on high velocity impact water entry projectiles. This was a new area of research for me. I made an appointment to visit a researcher at the Naval Surface Weapons Laboratory in Maryland to discuss water entry cavitations of projectiles. This researcher had worked in that area for many years. My visit led to a contract for me to use the facility to test my models on water entry phenomenon. During the same period of time, I used the LTV wind tunnel facility in Texas to obtain drag coefficients of my projectiles. For my projects, I tried to find the best people and facilities to assure success.

Throughout my professional career, I kept in mind that I should not neglect the human element and learn from my interactions with people. I learned to develop relationships with people in a different building either by joining their coffee pool or collaborating on a research project with someone in a different unit. Through these relationships, you will be able to learn a great deal about the overall health of the organization that may help you in the future.

Serving on organization-wide committees meets the same purpose. I attended numerous conferences in many countries around the world, served on many committees and panels, and chaired many of those committees and panels. Those contacts helped me to keep abreast of new developments in technology and enhanced my leadership and management skills.

My informal continuing education related to the human element and taught me over the years that, to be a good leader, you must know the people whom you manage. As an example, when I was Chairman of the Mechanical Engineering Department at Howard, a student came to me to complain that a faculty member would not give her an examination. She said that the Associate Dean of Engineering had told her to see her Department Chairman. The Associate Dean always deflected everything to the Department Chairman.

I knew much about the faculty member's personality and said to myself, "He must have gotten up on the wrong side of the bed this morning because that does not sound like him." I informed the student that I would talk to the faculty member. During my discussion with him, I learned that the student always played this game. She would arrive at his exams late with an excuse to postpone the exam to a later date. This time he would not postpone the exam, and yet she would not take it on time. Instead, she went to the Associate Dean to complain.

Experience also taught me that you must learn as much as possible about your own managers to be successful. They watch your behavior and test how you react in different situations. That information is passed up and down the leadership ladder and sideways to other organizations. The information affects your status in the organization. I am not saying that you must agree with the behavior of your immediate manager. If you do not accept your immediate manager's behavior you can fight it, but be prepared to justify and document your actions. Do not hold grudges because they may hurt you in the future.

Chapter 22

Technology Developments and Advancements

Throughout my life, I have seen rapid growth of technology development in written communications and copying, in oral communications, in storage of information, and in computations and analysis—from the simplest to the highly sophisticated. Here are my personal observations and experiences.

Written Communications and Copying Documents

New tools have been developed to prepare, copy, and distribute documents both within the internal and external community during my lifetime.

In written communications, one of the "simplest" developments of tools that I remember was the ball point pen. The ball point pen was first sold commercially in the mid to late 1940s. It became a replacement for the fountain pen. I purchased one through a mail order catalogue for thirty-nine cents, which was very expensive. At that time you could purchase eight bars of candy for forty cents. I believe that I was the first person in Sawdust to purchase a ball point pen. When Professor George Washington Farmer, our principal at the Sawdust School, saw my pen, he wanted to buy it from me. I did not sell it. However, there was a problem with this pen: it leaked ink when you were writing and caused smears in your work if you were not careful. I remember getting ink in my shirt pocket.

The typewriter was a very important tool. During my life time, the typewriter progressed from the old Remington with long mechanical key strokes to an electric powered one with an exchangeable ball containing English and Greek letters. Professor Farmer had an old Remington probably made in the early 1930s. It was used to type my sister Mildred's applications to attend college in late 1947 or early 1948. I watched letters being typed and the operation of the machine. My master's degree thesis and Ph.D. dissertation were typed with the IBM ball typewriter in the late 1960s. I still had to do my own graphics by hand with my drawing set. My instruments included rulers for measurements, French curves for curved lines, triangles for orientation and drawing straight lines, and inking pens of different openings for different thicknesses of lines. The inking pens were similar to tweezers—you placed a drop of ink between the tips of the pen and used an appropriate tool from your set as a guide to draw the line. In the late 1980s, computers and word processors began to replace typewriters and hand drawings at most organizations where I worked. Typewriters were basically obsolete by the late 1990s.

For duplicating or copying typed results, carbon paper, the blackboard, mimeograph machines, and the Xerox machine stand out to me. Carbon paper was used directly on the typewriter to make a copy. A sheet of carbon paper was placed between two sheets of paper before the document was typed. The letters "cc" stand for "carbon copy." Even in 2018, long after the typewriter ceased to be standard office equipment, some people still use "cc" to note a copy of a document.

The blackboard was a medium for teachers who had no other means to present their exams to students. I went to school from elementary through high school reading my exams from the blackboard.

During my college days, mimeograph machines were used to copy exams. The exam was typed on a stencil. The stencil was placed in the machine to make the number of copies needed. As late as 1975, I used the mimeograph machine to copy exams when teaching at Lowell Technological Institute in Massachusetts.

When I was a student, I made copies of documents with a machine that used thermal energy a couple of times. I believe the most important breakthrough in copying was the introduction of the photo copy machine from Xerox in 1959. The brand name became a VERB for photo copying, i.e., "Go *Xerox* this document."

Distribution of Documents

The U.S. Mail has been a means of distributing written documents as far back as the Pony Express, which carried mail across the country. The telegraph and railroad brought an end to the Pony Express.

When I was growing up, people used the telegraph to send messages. It usually had bad news, so no one wanted to receive a telegram. I believe that the telegraph was the fastest means of communicating written messages prior to the Internet. I telegraphed a message from England to the U.S. in the late 1950s and got a response the next day.

By the late 1980s, email, faxes, and the U.S. Mail were the dominant mode of distributing written communications externally. Current external communication modes include email, wireless telephone text messages, and social media such as Facebook and Twitter on the worldwide web. One can distribute information, post communications on blogs, or use other postings that have the capacity to capture readers' comments. However, many organizations and businesses are pushing to eliminate U.S. Mail and have all communications done electronically on the worldwide web. I receive correspondence weekly requesting that I go paperless on all of my accounts.

Oral Communications

I grew up in a rural area with no electricity or telephones. Oral communications literally meant that you spoke to the person face-to-face.

The radio became the medium for mass communication and entertainment. Our first radios were purchased in the early 1940s. These were battery powered radios with tubes. The non-chargeable battery was much larger and heavier than the radio. We placed the radio in the front room next to a wooden window so that we could anchor a wire antenna about twenty yards or more away in a persimmon tree. This was not a portable radio. However, after World War II, transistor development was proven successful. By the early 1950s, portable radios containing transistors were developed using small batteries. Around that time, my family obtained electricity and purchased a radio powered by electricity. Today, one can purchase portable radios that include alarm clocks as well as weather stations.

Another communication and entertainment medium is the television. I believe that the television was proven to be viable in the late 1940s. I saw my first television at the Gadsden County Fair in the early 1950s. It was a small black and white TV with a rectangular screen about one foot by one foot. Color TV became popular in the mid 1960s. One could purchase a TV in 2015 with a large screen that weighs eight pounds or less whereas the TV that I purchased in 1999 with a smaller screen is too heavy for me to handle alone. Further, software has been developed to connect a phone directly to the television.

The telephone has undergone significant developments. It has progressed from the rotary dial to a digital operation where you can store contact names and numbers, and it shows who is calling. It records messages from calls that are not answered, and displays the name and number of the caller.

Even more progress has been made with the introduction of the wireless or mobile phone. The mobile (cell) phone became available in the 1980s and has progressed to an all-purpose instrument— "intelligent phone" or "smart" phone—with a camera that shoots digital pictures and movies. You can send text messages or send and receive written documents through email. It is used as a navigation device, for purchasing, and for playing games, among the many things you can do with a mobile phone.

Other advances in oral communications include contact by computer with Skype and Gismo that I have used. Of course, we cannot forget video conferencing. As a faculty member at Howard, I used video conferencing to teach student teams with faculty at five universities around the world beginning in the fall of 2005. The universities were Howard in Washington; Virginia Tech in Blacksburg, Virginia; ITESM in Monterrey, Mexico; Technische Universitat in Darmstadt, Germany; and Shanghai Jiao Tong University in Shanghai, China. This was one of my most pleasing experiences as a professor at Howard—teaching students simultaneously in different time zones around the world from a laboratory that I developed. I acquired the funds from sources exterior to the University.

Computing

During my lifetime, I have seen exponential growth in computing. From my early years in grade school through entering college, my "computing" was using what I learned to manipulate numbers with arithmetic and algebra. The manipulations included addition, subtraction, multiplication, division, and square roots.

There were very noisy mechanical desktop calculators, the Munroe and the Friden, that could do simple arithmetic operations. However, I did not see or use one of those mechanical number crunchers until 1964 as a graduate student at IIT.

My first contact with scientific computing was in 1959 when I entered the Pre-Engineering Program at Florida A&M University in Tallahassee. My computer was a slide rule.

The slide rule was an instrument for all non-algebraic computing for an engineering or science student. The accuracy of the results depended on the user, the type of problem, and the result being sought. As an example regarding accuracy, I tried to solve a problem that used logarithms; my results turned out to be one hundred percent wrong. Slide rules were good for certain calculations but were not to be used for very sensitive computations. The National Bureau of Standards (NBS), now National Institute of Standards and Technology (NIST), published results related to very sensitive computations that are recorded in the book <u>AMS 1955</u> by the American Mathematical Society.

The next computer that I used was the large mainframe computer at companies and universities. The scientific computing language was <u>FOR</u>mula <u>TRAN</u>slating System or FORTRAN, developed in the mid 1950s. Prior to FORTRAN, computer programmers used machine language to code their equations. My early work with mainframe computers required a deck of cards as input in which holes were punched to provide the instructions. Thus, the term "punch cards" was used. I submitted my computing job to the mainframe computer through a card reader.

From 1965 until 1975, prior to working at Lawrence Livermore National Laboratory (LLNL)—previously named Lawrence Radiation Laboratory—I wrote my own computer codes and used punch cards. At Livermore, I submitted my computer code directly to the mainframe computer from a teletype machine in my office. I had the opportunity to become friends with Robert A. Hughes, an African American employee at LLNL, who was assigned to work at IBM in the documentation of FORTRAN in 1957. I learned much about the history of FORTAN from Bob.

I used the teletype machine to submit my jobs until I left LLNL in 1988 to become Chairman of Mechanical Engineering at Howard.

The first portable calculator that I used was the 9100-B Desk Top Unit made by Hewlett-Packard (HP) when I was employed at Sandia National Laboratories (SNL) in Albuquerque. It was similar in size and shape of the Munroe or Friden mechanical calculators. I purchased an extended memory package for the HP 9100-B to digitize analog data and analyze the results on my sea voyages with oceanographers from Texas A&M University in 1971.

The next year, 1972, I saw a demonstration at SNL of the HP-35 pocket calculator that was developed to replace the slide rule. I taught at Lowell Tech in Massachusetts from 1973 to 1975, during the transition from the slide rule to hand calculator. I had to develop my exams so that students who used slide rules had the same advantage in computing as those who used electronic calculators.

In the late 1980s, personal computers came into use. In the 1990s, laptop computers and workstation computers were used by many people. With the development of software by numerous companies and the introduction of workstation computers, mainframe computing diminished. In these early years of the 21st century, we have notebooks and mobile phones that satisfy the computing needs of most people. I believe that the development of computers is far ahead of software development in scientific computing.

Information Storage

During my lifetime, I have seen the development of numerous media for storage of information. From the time I was a child until my first professional position after I earned the Ph.D. degree in January 1970, the media for storage of information was printed or "hard" copy. Printed information included but was not limited to newspapers, books, encyclopedias, professional journals, research reports, microfilm, pictures and negatives developed from still cameras, tapes on reels from movie cameras, vinyl records and albums, punch cards, and printouts from computing.

My first experience with electronic data storage was on the HP Desktop Electronic Calculator. I purchased it to analyze data from my voyages with oceanographers from Texas A & M University in 1971 while I was employed at Sandia Corporation. Although I used mainframe computers, it was not until I moved to California in 1975 to work at Lawrence Livermore National Laboratory that I was able to store all of my information on the computer system with photo storage developed by IBM. From that time on, I saw storage systems progress from punch cards to reel tape to photo storage to disk drives, to floppy disks, to compact disks, to flash drives.

Today, one can find information on the world-wide-web that was impossible 30 years ago. Prior to the web, one had to physically obtain information from libraries, newspapers, encyclopedias, and books on a particular subject. This information is now available on the Internet with a click on an electronic device. One can use the mobile phone or computer tablet to search for any information and get results immediately. We now have a new verb, "Google," to gather information. Google it!

However, not all of the information from the searches may be true or accurate. Artificial intelligence (the ability of computers to perform functions that normally require human intelligence) can display false written and video information to purposely mislead the public. Anyone can put just about anything on the world-wide-web.

I am not aware of any means that have been mandated by governmental agencies to prevent disclosure of false information on the web. This should be of concern. Everyone should support strong development of technology and restrictions to prevent the display of false information.

High speed computers and large capacity information storage systems have been developed and this technology development continues at a rapid pace. With artificial intelligence, we now have robots (machines) that can do many tasks which required human intelligence a few decades ago. My thoughts relate to the question, "When will machines be able to totally replace humans?" If that comes to be, what will happen to the world as we know it? Will humans become extinct?

Epilogue

I have had a very challenging but rewarding life. Looking forward, I wish to impart my thoughts on what I think may be helpful to current and future generations.

I have been a self-starter throughout my life, and that is one of the things that made me successful. Most importantly, my success was due to values that were instilled in me by family and neighbors. Those core values include respect for others, honesty, responsibility, resourcefulness, respect for hard work, courage, belief in education, and belief in oneself. Those and other values are reflected in what I have written in this memoir.

My philosophy has been that if you see something that would be helpful to others, go out and do it. Help others, be circumspect, teach them but do not let them take advantage of you. Believe in yourself but listen to others who can help you. Learn from generations that came before you; question them about current situations, and things that they have experienced; do not think that you know more about life than they do.

Assess all circumstances relating to people you meet and carefully choose your friends and acquaintances. Some acquaintances want only what they can get from you; do not call them friends. Surround yourself with people who can help you and those you can help. Always keep in mind that there will be others who want to hurt you and take advantage of what you have if you let them.

Be patient; everything you want cannot be obtained immediately. And, set high goals for your life and work hard to fulfill those targets. The fulfillment of your goals will determine how successful you have been in your life.

I set and achieved goals that no one in my community in Sawdust would have thought possible when I was a child. Who would have thought that

I would someday serve in numerous leadership positions in engineering, science, and education at national laboratories and universities, become Chair of the National ASME Mechanical Engineering Department Heads Committee in the United States, Chair of the ASME Committee on Accreditation of Mechanical Engineering Programs, and serve as a Consultant on numerous Science and Education Programs that were important to the nation?

However, one of my most rewarding experiences after I earned my college degree was how a generation of men who had sons and daughters my father's age in Sawdust respected and treated me. I visited my parents and those men—Willie Campbell, Spencer Richardson, Harry Gilliam, and Laura "Mr. Bita" Porcher. I would sit on the porch at my parents' house with one or more of them and have discussions about science and the state of the world. They had followed my life and accomplishments, believed in me, and knew that I was an achiever. I loved our discussions.

I would also visit Aunt Laura and Uncle Rubin Jordan who were also members of the above generation. Uncle Rubin was wheel-chair bound and did not travel. We would sit on his back porch and have discussions about life. He did not know his birth date. When he related things that he had observed when he was a child, I surmised his age. He was probably ninety or more years old the last time I visited him. The point here is that you get an appreciation about living by talking and relating to older generations. Those relationships certainly helped shape my outlook on life.

As I reflect on my life, I think about what life was like for my generation compared to generations that followed me. I grew up on a farm. All children five years and older had to work on the tobacco farms during the summer to help make ends meet. Today that would be called child abuse, and I do not support child abuse.

Although formal education was emphasized in the black community, many young boys dropped out of school before they completed middle school. I do not recall a high dropout rate for young girls. The families wanted their daughters to obtain credentials to become teachers and their sons to take over their farms. Hence, high school was not a priority for the boys and they were encouraged to learn the necessities of successful farming at an early age.

Many of the boys had to work on the farm during the school year and did not get promoted to the next grade—due no doubt to a high rate of absences and too many missed lessons that could not be made up. Some of the families lived on white farmers' properties and the boys had to work there during the school year. Consequently, young boys remained in lower grades until they showed no interest in school. I saw families whose oldest son did not finish middle school yet their youngest sons finished high school. On the other hand, I also saw families whose oldest son finished high school and the next two sons in that family finished only sixth grade.

Education during my generation was more than formal school work. We were also taught family values and survival techniques in the Jim Crow South and that included farming and understanding human behavior. However, I must say that all of my six siblings attended college and three obtained Master's degrees. I earned the Master's and Ph.D. degrees in engineering science. Further, the small community of Sawdust, consisting of fewer than fifty black families during my early childhood, had at least four people in my generation with roots in Sawdust—Agnes Phillips, Lewis Thigpen, James Lloyd Milton, and William Lloyd Nealy—to earn the Ph.D. degree prior to the year 1975. James Lloyd Milton and William Lloyd Nealy are my relatives. I also think that there may have been a grandson of Harry Gilliam, born during my generation, who may have earned a doctorate. This shows how important education was in the black community in Sawdust.

It was said that everyone in Sawdust was related either by one side of the family or the other. Thus, we had an extended family of distant cousins and many families in the black community who looked out for the welfare of their neighbors' children. Family values and care of children by the local community provided protection in the Jim Crow South and helped to instill ethics and responsibility to my generation.

Life is more difficult for the modern generation—youth and young adults. They have to cope with more crime and drugs. They have more formal education and more wealth. I believe that they have been overindulged— "spoiled"—without being taught how to survive in the community. The parents wanted their children to have more material things than had been available to them. Consequently, this generation is more materialistic, selfish, and less appreciative than my generation.

I believe that this behavior came from the leadership in our country as well as from the parents of the modern generation. During the Reagan Administration, there was emphasis on selfishness. It is no mystery that the teenagers during that era developed strong, selfish attitudes in general. But their children—this new generation—appear to have taken selfishness to a higher level. I call them the "Me Generation." Further, I have seen many parents listen to what their children say and then act as if their children know more about living and survival than older generations.

I have observed that many in the modern generation's poor and middle class families do not respect what their families have sacrificed to provide materialistic things. These young people believe that their parents, surrogate parents, and other relatives will always be there with resources to satisfy their wishes. They do not respect money. I have seen this in those whom I have helped. Further, they have difficulties in choosing friends who are supportive and not out to prey on or take advantage of what they have.

One thing that children in the current generation do not have is the extended family to consult. Consider the old proverb, "It takes a village to raise a child." For today's youth, there is very little "village" or extended family. They have not been taught family values that were most important in my generation. Yet family values are still very important today.

I believe that things are worse not only for the modern generation of poor and middle class African American families, but for all generations of Americans under President Trump's Administration, beginning in January 2017. Trump is a liar, cheat, and racist whose three years in office have revealed dictatorial behavior and support of white nationalism. He now calls himself a nationalist. By his words and actions, his administration has devalued Black, Brown, and Muslim lives. Who will be the next to have their lives devalued? As a racist, he has worked with the support of the Republican Congress during his first three years to undo accomplishments of his predecessor Barack Obama, the first black President of the United States. President Obama's policies helped ALL people in the country.

Trump's policies are divisive to our country and the world. This is a tough time for our country. Trump is supported by the Republican Majority Leader in the Senate, Mitch McConnell, and a majority of the Republican Congress in both the House of Representatives and Senate.

Trump has an agenda and policies that could set us back more than one hundred fifty years when the country was divided and led to the Civil War.

As I write this memoir, the Republican Congress has given up its role for Checks and Balances required by the Constitution, the rule of law, and is a hostage to Trump. This is a characteristic of a dictatorship. I encourage all who do not accept the fascist and divisive activities to register to vote, go to the polling place, and vote before it is too late.

In this memoir, I have discussed my life and some of the many influences that shaped it and helped me to be successful. Success does not come as a given in a poor uneducated family. You must work hard and opportunities may follow. I have had many opportunities and have taken advantage of those opportunities. Those include opportunities to work, develop a career, and help others. Those opportunities have been depicted in this book.

I have worked since I was five years old. Seeing no opportunities to improve my status in life, I volunteered to serve in the U.S. Army as a teenager. After returning from active duty in August 1958, life was still difficult for me as a black person in Florida. I took menial jobs but still searched for opportunities to improve my status in life. I entered college in the fall of 1959 with only enough money to pay tuition for one semester. I worked every night to support myself. Through my years in college, I found that numerous opportunities existed if I worked hard, and I received student loans, scholarships, and fellowships to earn the Bachelor's, Master's, and Ph.D. degrees.

My life has been built around family values, being strong, hard work, formal and informal education, having friends, and helping others. My contribution to helping others takes on many aspects, including financial support of charities, churches, and scholarship funds at universities and professional societies. In addition, I help individuals in need through monetary contributions. I am also engaged in volunteer work.

There are so many needs waiting to be addressed. If each of us does what he or she can, and stretches that help even further than they think they can, all of us will rise. And our communities will be transformed from sawdust into giant, solid oak trees.

APPENDIX

Family Trees

LEWIS THIGPEN'S PATERNAL LINEAGE
(1st of 2)

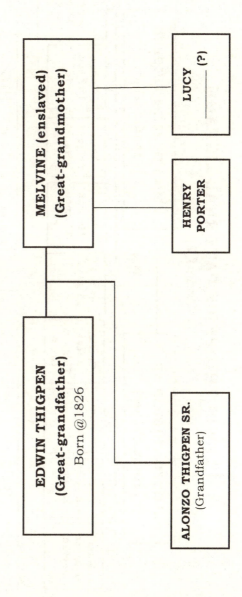

LEWIS THIGPEN'S PATERNAL LINEAGE
(2nd of 2)

ALONZO THIGPEN SR. (Grandfather) — **EMMA GILLIAM THIGPEN** (Grandmother)

(13)

Laura Thigpen Jordan (12)
- Merrit Jordan Sr.
- Ellie
- Zellie
- Johnnie
- Rubin, Jr.
- Joe
- Meadie "Bunch"
- Malzeprie "Scrap"
- Lonnie
- Ruth
- Addie "Scoot"
- Burnice "Bill"

Lucy Thigpen Rolax (10)
- Clarence
- James
- Emma Lee
- Lucile
- Neaner Mae
- Robert
- Annette
- Catherine
- William
- Fred

Johnnie Thigpen (8)
- Eddie
- Alfred
- Spugeon
- Ellis "Tugar"
- Andrew "Abe"
- Mary
- Joe
- Gertice "Toe"

Carrie Ardean Thigpen Gunn (4)
- Essie
- Willie Mae
- Adell
- Ruby

James Thigpen

Mary Melvine Thigpen Paul (4)
- Quinton
- Winfred "Int"
- Waymon
- Dorothy

Addie Thigpen Hall (2)
- Lennon
- Donald "Pat"

Alonzo Thigpen, Jr. (7)
- Leatrice
- Mildred
- Gladys
- Amos
- **Lewis**
- Isabel
- James W.

5 Others (did not live past birth)

300

LEWIS THIGPEN'S MATERNAL LINEAGE
(1st of 2)

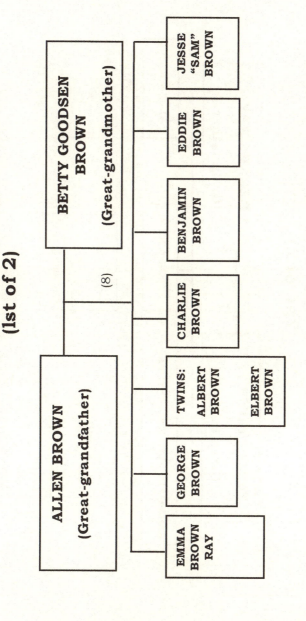

LEWIS THIGPEN'S MATERNAL LINEAGE
(2nd of 2)

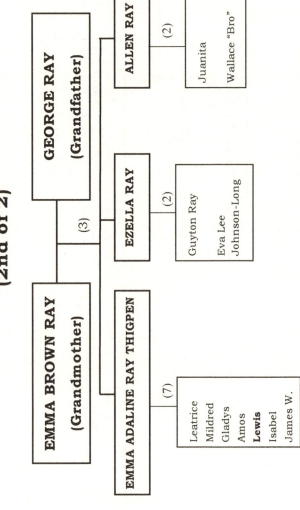

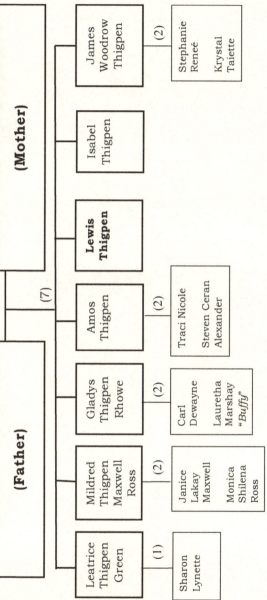

Index

A

Abey, Albert A. 257
Abidjan, Ivory Coast 217
Accounts Clerk in the food service department 15
Adams, Willie 97, 100, 104
Africa 217
African American newspaper, the Pittsburgh Courier 57
AFRO American Life Insurance Company 14, 30
Agnew, Spiro 272
Albuquerque airport 114
Alerts on base at Ayers Kaserne 80
Aloe Vera 40
Amsterdam, Holland 209
Apalachicola National Forest 187
Arc de Triomphe 209
Armstead, Amanda (great great aunt) 12
Army Reserves 49, 98
Artificial intelligence 289
Aruba 201
Asia 196
Assistant Principal in Broward County 15
Atomic Energy Commission (AEC) 201
Auckland, New Zealand 219
Auschwitz concentration camp 213

Austin, Geneva 108, 113
Australia 196
Austria 207
Ayres, Anna Marie 257

B

Baker, Hailey Leroy 107, 108, 254
ball point pen 283
Barcelona, Spain 208
barefoot 27
Barrow, Alaska 257
Basic Training 70
bed pans 17
Beef 263
Belgium 207
Bell, Alvin 87
Bell, William 264
Bergen-Belsen concentration camp 80
Bernstein, Barry (Professor) 123, 126, 127
Berry, Charles Edward Anderson (Chuck Berry) 70
Best man 141, 254, 255
Betty Brown Place 6
bicycle 33, 44, 52, 191, 210, 222
Bid Whist Tournament 61
Big Ben 209
Big Snow 121
birther 276
blackboard 284

Black, Carrie (cousin) 13
black panther 22
Blountstown, Florida 14
blues songs that have moved me 264
boiling a frog 50
boil on my neck 21
Bolita 57
bowling alley 84
Bradley, William Lee Conley Broonzy (Big Bill Broonzy) 264
brains and eggs for breakfast 38
Brazil 162, 205, 207
breaking the field 35
bridge across the River Thames 209
Britt, Helen 108
brogans 3, 27, 42
Bronx, New York 110
Brown, Allen (my maternal great grandfather) 6, 12
Brown, Betty (my maternal great grandmother) 6, 13
Brown, Eddie (uncle Eddie) 278
Brown, Mary (great aunt) 13
Brown, Robert Clifford (Washboard Sam) 264
Brown, Silas (my maternal great grandfather's brother) 12
buck 4, 56
buck barrel 56
Buckingham Palace 209
Buford, Jimmy 105
Building Construction 14
bull fight 199, 208
bull terrier named Glad 34
burlap sack to catch fish 45
Burnett, Chester Arthur (Howling Wolf) 118
Bush, George H. W. 274
Bush, George W. 274
Butchering hogs 36
Butler, Mrs. Eva Simms 63
Butterfield, Paul 118

C

Campbell, Jesse \ 279
Campbell, Jesse (third cousin) 23, 40, 42
Campbell, Susie (cousin Trudy's daughter) 4
Campbell, Trudy (cousin) 4
Campbell, Willie 18, 26, 48, 76, 280, 292
Canada 196
canning 6, 7
carbon paper 284
Carrabelle, Florida 187
Carter, James Earl 272
Carter Parramore High School 14
castor oil 39
castration of pigs 39
Castro, Fidel 270
catching fish in a large burlap sack 45
change in leadership 157
Chawla, Ramesh 177
Chef Boyardee Spaghetti with meat sauce 28
Chemistry Department 99, 141
Chiarulli, Peter (Professor) 120, 122, 126
Chicago, Illinois 11, 116
Chicken hawks 47
chickens 20, 47, 50, 53
China 213
china berry 40
Chinese food 262
Chin, Raymond C. Y. 144, 154, 194, 197, 257, 262
Christmas 28, 56, 189, 225
Citizens Bank 14
Civil Investigating Department (CID) 72
Clark, Fannie 189

Clark, Mrs. Ola 61, 189
class action suit 135
Clinton, Hillary Rodham 216, 276
Clinton, William Jefferson 214, 215, 274
cloakroom 19, 32
Clydesdale horses 4
coffee tree 18
cold storage 38
Combat training exercises 78
communication modes 285
Communications Committee 74, 76
Community Center 19
Community College in Tallahassee 14
Community service activities 189
Company Commander 72, 76
Company Store 24, 28
Coney Island 110
Constitution Hall 109
Continuing education 280, 282
corn shuck tea 40
Corporal Sergeant 70, 87
cottonmouths/water moccasins 187
cows dropping calves 21
crackling bread 38
cracklings and pork skins 38
Currency inflation in Brazil 207
curriculum 31
Cypress Inn 61, 75, 187
Cypress Pond 19, 45, 46, 61
Czech Republic 207

D

dashiki 8
Davis, Angela 255
Davis, Steven S. 112
day room 83
Death Valley 116
Dental care 13, 68
Deputy Clerk in the Quincy Courthouse 14
Desert Storm 279
discrimination complaint 167
discussions with older men 280
dishwasher 92, 96
Distemper (a viral disease) 39
Ditches 45
DMZ between North and South Korea 216
Donaldsonville, Georgia 5, 53
Downing, Lewis K. (Dean of Engineering at Howard) 109, 170
Doyle, Mrs. Lillie Mae (my first teacher) 18
Drakeford, Mrs. Carolyn 195
Dukakis, Michael 274
Dumb Dumb 71

E

Earthquakes 221
Easter holiday in 1956 75
eastern and western style toilets 213
Ebony Magazine 254
Eddy Stone 119
Edwards, Marcus 102
Edwards, Newell 102
Eiffel Tower 209
Eisenhower, Dwight D. 83, 270
elderberry bushes 40
electronic data storage 289
email 285
England 207
English composition 63, 98
Enlisted Men's Club 84
entrepreneurs 57
Europe 86, 196
excruciating pain 68
Experimental Rock Mechanics 143
experimenting with new money crops 5

F

fake Rolex watches 215
family sayings 262
FAMU 14, 68, 96, 104
Farmer, George Washington (Professor) 19, 26, 33, 43, 60, 283
Farmers' Almanac 35
farming 35
Father-Son Banquet 50
fear of roosters 20
Federal Aviation Administration (FAA) 106
Ferraro, Geraldine 273
fertilizer distributer 36
fight back 35
First Sergeant 71, 73, 84, 86
fish fry on the day after Christmas 225
fishing lines 32, 44
fish stews 7
five-year Strategic Plan 147
Florence, Italy 210
Florida A&M College 14
Florida Atlantic University 15
Florida Caverns 56
Florida State Hospital in Chattahoochee 15
Florida State University (FSU) 96
flour sacks 8, 38
foot-powered pedal-driven sewing machine 8
Forbidden City 214
Ford, Gerald R. 272
Fort Dix, New Jersey 76
Fort Jackson 70, 87
Fort Knox, Kentucky 70, 76, 82
FORTRAN 124, 287, 288
Four Corners, New Mexico 198
Fowler Hall 118
France 207
Francis, Mrs. Ruby Gilliam 63, 189
Frankfurt, Germany 211, 215
French food 262
freshly dipped snuff 39
Fried quail 264
Ft. Lauderdale 15, 140, 202, 225

G

Gadsden County 3, 5, 6, 16, 48, 187, 225, 286
Gadsden County Art Association 15
Gainesville, Florida 11, 18, 36
Gas pipeline pumping station 93
Gates, Robert 216
General Unknown 99
George Diamonds Steak House 192
German ancestry 10
German reading course 124
Germany 207
ghost story 22
GI Bill for Korean War Veterans 14
Gilliam, Anaka (great aunt Anaka) 11
Gilliam, Carrie (great aunt Carrie) 11
Gilliam, Harry 50, 280, 292
Gilliam, Laura (great aunt Laura) 11
Gilliam, Mrs. Syneda (midwife) 16, 21
Gilliam, Samuel (cousin) 32, 49, 59
Gilliam, Samuel (paternal great grandfather) 11
Glakpe, Emmanuel K. 174, 195, 260
Glass Bottom Boat Tours 56
Gliwice, Poland 212
global warming 221, 224
Glory Road 225
Golden Rule 261
Goodyear Foundation Award 109
Gorbachev, Mikhail 273
Gore Jr., Albert 274
gourds 47
Graduation Ceremonies 113
Gramophone 61
Grant, Raymond 63
Great Recession 275

Great Wall of China 214
green back dollar 208
Greensboro High School 14
Green, Sharon L. (my niece) 113
Greyhound bus 87, 91, 100, 104, 116, 139, 198
guard duty 71, 85
guest house 203
Gulf of Mexico 133, 187
Gunn, Adell (first cousin) 11
Gunn, Brister (my great-grand uncle) 10
Gunn, Carrie (aunt Carrie) 11, 18, 54
Gunn, Essie (first cousin) 11
Gunn, Ruby (first cousin) 11, 22, 30, 37, 45, 48, 56, 60, 61, 75, 94, 117, 133
Gunn, Willie Mae (first cousin) 11, 45
gunpowder and milk 40
Gyroscope 71, 76

H

Hall, Addie (aunt Addie) 11, 18
Hall, David (uncle Esau) 18, 36, 58
Hall, Donald (first cousin) 18, 20
Hall, Lennon (first cousin) 18
hand-powered pump 18, 19
handshake from someone 5
Harlem, New York 111
harrow 35
Hartford, Connecticut 11, 67
Hedstrom, Gerald W. 257
Heilbronn, Germany 207
Hercey, Zeora 255
hiccups 40, 117
hidden agendas 157, 165
Hilliard, Thomas 118, 254
Hippy Wagon 141
Hitler, Adolph 16, 27, 125
hobbies 186
hog hoof tea 40

hold your breath and drink water 40
Holland 207
home made candy 13
home remedies for both animals and human 38
Hoover, Herbert 16
hot foot 82
Howard, Darnley E. 112
Howard University 104, 155
Hughes, Robert A. 288
Humphrey, Hubert 272
hunting, trapping and fishing 5
Hurricanes 221
Hussein, Saddam 274
Hyde Park, New York 111
hydrostatic lock 81

I

ice box 17
Ice Penetrating Sonobuoy 133
ice plant 7, 38, 48
Idaho Falls, Idaho 153
Illinois Institute of Technology (IIT) 116
Indigenous people 134
International Crises 82
International Language 208
International Soccer Tournament 200
Isaac, Jane (aunt Jane Isaac) 12
Islands in the Caribbean 201
Islands in thePacific Ocean 196
Italian food 262
Italy 207, 210
Ivory Coast (Côte d'Ivoire) 217

J

Jackson, Andrew 276
Jackson, Mellon 25
Jackson, Mrs. Amelia 6
Jacksonville 15, 70, 94
Jamaica 201

Japan 213
Jazz and Technology 108, 109
jelly and fruit preserves 6
Jenkins, Lucius (ice man) 48
Jim Crow South 10, 32, 44
Joe Louis 60
Johnson, Eddie L. 85
Johnson, James H., Jr. 158, 169, 177, 195
Johnson, Lyndon B. 271
Jordan, Alice (cousin) 32
Jordan, Laura (aunt Laura) 11, 278
Jordan, Lonnie (first cousin) 278
Jordan, Rubin, Sr. (uncle Rubin) 292
Juneteenth 28
Juniper Creek 5, 42, 46, 187
junk man 27

K

kangaroo and emu 219
Kennedy, John F. 101, 270
Kennedy, Robert 272
Kenya 276
Kerosene lamps 17, 20
Khrushchev, Nikita 271
King, Jr., Martin Luther 272
King, Mrs. Hazel 63
King, Riley B. (BB King) 75
Kingston, Jamaica 204
Kirch-Göns, Germany 77
kitchen 6, 17, 19
Kite, Frank 141, 255
Ku Klux Klan 10

L

Lake Doe 55
Lakeside Village Apartments 142, 154, 155, 222, 259
Lake Talquin 94, 187
Lancaster County Seed Company in Pennsylvania 57

lard cans 38
large mainframe computer 287
Lawrence Livermore National Laboratory 141
Leatrice's 85th birthday 227
Lebanon Crisis in 1958 279
Leffall, LaSalle D., Sr. (Professor) 53
leisure time 194
lighter'd 39
Lincoln, Abraham 19, 225
Lincoln Hotel 120
Little Joe 81
Little Richard 75
Local Tailor, Barber and Kitchen Police 83
London, England 209
Long Island, New York 111
Long Term Visiting Staff Member at Los Alamos National Laboratory 170
Lorenson, Ray 257
Los Angeles, California 28, 58, 116, 184, 219, 264
Louisville, Kentucky 74
Luau in Honolulu 198
lye soap 38

M

Madry, Claudia (Naud) 27
Madry, George 118
major challenges 9
make my own toys 40
making a baseball 42
March of Dimes charity 61
Marseille, France 208
Martin Luther King Jr. Blvd 12
Mason-Dixon Line 68
Mason jars 6, 38
Mathematics and Science 190
Matrix Organization 143

Index

Maxwell, Janice (my niece) 8, 113, 183, 203
Maxwell Strom's farm 6
Mayo Flournoy's Rolling Store 21, 22
Mays, Willie 96
mechanical desktop calculators 287
Mechanical Engineering Department Handbook 167
Mechanics Department 113, 120, 121, 126
Mediterranean seaside 208
Melbourne, Australia 219
Melting of glaciers 224
Melvine (my paternal great grandmother, an enslaved woman) 10
memberships in professional organizations 192
Memorable Teachers in High School 63
Merida, Mexico 200
messes 38
Mexican food 263
Mexico 199
midwife 16, 21
Milan, Italy 210
Miller, Pete (Associate Director at Los Alamos National Laboratory) 170
Milton, Daniel (cousin) 75, 139, 254
Milton, James Lloyd (cousin) 100, 254
mimeograph machines 284
Mitchell, Archer S., Jr. 118, 194, 199
mobile phones 288
Mondale, Walter 273
Montego Bay, Jamaica 203
moonshine 4, 27, 34, 75, 138
Morganfield, McKinley (Muddy Waters) 118
Morrison, Frank 151
Morrisons Cafeteria 97, 100

Mother Blues 118
Mountplesant 10
Ms Rendy 6
mulatto 10
mule-drawn cultivator 36
Mullet fish sandwiches 20
my father 5, 27, 278
my fifth birthday 28
my first flight on an airplane 209
my mother 3, 9, 12, 225, 226
my siblings 9, 14, 15, 263
My Travels 196

N

NAACP 10
Naftzger, Robert 120, 191, 194
Nasser, Gamal Abdel 83
National Airlines 114
Native American ancestry 11
Natural environmental events 221
Nazis 80
Nealy, Essie Gunn 107
Nealy, William Lloyd (second cousin) 139
Neff, Margaret Jean 140, 141
neighbors 24, 32, 36, 218, 221, 227, 264, 291
Nelson, Jonathan P. 105, 114, 119
New awakening and a new experience 156
New Farmers of America (NFA) 50
Newspapers and Advertisements 28
New Zealand 219
Niagara Falls 197
Nice, France 208
nicknames 6, 16
Nielson, Steven 260
Night Cook on the U. S. N. S. General Alexander M. Patch 77
Nixon, Richard M. 272
non-academic curriculum 33

Noriega, Manuel 274
Norris, Mr. 63
North America 196
North Carolina 10
Number 10 Downing Street 209

O

Obama, Barack H. 275
Ocala, Florida 55
Oceanographers from Texas A&M 133, 201
Ocho Rios, Jamaica 203
old age pension 13
Old Town Chicago 118
Osaka, Japan 213
Osama bin Laden 275, 276
Ostrava, Czech Republic 211
Oswald, Lee Harvey 271
outdoor auditorium 19
outdoor toilet 12, 18
overalls 27
Overhoultz, Record Shop Owner and DJ 20
Owens, John 111, 254
Owens, Mary 120, 255

P

pallet 36
Palmer House Hotel 117
Palmer, Roy B. 108
Panama City, Florida 27
Paris, France 209
Parramore, Robert 7
Passes and Leaves 84
passion for new places 196
Patterson, William 255
Paul, A. D. 25, 189
Paul, Mary Melvine (aunt Mel) 11
Paul, Quinton (first cousin) 11
Peace, Romaine 195
perlau 7, 38

Peterson, Alan 141
Peterson, Lois Kieffaber 141
Physical fitness training (PT) 78
Pipe and Hat, my father's signature 3
pit stop 217
Placement exam in mathematics 96
planning to retire 193
planter 36
poems 54, 190, 261
poison ivy 39, 40
Poland 207
Police brutality in Milan, Italy 210
Polynesian performers 198
Poncho Villa 199
Pony Express 285
popguns 32, 40
Popular Science magazine 32
Porcher, Laura 292
Porter, Henry (my great uncle) 10
pottery 42
Poughkeepsie, New York 109, 142
practical jokes 47, 82
Prague, Czech Republic 211
pre-engineering student 14
prejudice 72, 74, 156
pressure cooker 6, 38
Prince Albert Pipe and Cigarette Tobacco 3
Professor Levans 127
Professor Markovin 127
Professor Richter 124
projectile penetration 131
propeller-powered U.S. fighter planes 27
Providence Road 31, 101, 225
prune juice 39
puddle jumper 114
pulpwood 93
punch cards 287

Q

Quayle, Dan 274
Queens, New York 110
quicksand 46
quilting party 8
quilts 7, 8
Quincy 10, 12, 15, 101, 226

R

racial profiling 100
racism 9, 84, 156
racism and subtle discrimination in the Army 84
radio 285
Railroad Mills Snuff 39
Rambeau, Hazel Ray (cousin) 53
Randy's Record Shop 61
Rap sessions 59
ration books 8, 24
Ray, Allen (uncle buddy) 6, 12, 30, 187
Ray, Emma Adaline (my mother) 6, 12
Ray, Emma (my maternal grandmother) 5, 12
Ray, Ezella (aunt Ezella) 6, 12
Ray, George (my maternal grandfather) 5, 12
Ray, Juanita (first cousin) 30
Ray, Wallace (first cousin) 30, 33
Reagan, Ronald W. 273
Reardon, Patrick 260
recoilless gun 132
Reform School 34
Reiss, Robert 194, 198, 255
respiratory illnesses 39
Rhowe, Carl Dewayne (my nephew) 202, 279
Richardson, Spencer 292
Rise and Fly 62
Rock and Roll music 70
Rockefeller, Nelson 272
Rodean, Howard 144
Rolax, Amanda (a friend) 49, 94
Rolax, Charles (second cousin) 34, 46, 59, 62, 75, 94, 100, 139, 254
Rolax, Henry (uncle Henry) 29
Rolax, Herschell (second cousin) 108
Rolax, James (first cousin) 278
Rolax, Lucy (aunt Lucy) 8, 11, 278
Rolax, Pierce (Mr. Sonboy) 49
Rolax, Robert (first cousin) 54, 278
Rolax, William (first cousin) 8, 140, 278
rolled cigars 6, 30
Rome, Italy 210
Roosevelt, Franklin D. 16, 31, 111, 190, 269
Ruby, Jack 271
Rudd, Edward 9
Rudd, Willard 10
Rug Doctor 259
Rush, Otis 118

S

Sabbatical 170
Sadat, Anwar 119
Sandia Mountain 201
San Diego, California 117
Santa Claus 28
sardines 40
sassafras tea 39
Saturday night dances and fish fries 20
sausage casings and chitterlings 37
sausage meat 38
sausage meat grinder 38
Sawdust Community 3, 16, 51, 60, 280
Sawdust School 18, 26, 28, 34, 50, 58
scary story 22
School Boy Patrols 56
School-House-turned-Dance-Hall 20
Scientific computing 287

Seafood 263
search for an apartment 142
Seismic Monitoring Program 144
Seoul, South Korea 215
Service Club 84
shade tobacco 4, 9, 67
Shanghai, China 215
Shanghai Jiao Tong University, Shanghai China 181
Shanks High School 14
sharecropped 3, 9, 12, 53, 61
Shaw, Jimmy (distant cousin) 59
Sheppard, Kennon 9
Sheppard's mill in Greensboro, Florida 57
short sheet 82
shrunken head 134
Siegel, Mark Paul (Corky Siegel) 118
Signifying Monkey 59
Silver Springs State Park 56
Simone, Nina 108
simulated combat 80
Sit-Ins 99, 101
Slaughtering and butchering hogs 36
slide rule 287
Slipping and Sliding 75
Smith, Sonya T. 176
smokehouses 7, 18, 21
Smokey 22
Snipe Hunt 47
social media 285
Social Security 13, 16, 193
Solar eclipse 224
sonic speed 41
Sooner 34
soup bone 7
South America 196
South Carolina 70, 87, 113, 140
Southern food 262
South Korea 213
Spain 208

Spanish Club 56
Spanish flu 5
Special Honors 112
Special meal on New Year's Day 264
Spencer, Richard (VP Sundstrand Aerospace) 172
spider webs 39
Stevens High School 14, 30, 63, 68
Stevens, Russell (County Agent) 55
stick ball 58
Stonecipher, Harry (President and CEO Sundstrand Aerospace) 173
Stout, Ray B. 121, 127, 154, 194, 255
Stubbs, Mary Frances 195
Suez Canal Crisis in 1956 279
Sugar mill 26
Summer camp 104
Sunday school superintendent 189
superstitions 57, 264
surrogate children 183

T

Tailor Made Suits 83
Talquin Electric Corp 61
tan khaki work pants and shirts 3
Tao, L. N. (Professor) 122, 127
Tate's Hell 188
Technische Universitat Darmstadt, Germany 181
Tecnologico de Monterrey (ITESM) Monterrey, Mexico 181
Telephone 286
Television 286
Tennessee Ernie Ford 24
Terracotta Warriors 215
Texas A&M's ship, The Alaminos 201
The 4-H Club 55
The greatest Polish joke I've ever seen or heard of 213
the human element 281, 282
The Termite 26

Index 315

The three R's 31
Thigpen, Alfred (first cousin) 278
Thigpen, Alonzo, Jr. 3
Thigpen, Alonzo, Sr. (my paternal grandfather) 3, 12, 17
Thigpen, Amos (my brother) 9, 14, 35, 61, 94, 101, 117, 133, 207, 208, 278
Thigpen, Edwin (my paternal great grandfather) 10
Thigpen, Ellis (first cousin) 278
Thigpen, Emma Adaline Ray 3
Thigpen, Emma (my paternal grandmother) 14, 17
Thigpen family farm 4, 16, 18, 45
Thigpen, Gladys (my sister) 8, 14, 22, 30, 32, 37, 48, 50, 56, 60, 61, 94, 187, 202, 225, 262
Thigpen, Isabel (my sister) 8, 15, 53, 183
Thigpen, James (uncle James) 11
Thigpen, James Woodrow (my brother) 5, 13, 15, 21, 113, 140, 188, 190, 225
Thigpen, Johnnie (uncle Johnnie) 11, 278
Thigpen, Larfield (second cousin) 279
Thigpen, Leatrice (my sister) 8, 14, 45, 110
Thigpen, Lewis 13, 16, 150, 153, 169, 184
Thigpen, McKinley \ 279
Thigpen, Mildred (my sister) 8, 14, 28, 183, 189, 202, 284
Thigpen Road 12
Thigpen, Spurgeon (my first cousin) 12
Thigpen, Stephanie (my niece) 201
Tiananmen Square 214
Tijuana, Mexico 117
Time Magazine 32
Tobacco poultices 40

Topoleski, Eugene 119, 123
to survive with limited resources 40
Tour to Kyoto, Japan 214
Tower of London 209
Trailblazing 5
traps to catch birds 40, 41
traveling convenience store 7
Travel to Poughkeepsie 109
trigonometry 98, 99, 102
Trinidad and Tobago 201
Truman, Harry S. 31, 84, 94, 269
Trump, Donald J. 264, 276
Trying to find myself 91
trying to herd cats 159
Tuition scholarships 107
Turner, Michelle 185
Turner, Tina 185
turning plow 35
Twentieth of May 28, 225

U

Uncle Tom 70
Union Chapel AME Church 27, 29, 189, 226, 262
United States 83, 86, 198, 214, 278
University of Maryland 190
University of Massachusetts at Lowell 137
University of New Mexico 256
University of Ostrava 211
unprocessed spices 7
U.S. Mail 285
U.S.N.S. General Alexander M. Patch 76, 87

V

Vassar College 111
Video Conferencing 175, 286
Vienna, Austria 211
Vietnam War 279
Vira, Naren 213

Virginia Tech 175, 181
Volcanic eruption 223

W

Walker, Aubrey 108, 254
Walker, M. Lucius, Jr. 112, 135, 156, 170, 194
Wallpaper 28
wash pot 38
Watkins, Charles B., Jr. 135, 254
West Germany 70, 74
White bully in Sawdust 101
White island in the middle of a Black neighborhood 120
Whitfield, Rebecca (great great aunt) 12
Whitworth, Horace A. 212, 214, 219
Wiggins, Ms Marilyn 63
wild game 7, 262
Wilson, Nancy 108
Windsor, Connecticut 67
winter nights 28
wood burning stove 17, 19, 50
wooden boomerang 220
Worchester Polytechnic Institute 138
workbook 32
World's Fair Brussels, Belgium in 1958 210
World War II 7, 17, 24, 27, 54, 70, 75, 80, 213, 278, 285
world-wide-web 289
written contract 5

X

Xerox machine 284
Xian, China 215

Y

yard brooms 27
YMCA 117
York Harbor, Maine 137

Made in the USA
Las Vegas, NV
14 March 2021